With the compliments of
John B Ewan,
15-11-63.

The
Good Housewife's
Encyclopedia

Uniform with this volume:

THE GOOD COOK'S ENCYCLOPEDIA

THE GOOD HANDYMAN'S ENCYCLOPEDIA

The Good Housewife's Encyclopedia

EDITED BY PAMELA FRY

SPRING BOOKS · LONDON

ACKNOWLEDGEMENTS

In compiling and writing this book, my task was made much easier by the panel of experts who prepared the home maintenance, decorating and gardening sections, as well as the many individuals and organisations who were so very co-operative in providing me with both advice and material. I would particularly like to thank the following:
Blue Band Luxury Margarine, Cadbury Brothers, The Cheese Bureau, Colman's Mustard, Colman's Semolina, The Nestlé Cookery Service, Oxo Limited, Royal Society for the Prevention of Cruelty to Animals, St. John Ambulance Association, Stork Cookery Service. Diagram of holding bird (Fig. 34) by Courtesy of Spratts Patent Ltd.

WESTBOOK HOUSE · FULHAM BROADWAY · LONDON

Printed in Czechoslovakia

T 1230

CONTENTS

HOW TO MAKE A HOUSE YOUR HOME

EXACTLY HOW do you make a house a home? By filling it with expensive furniture, and all the latest modern conveniences and gadgets? Well, that would be very nice if you could afford it — but I do not think it has much to do with creating that particularly warm and cosy atmosphere which most of us think of when we use the word 'home'.

A real home is not just the place where a family lives; it should also fit in with and reflect their lives and personalities. It is a place for old memories as well as new ideas; comforting and welcoming, it is above all a place which truly meets the needs of its inhabitants.

In the old days, families often lived in the same house for generations — if not for centuries. The house became part of them and their history. The inkstains on the schoolroom table, the initials carved on the apple tree, the cushions so lovingly embroidered by Great Aunt Matilda, the gate so often broken and mended by succeeding generations of schoolboys-into-fathers — all these were part of home.

Today, for many of us, the old slow methods of tradition are no longer possible. The world is on the move, and very few people now spend their lives in or even near the place where they were actually born. Most young couples begin married life in a tiny flat or even in one room.

If you *are* living in this sort of a home, you may feel rather discouraged. But no matter how small and apparently inadequate it may appear to be, the old principles still apply, and miracles can still be performed, providing you have the necessary will and imagination.

The art of homemaking has not been lost. In spite of (and perhaps because of) the high pressure mechanised world in which we live, more and more people are learning the pleasure of planning, decorating and maintaining their homes themselves. In the face of all the limitations imposed by lack of space, money and even time, miracles really are being performed. Built-in or renovated furniture, vibrant colour schemes, proper lighting and clever design are being used to transform even the ugliest and most unpromising rooms. Modern methods and materials help to make the job easier than Grandfather would have believed possible.

There is more to the story than this. People are learning to do-it-themselves, not only because it adds so much to the joy and satisfaction of genuine homemaking, but because it is, above all, *practical.* The truth of the matter is that in this age of increasing specialisation and little or no domestic help the more self-reliant a family becomes, the more easily and happily their home will operate.

It is not only quicker, cheaper and more satisfying to do your own decorating and alterations, as well as a great number of minor household repairs, but it also provides you with valuable ammunition when the 'expert' does have to be called in on some more complicated job. The more one knows about the task at hand, the less likelihood there is of being overcharged or discovering too late that an expensive job has been carelessly or inadequately done.

This book is an all-round practical handbook which has been designed to meet the needs of everyone who is interested, or thinks he would like to *become* interested, in the techniques of do-it-yourself. Not only with regard to home maintenance and decoration, but in all the other vital aspects of family life — housekeeping, first aid and accident prevention, the care and training of pets, shopping, cooking, entertaining and gardening.

You will find these pages packed, not only with practical information, but also with all sorts of new and exciting ideas: how to run a successful barbecue party; how to solve the problems presented by a dark or badly proportioned room; how to make beautiful curtains out of the cheapest material imaginable; how turn your bathroom into a place of sheer luxury or your garden into a minor paradise, complete with pool. In other words, I have compiled this book with the intention of providing as much down-to-earth information as could be packed into its pages. But more than that, I hope it also succeeds in whetting your appetites to learn the fascinating art of truly *creative* homemaking.

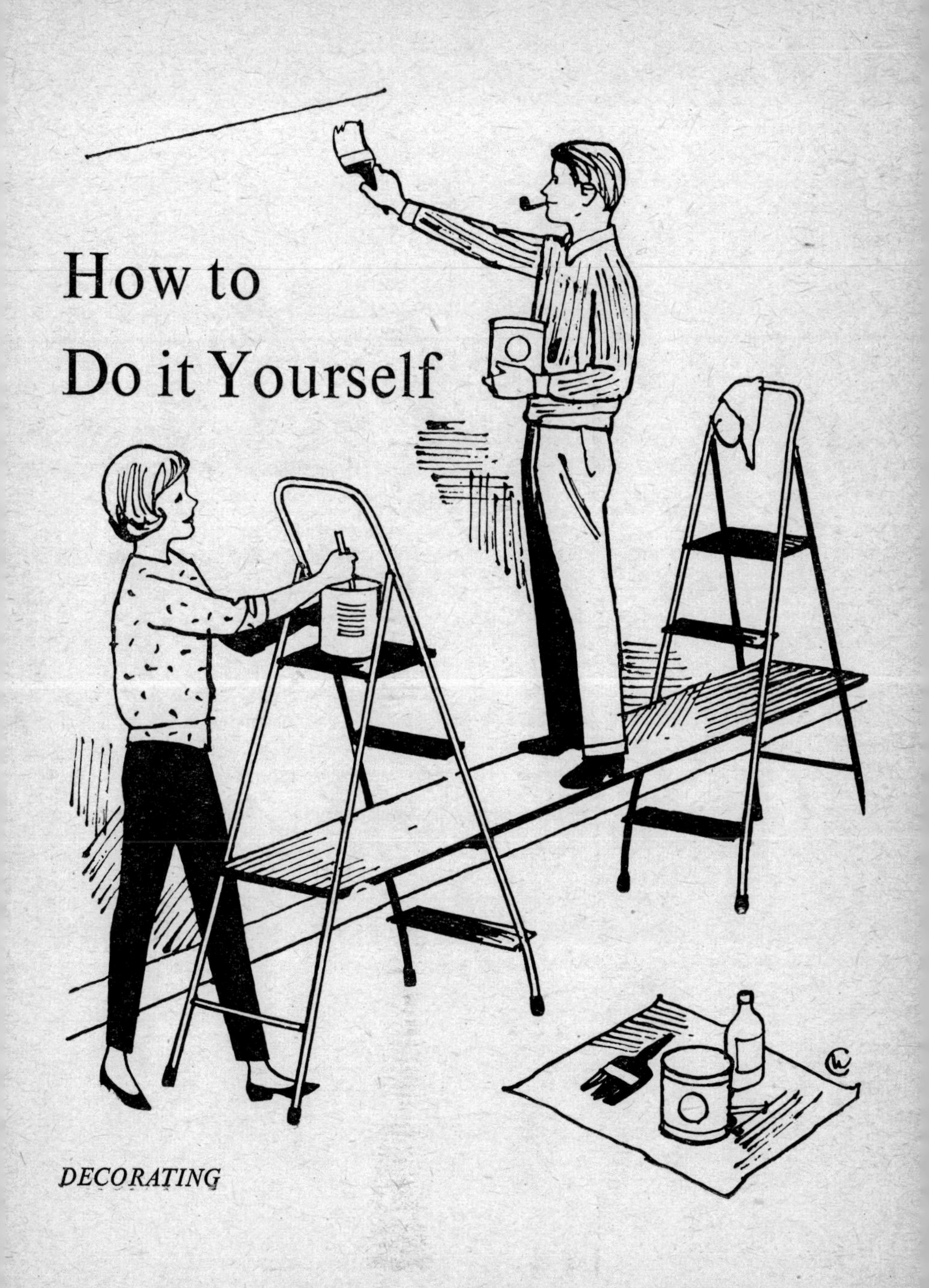
How to
Do it Yourself
DECORATING

DECORATING AND FURNISHING

WHETHER YOU are just starting your first home, or have had many, you will enjoy making it a prettier, more comfortable and pleasant place in which to live. Improving a home, especially if you do a lot of the work yourself, can be a most rewarding and at the same time economical hobby!

One of the hardest things to learn is deciding which jobs you can successfully do yourself and those which you must leave to the experts. To some extent this will depend on your own particular talents and capabilities — one person is able to tackle most jobs around the house, another is very good at one or two specialised things. Generally speaking, a plumber must be called in for anything to do with water systems, installations of baths, sink units, etc. Central heating, gas and electricity are other subjects which need the advice of trained engineers, and certain floorings have to be laid by an expert.

It is possible to go to classes, organized by local councils, on many subjects connected with the house — soft furnishing, painting and decorating and furniture making for example. If you have time, these are well worth attending for you learn a great deal while making something under expert supervision.

In this section the term 'do-it-yourself' is all-embracing and covers general advice on spending your money wisely, making your choice from various equipment on the market as well as actually making and mending things yourself.

HOUSES AND FLATS

HOME DECORATING is not just a question of painting the inside and outside of your home. Your choice also depends on where you live and the sort of property you have. Area is largely dictated by your family's needs and the proximity to office and schools, and the type of property available is in turn again dictated by the area, but if you are lucky enough to have *carte blanche* perhaps the following suggestions for dealing with various types of property will help you to make up your mind. Or, if one of the problems is *your* problem, they may help you to solve it.

The New House or Flat:

This section can be divided into two groups: the custom-built house or bungalow (i. e., one which you have built expressly for you) and the 'off-the-peg' house or flat (one which has been built by a property company and sold more or less as it stands).

If you are having your house built it is wise to employ an architect to design it for you. He will see the plans and specifications are met by the builder, and together you will be able to plan a workable house for yourself and your family. If you cannot afford architect's fees (about 8 per cent of the value of the house), choose a reliable builder, plan the house together with him, but adopt the habit of dropping in on the building site occasionally unannounced, to make sure all is going well!

An 'off-the-peg' house or flat is usually chosen by a visit to a show house or flat of similar design on the estate or in the same block. If you see this early enough, and work has not really started on the one you will be inhabiting, it is often possible to make some alterations and modifications, but these will cost you extra.

The inside walls of a new property are usually finished with distemper, as they go on 'sweating' for at least six months after plastering (although some builders hang wallpaper immediately) and the woodwork primed, undercoated and topcoated with gloss or eggshell finish paint. Certain advantages may be incorporated such as half-tiled walls in bathrooms and kitchens, central heating, some parquet floors, and thermoplastic or other tiles in the bathroom and kitchen. So perhaps you will not have to actually 'do it yourself', as far as the decorating is concerned, for some time, but you still have to make up your mind on colour schemes as well as coping with curtains, carpets and other floor coverings.

It is always wise in a new flat or house to keep the colour schemes simple until you have lived there for a year or more and have the 'feeling' of each room. Remember that small rooms seem more spacious if they are all painted one pale colour. Consider having all the woodwork painted white throughout to start with and many of the walls as well. If this sounds too stark, try bathroom walls pale pink, kitchen all pale blue or yellow, living room and hall pale grey and the bedrooms pale pink or lilac.

The advantages of a new house or flat are fairly obvious. You get a clean, pleasantly decorated home from the start, often incorporating some of the best modern equipment available. A vacuum cleaning system, for example, can now be built-in with the house. It has space for the cleaning hose to be fitted in each room, and all the dirt is sucked through to a central disposal point. You can have the best of central heating systems, some of which are only suitable for building into new houses as they, like the vacuum cleaning system, have to be built into the walls with the plumbing (*see* CENTRAL HEATING, *page 49*).

Last but not least is the monetary advantage. It is much easier to get a mortgage on a brand-new house or flat, often up to 90 per cent, and many property companies building 'off-the-peg' houses and flats are able to offer good mortgages as well. The problems are less obvious. Often the price of a new house is really astronomically high for the amount of accommodation. To get the perfect house, you really need to be almost a millionaire, otherwise you have to make a lot of compromises. You are able to make some alterations with a ready-built new house, but only minor ones, so that where you would prefer a separate dining and living room, you often have to accept a complete open-plan living-dining room, with the kitchen half open to view into the bargain. Rooms are often very small and the only way to deal with these is to build in a lot of the furniture. Fortunately many architects and builders have woken up to the fact that a house must have cupboards! Another fault with most modern houses is the large expanse of glass which keeps building costs down, and makes your heating costs go up! If it is possible these large 'picture windows' should be double-glazed. (This can be done later by the amateur, *see* WINDOWS, *page 141*), Soundproofing is another worry with a modern house, which is often quite a difficult one to overcome.

The Old House or Flat:

The term 'old' may mean that you find yourself with a Victorian horror, a Georgian gem, a country cottage of charm, a drab beige box-like flat built in the 'twenties or an average 'between-the-wars semi'. And each will have its own problems and need a slightly different approach.

Even if you can afford to re-decorate throughout before you go into the house or flat, it is still sometimes better to 'hold your horses'. Until you have lived somewhere, you cannot possibly know what alterations you will want to make. Structural alterations and amendments to the plumbing can quickly run away with the money, and ruin all the decorating you have already done. So just make your new-old house livable and go in with a few scrubbing brushes and brooms to control the dirt of years, and wait for a few months before beginning to decorate.

First think about water systems and heating (although you will not really know how much heating you require until you have spent a winter in the house). Some solidly built old houses only need some of the fireplaces taken out and replaced with slow-burning air-circulating combustion stoves, and smaller rooms and bedrooms heated with electric or oil convector heaters. Other old houses need insulating completely and central heating installed before another winter can be faced (*see* CENTRAL HEATING, *page 49*). Efficient hot water systems will largely depend on the plumbing, type of house, number of baths, basins, etc. In any case you will probably have to call in expert advice for this. Next consider electricity. Most old houses have insufficient light and power points. These should be placed after a great deal of thought so as to give maximum efficiency.

Now think of structural work, whether you intend to knock one wall down to make a large room, or build a new wall to divide up a large room. A word of warning — before knocking down any walls, make sure they are not the main load-bearing ones of the house, otherwise you will be heading for disaster! Many old houses have far too many doorways, some of them completely unnecessary, causing draughts, and some of these can be easily bricked up on one side, making a flush wall, and turned into a pleasant alcove on the room side, with shelves and cupboards built into the resulting recess. Fireplaces can be ripped out, new windows made, sometimes whole rooms added on before you get down to the actual decorating.

The *advantages* with an old house or flat are they are sometimes more soundly built than a new house; they can have a great deal of atmosphere and charm, are often surrounded by a mature garden and are in many cases cheaper than their modern counterpart. Rooms are often much more spacious, walls are soundproof and often can be furnished with a delightful mixture of secondhand furniture. The scope for alteration and decoration is often endless.

The *problems* are varied. Firstly it is often quite difficult to get an adequate mortgage on an old house so that your capital is swallowed up, leaving you with very little for repairs and alterations, and there are often essential repairs which have to be done immediately. They often need re-wiring, and old roofs and pipes have a habit of springing a leak, usually in the middle of the night! Also the installation of a new boiler often causes old pipes to crack with the new efficiency of really hot water. An old house may prove really difficult to heat, and in any case the work of renovating and repairing will be an uphill one.

Converting a House:

The term conversion can cover almost anything these days from buying an old barn and making it into a three-bedroom house to knocking a wall down to make two rooms into one! But the two major types of conversion are the modernisation of old property and the dividing of large houses into flats. Before you can attempt either you will need to get planning permission from the local council, so it is wise to make sure whether you will be able to get this before you buy the property. If there are very heavy structural alterations you will need the advice of a good builder, or you may have to bring in an architect who will provide plans for you to see and to show the authorities if necessary.

Before embarking on a conversion, think twice! Is it going to be a really practical proposition? If there is a great deal of building work to be done you will either need to be an enthusiastic do-it-yourselfer, prepared to try your hand at anything, or need to have plenty of money! First estimates on conversions are often apt to be too low, as all sorts of unseen problems can develop once a building is taken apart. Many builders are even chary about giving one and certainly confine it to an approximate estimate. If the cost of the original building, plus the cost of conversion, is going to be much more expensive than the building of a new house, you will have to think whether the advantages of position, well-weathered brickwork and general charm are really worth paying for.

Other points to take into consideration before jumping in with both feet are: is the house on main drainage (in the case of a country cottage) or will a cesspool have to be dug? Are electricity, water and gas all laid on? If the road is not made up, what sort of road charges will there be if it suddenly has to be? If converting a house into flats, make sure that it is large enough to turn into self-contained flats with adequate bathroom and kitchen facilities. Make sure too that the plumbing can be altered to give separate water heating systems for each flat. If you intend to live in the property, another point to consider is where you will live while the actual conversion work is going on, as normally it is impossible to live somewhere with the walls literally caving in around you.

The British Government does give grants to assist in the modernisation of old houses. They are intended to help put in a bathroom, lavatory, food store or hot water system if these things do not exist already. Usually they amount to one half of the cost up to a maximum of £155. There is also a system of grants for the conversion of a large house into flats and as a rule this will account for half of the total cost up to a maximum of £400 on *each* dwelling. This means that if you are converting a house into three flats with an expenditure of over £800 on each, you could receive up to £1,200. The local authority has the right to give these grants, and in the case of converted flats they can control the rent for a specific time after conversion.

THE EXTERIOR OF THE HOUSE

Choosing the Colours:

Decorating the exterior of your home not only protects the fabric of the building, it also helps to make the house look more attractive and if tastefully decorated gives a favourable first impression of the occupants, and makes the view for the passer-by much more interesting.

Choosing your colour scheme depends on the house, its position and your own personal taste. A house which is architecturally beautiful only needs a simple colour scheme to show up its natural beauty — a Georgian country-house, for example, with a plaster façade, can be painted white and the shutters and door a rich blue. Or the house could be painted pale grey, with deeper grey shutters and a coral-red front door. A small Regency cottage in town or country can be painted a warm rich pink with white shutters, window frames, eaves and door. The window frames, curved porch and door of a Queen Anne house are best painted in a neutral colour — white, pale grey, greeny-grey, to protect the wood and sharpen the mellow colour of the brickwork. Similarly the delicate tracery of a wrought-iron balcony is shown to its best advantage when it is painted black against a background of white, silver-grey or pale blue. Tudor houses look best when treated traditionally — the beams black, the walls white or left the warm mellow red of the natural brick, paintwork on window frames and gutters black or white.

Unless your house stands completely alone its colour scheme has to be considered in relation to those around it — a violent clash of colours is not very pleasant for the neighbours opposite, especially when the two houses join each other! A wise rule to follow when painting the outside is never to choose more than one strong colour, and use it in conjunction with a neutral colour such as white, black or grey. You can also use two tones of one colour (pale blue with bright blue, pale grey-green with soft leaf green, etc.) together very successfully.

It is possible to play such *'trompe l'oeil'* tricks with colour, that a badly proportioned house can be made to look quite well balanced! A stucco-fronted Victorian town house can be improved if the stucco is painted pale grey, window frames and window surrounds and pillars supporting the portico are painted white and the wrought iron is painted black, with the front door in a bold blue, mustard yellow or coral red.

A pebble dash semi-detached suburban house can look very elegant if the pebble dash is painted pale grey or white, the woodwork black and the front door a bold yellow. Alternatively the pebble dash can be painted a pale pink, the woodwork white and the front door pale grey or black.

A modern part-timbered house needs a simple colour scheme to show off the wood boarding to advantage. This, by the way, can be treated with a special preservative. Paint the window frames, eaves and pipes a neutral colour or white and paint the front door a cheerful colour.

Choosing the Paint:

Most manufacturers have special types of paint for doing outside decoration as it needs to stand up to the weather. There are special rust-proof primers for metal, cement-based colour washes for pebble dash walls, emulsion or oil paint for rendered walls and coloured washes for bricks, as well as strong enamel for woodwork. There is one special enamel which dries so quickly that the paintwork is not spoilt, even if it begins to rain when you are half way through painting a window frame.

Decorating the Outside:

You will need some basic tools before you can start decorating *(see* TOOLS, *page 86)* and in addition to the usual brushes, scrapers, etc., you will need paint kettles, a hook (to hang paint kettle on the ladder so you have one hand free to hang on with!), a blow lamp or electric paint stripper, bucket and sponges for washing down purposes, and ladders and steps. The ladder should be of the double extension type, which can be made into two ladders if necessary. Be sure to have a ladder which is long enough to reach the highest part of the house with ease, otherwise you may end up in hospital after trying to reach up those extra two inches! Also make sure that ladder or steps are placed on a firm base before mounting, and ladders should be as near vertical as possible when placed in position. A pair of 5 ft. steps should be high enough to enable you to get at all the lower parts of the house. Where the stacks are rendered or pebble dash they will need painting — to reach them you will have to make a roof ladder *(see* ROOFS, *page 126).*

Inspect the areas to be decorated for faults, and for repair where necessary, before painting. Just as when painting the inside of the house, it is the preparation which is long and laborious, but it is essential all surfaces are thoroughly prepared before painting actually begins, otherwise all your efforts are wasted.

Renew missing or loose putty in window frames, cut out and replace unsound timber in doors and frames. Fill and make good any cracks or blisters in cement rendered and pebble dash walls. Inspect metal windows for rust spots and loose putty, tighten any hinges if necessary. Wooden hinged windows may need new hinges or the screws may need renewing with slightly longer ones than originally used. Check joints in this type of window and in sash windows and tighten if necessary.

To Renew Putty:

Clean and apply a coat of primer, using a rust-proof primer on metal windows and then re-putty, using a putty knife. If there are gaps between wooden window frames and the brickwork, this should be made good *(see* WALLS, *page 132).*

Clean the inside of the gutters of all leaves and rubbish, brush with a wire brush and then give a coat of bituminous paint, being careful to keep this to the inside of the gutters only. Do not drop any on existing paintwork as this will affect it.

Brush metal drain pipes with a wire brush to clean, and apply a coat of special rust-proof primer. If you have, or can borrow, a power tool the job of cleaning rust spots from metal windows, drain pipes, etc., is a lot easier and quicker. The best attachment for this job is three different sizes of wire brush. A power tool with the proper attachments can be used to sandpaper woodwork as well.

Walls and paintwork should be thoroughly washed down to get rid of dirt and grime. If you have a badly stained wall, try the following method to remove it: Wash the wall down with a solution of spirits of salts using 1 pint of spirits of salts to 4 gallons of water. Take care not to splash this liquid on the skin as it can be very painful. After using the mixture on the wall, wash it down thoroughly with clean water until it is free of any salt deposits (a hose played on the wall is the best way to remove it).

Next rub the paintwork down with sandpaper or a pumice block. Edges of flaked areas should be 'feathered' and the areas 'filled' with undercoating. Any areas treated this way should be sandpapered again after they have dried out. If the paintwork is very bad, it will be necessary to strip completely. Either use a blow lamp, holding it 6 to 7 inches from the surface, using the tip of the flame rather than the middle, or an electric paint stripper. You can use one of the liquid paint strippers now on the market. After stripping, rub down with sandpaper, fill any holes or cracks, treat knots with shellac knotting and then apply a coat of primer. Hardwood window sills should be rubbed down, filled, then given a coat of primer.

Remove any moss growth with a scraper and wire brush and then scrub with one of the proprietary brands of fungicidal washes. On rendered walls it is not wise to use a blow lamp on these growths as the heat is liable to crack the rendering.

All this preparation must be done thoroughly before you can start on the actual job of painting. If it is possible, remove external fittings such as letter box, door knobs, etc., at this stage. Just before painting, dust off all surfaces with a dusting brush and apply the undercoat, starting at the top of the house from the gutters and working down to ground floor level. Never rely on a topcoat to cover up the previous colour, so see the undercoat is evenly applied. To do this, brush it well out as you go. It is not wise to leave an undercoat exposed to the weather for long periods, so if it is not possible to complete the whole area in a reasonable time, break the work up into sections and complete one at a time.

Allow the undercoat a reasonable time to dry out and then sandpaper with a fine grade of paper, dust off and apply the topcoat. If you decide to apply two top coats don't forget to sandpaper lightly between the application of the first and the second.

Care of Your Brushes:

Always clean your brushes after you have finished with them each time. Do not leave them in water! Hang up to dry after shaping the bristles while they are still wet — don't attempt to stand them up to dry or the bristles will go an odd shape. Wash out your paint kettle with either paraffin or white spirits. If you do let paint dry in the kettle it can be burnt out, but it will shorten its life quite considerably.

THE INTERIOR OF THE HOUSE

Colour Schemes:

Choosing a colour scheme is not only confined to wallpaper and paint! A good decorative scheme is one which accounts for walls, ceiling, woodwork, floors, curtains, furniture and accessories, causing them to blend together to create a pleasing whole. This effect may be achieved in many ways and in many styles according to the type of home and furniture, the likes and dislikes and the personalities of its owners.

Good decoration begins at home, in the room which has to be decorated, and with you and your family who have to live in it. The majority of rooms are far from perfectly proportioned, but clever use of colour, design and pattern can do a lot to help rectify this. For example, you can make a room seem larger by painting walls and woodwork all one shade, or by painting the skirting to tone with the floor covering to give an impression of a larger floor area. You can make ceilings almost disappear by using pastel tints of blue-grey or grey-green, or by painting a paler shade than the walls. In a tall room, you can make the ceiling seem lower by painting it a darker shade than the walls, or by papering it with a distinctive paper. In an attic you can lose an awkward-shaped ceiling by papering it all over to match the walls. You can lose an ugly cupboard or exposed piping by painting them the same colour or a shade lighter than the surrounding area. You can make a long narrow room seem better proportioned by papering the narrow wall with a different paper than the other walls. Or, if the window is in the narrow end, try hanging full length, dramatically designed curtains at the window, and continuing them well beyond the window area. You can make a box-like room seem much more elegant by papering or painting one wall a different shade, or by treating the alcoves on either side of the fireplace in the same way, and then adding a curved cornice where walls and ceiling join. You can make a cold north-facing room appear bright and sunny by using cheerful yellows, oranges and reds, or a hot room feel cool by using blues and greens. You can exploit and magnify every scrap of light which creeps into a basement by painting the walls a shiny white or a very pale yellow. You can make living rooms, bedrooms and workrooms restful, halls and kitchens welcoming, playrooms gay (and at the same time easy to clean with washable paints and wallpapers) and bathrooms luxurious. You can also use your decorations, carpets and curtains as a muted background for beautiful furniture, or you can create such a fabulous decor that nobody notices the furniture is composed of junkshop finds mixed in with a few modern pieces.

In fact choosing a colour scheme, whether you are starting completely from scratch, or whether you have to 'work in' existing furnishings is a great adventure. But there are so many good paint colours, well-designed and inexpensive wallpapers, floor coverings and fabrics to choose from that it is sometimes difficult to know where to start.

If you have complete *carte blanche,* it is wise to think of the style of house or flat you have and decide if you are going to use very modern decor and furnishings, period decor and furnishings, or a mixture of both. Then start looking at colours, grouping them together to see which ones mix well together. Manufacturers' paint chips often help, and you can spread these out and work out a colour scheme or two. If you can't get paint chips, try mixing scraps of ribbon together or reels of sewing cotton. Or you might get inspiration from a local dress shop window or hat department, or from the colours in a piece of fabric or a favourite dress. In fact, choosing a good colour scheme is rather like choosing clothes. For example, start with a bottle green suit, add a pale blue blouse and a blue, white and green rose print silk scarf, add a shiny black bag, a sharp accent of white gloves, pretty pinky-red lipstick and nail varnish, an emerald green brooch and a white hat for sunny days or one in a darker shade of blue than the blouse for dull days. To translate this into terms of a room scheme, the bottle green suit becomes the carpet, the pale blue becomes the walls, the blue, white and green silk scarf the curtain fabric, the white accents the woodwork and a white rug in front of the fire, the black bag one special leather chair, the pinky-red is the cushions and is perhaps echoed in a picture, and the white and blue hats are lampshades. The brooch — one precious ornament. You can see how these two types of planning are closely related to each other.

If you are not starting from scratch, and already have a predominant colour in the room, in a floor covering, a three-piece suite, a curtain fabric, a fireplace, etc., you will have to build your colour scheme round it, either attracting attention to it by playing down other colours and surfaces or detracting from it by making something else the focal point of the room. When planning a scheme remember that heavy colours such as dark blue and green, browns, dark reds, need plenty of white paint and accents to keep them light, and strong colours need to be offset with whites and neutrals. Never put too many colours in a room or the effect is terribly jazzy and unrestful. Several tones of one colour are often much more effective than all the shades of the rainbow, but even these have to be carefully highlighted with accents of a strong colour or white. Remember to look at colours in artificial light and daylight before finally making up your mind as colours change in different lights. Finally, think of the colour scheme in relation to the rest of the house. If each room is decorated in completely different colours the effect from room to room can be very 'bitty'. It gives a pleasant feeling of continuity if one colour can be carried through from room to room. It need not necessarily be on the same surface each time. For example, a terracotta wall in the dining room could be echoed in the curtains in the living room, in the floor coverings in the hall and stairs, in pots and accessories in the kitchen, and yet mixed with different colours in each room. Once you have chosen a colour scheme the next consideration is texture and pattern. You find texture in the weave of the upholstery fabric and curtains, in the carpet and other floor coverings, in stippled walls, embossed, textured and flock wallpapers, in brickwork, and in the grain of wood. Pattern is usually found in wallpapers, fabrics and floor coverings. One of the pitfalls in planning a decoration scheme is the use of too much pattern. Generally speaking there should never be more than two different patterns in one room, and then they should be used with utmost discretion and never put next to each other. For example, if the walls are all to be papered with a patterned wallpaper, the curtains and carpets should be plain with textured upholstery fabric and perhaps a few cushions with a design on them; or plain walls, patterned curtain fabric, a textured carpet and one patterned chair and all the rest plain, or a patterned floor, plain curtains, three plain walls and one patterned wall.

If you find difficulty in visualising how the finished room will actually look, ask for fairly large samples of wallpapers, fabrics, etc., and then fix them inside a shoebox in roughly the position they will occupy in the room. This will give you a three-dimensional idea of your scheme, although the difficulty lies in scaling down the designs in your mind to the proportions they will have in the rooms.

ROOM-BY-ROOM IDEAS

The Attic, Basement and Cellar:

ATTIC: In many houses there comes a time when you find there simply isn't enough space, and you have to decide whether to move or try to make an extra room. It is sometimes possible to make another 'room in the rafters' in many houses, and the attic with the addition of extra or new windows, a safe floor and new pull-down ladder (or open-tread wooden staircase) can become a very attractive new room. Sloping ceilings can add greatly to its charm and papered all over (ceiling included) with a small patterned floral paper, or *toile de Jouy*, etc., it will make a very pleasant spare bedroom or a girl's bedroom. Completely decorated as a ship's cabin, with bunk beds, lockers under the windows and a colour scheme in navy blue, white and yellow, it can be used as a bedroom or playroom for boys.

With shelf-lined walls, a desk and comfortable chairs it becomes a quiet study (especially if you can pull the ladder up behind you and work completely in peace). Fitted up with units, sewing cupboards, ironing space, Hi-fi and record storage it can become a family hobbies room or workroom. And if the best view from your house is seen through the attic windows, why not turn the attic into a sitting room? If you have a very large house it may even be possible to make the attics into a self-contained flat to let, or into a bed-sitter with cooking facilities for a grown-up daughter.

BASEMENT: The basement often already houses the kitchen, and it is usually practical to make one of the other rooms into a dining room. Sometimes this room is dark and rather airless, in which case it is practical to try to make the window a little bigger, even perhaps to make a large picture window, particularly if this can look out on to the garden. Alternatively, if the outlook is really grim, hang venetian blinds at the window with frosted glass behind. If it is very dark, you can close up the window completely (installing ventilators to give fresh air) with a hardboard panel with a blown-up picture of a pretty view. You can make a false window running the length of the wall, using reeded Perspex, lit from behind with electric light. Have rich curtains at either side (which need not necessarily pull).

Often the basement is the obvious place to have the utility room and this can be fixed up for washing, ironing, etc., and with adequate heating and lighting it can also have a workbench.

In a house without a garage, it is often possible to convert the front part of the basement to a garage, by digging away the front garden and making a sloping drive.

With a very large house, the basement can often be converted into a completely self-contained flat, making an extra room if the staircase if removed.

CELLAR: The cellar does not always provide an extra room as such because it is cold and damp, but it is very often useful for the installation of central heating, as there is plenty of storage space. It is also possible to turn the cellar into a neatly equipped laundry, especially if you are lucky enough to have an automatic washing machine and dryer. It can also be fitted up with a carpenter's bench and used as a workroom, or if your hobby is photography or ciné filming, you can turn it into a photographer's darkroom and film-cutting room. Sometimes it can be used as an extension to the pantry, and with slatted shelves you can store apples, tomatoes, preserves, etc. Or why not use the cellar as a cellar and take up making home-made wine as a hobby? Also the cellar can be a very unusual and amusing place to have a party!

THE BATHROOM

IT IS SAID on the Continent that the Englishman lies in his bath for hours, but seldom washes himself! Whether this is true or not, anyone who enjoys soaking in a bath likes to do so in pretty and comfortable surroundings.

If you have bought an old house without a bathroom there are Government grants to help you install one (*see* CONVERTING A HOUSE, *page 14*) and to help you install a water system, if there isn't one already, to provide that stream of constant hot water!

It is the final luxury touches which give a bathroom its personality. You can give it an Eastern touch with a woven straw Ali Baba linen basket and tall minaret-shaped bottles, or a fluffy feminine look with pretty cosmetic bottles, flowery towels and a pair of bathroom scales upholstered with nylon fur. You could even go as far as installing radio and television, and for business executives there is always the telephone!

Colour Schemes:

When it comes to decorating the bathroom, don't make it too clinical. If you want to have ceramic tiles, which are very practical, try putting one or two pretty flower-designed ones in at random amongst tiles of a plain soft colour, or let in a panel of boldly designed ones behind the bath. Tiles provide a durable easy-to-clean damp-proof surface, but you can also use one of the laminated plastics in a soft glowing colour or pretty design on your bathroom walls, fixed on battens plugged to the wall. Or use one of the self-adhesive plastics or a washable wallpaper or a vinyl wall covering which you stick on like wallpaper, using a special solution. If condensation is your problem use a matt, flat or eggshell finish paint specially recommended for steamy atmospheres, or brush with a special anticondensation compound before covering with its own special paint. You can even stick marble-effect vinyl tiles to the bathroom wall as well as the floor.

You can make a small bathroom look larger by using mirrors on the walls and sometimes this can be very effective, but they are not very practical in a very condensation-prone room as they tend to aggravate the condition. One way of helping to beat the condensation problem is by having an adequately heated bathroom, as this is usually half the cause; hot steam coming into contact with cold bathroom walls quickly settles as a mist on the cold surface and then starts to run down. *(For more details see* VENTILATION, *page 131.)*

The colour scheme for your bathroom will depend on many things: the colour of your bath and basin, your own personal tastes, the rest of the house, etc., but remember you have to look at yourself in the bathroom mirror first thing in the morning! The warmer colours of the spectrum are kinder than the cold ones, and tend to look less clinical. A cold-looking bathroom can be brightened very quickly with a coloured ceiling, or a pretty papered one (after all, you look at the ceiling when you are lying in the bath), and gay towels and curtains which tone in with its colours.

Conversion – the Bathroom-Laundry:

In some houses, particularly old converted ones where a bedroom has been made into a bathroom, the bathroom is very large. If you are limited for space in your kitchen, you can always make the bathroom do double duty as a laundry — in fact in some modern houses bathrooms are being designed to be dual-purpose. If you have space you can build a counter all along one wall to take washing machine and spin-drier under it, using the shelf for talc, bath salts, etc., and building in the handbasin at the end.

Baths:

Once you have the hot water the most important thing in the bathroom is the bath. If you are installing a new one you will have difficulty in choosing, for there are so many to choose from to suit all types of bathroom and all pockets. You can have a long low bath reminiscent of Roman times, about seven feet long with three control buttons on the side for hot, cold or warm which brings water of the right temperature gushing in from a tap at the other end of the bath; you can have baths with stainless steel safety handles for elderly people and children, baths with built-in showers, baths with taps on the corner for a home where the plumbing is difficult and space is limited, and for really small homes a tiny triangular sunken bath or a ship's bath with a 'step' in it so you bath in a sitting position! And the colour selection is even bigger — delicious pale turquoise or powder blue, soft lilac, deep rose, dove grey, citron yellow, deep aubergine or even black. And these coloured baths with matching handbasins, lavatories, etc., cost very little more than the standard white.

Handbasins:

Handbasins are now so well designed that they are a joy to clean. No longer are there any corners to trap dirt and soap and the pedestal is long and slim. Some handbasins now have a large flat area on either side which provides ample space for tooth mugs, talc, bath oil, etc., and does away with the need for a bathroom shelf. If you are lucky enough to have a large bathroom it is worth thinking about having two handbasins, which will certainly ease congestion in the bathroom in the morning. Or if you have several children you can buy a low child-sized basin especially for them. If you want a really glamorous handbasin you can buy one with roses or bunches of flowers or birds on it, and one Italian designer even made a bath and basin with a swarm of butterflies on the bottom.

Showers:

If you feel like indulging in the luxury of a shower you can have one built above the bath, and protect the rest of the room from splashes with a reeded glass panel mounted on stainless steel, or more simply by a plastic shower curtain. Or you can have a separate compartment for the shower glassed in with plain, decorated or frosted glass, with tiled walls and floor, or mosaic or plastic. Alternatively the shower can be a separate little room.

Medicine Cabinets:

In most homes the medicine cabinet lives in the bathroom and also houses shaving equipment and has a mirrored door. Medicine cupboards should all have locks, especially in a home where there are children, and all poisons, pills, etc., should be locked safely away. For this reason it is not very practical to have a double-duty medicine cupboard — much better to have a small cupboard in the bathroom with a mirror for a door which pulls out on a hinge to almost any angle, and the shelves inside to hold bathroom equipment. The medicine can then be kept safely elsewhere.

Lighting:

Lighting in the bathroom to be really ideal should be of two types: a soft fluorescent glowing through a glass panel in the ceiling and a good light over the handbasin for shaving and making-up. Ideally the light switch should be outside the door, or certainly nowhere near the bath or basin, so you are not tempted to switch on or off with wet hands.

Heating:

If you are lucky enough to have the hot water storage tank in the bathroom you will either have, or be able to make, a heated linen cupboard. Alternatively you can create one by fitting a special electrical element into a cupboard. If there is no space you can have a heated towel rail either by running it off the hot water supply or buying an oil-filled radiator with a towel rail above it which works off the electricity, or by buying an electrically heated towel rail. These will all help to heat the bathroom too. If you don't have central heating, nor the hot tank in the bathroom, much the safest form of bathroom heater is the infra-red type which fixes high on the wall and has a covered element, but again take care not to switch on or off with wet hands.

THE BEDROOM

EVEN THOUGH it is mentioned in the furniture buying section, it is well worth repeating here: don't economise by buying a cheap bed, even if it means keeping your clothes in a suitcase for the time being! After all, you spend about one-third of your life in bed, so it may just as well be in comfort! A bed should not be too soft, but neither should it be too rigid, and the only way to buy one is to go and test all the beds in the showroom until you find one that suits you. If you are a very different weight from your husband, or you like a hard mattress and he prefers to sink into a soft one, there are two possible answers. One is to buy twin beds, the other to have one base and two mattresses which are joined together down the centre by a special zip-fastener construction. Whether you choose a bed each, or a communal one, remember a 4 ft. 6 in. is the smallest for mutual comfort — a 5 ft. is much better. You can have much wider ones, or go in for a film-star glamour with a circular or oval bed, but these will need special linen, blankets and quilts to fit. Twin beds should be 3 ft. 6 in. wide for adult comfort, and they can be joined by one long headboard if you like a more streamlined look. If one of you is over 6 ft. tall you may find the average 6 ft. 2 in. bed too short, but longer ones can be ordered.

Although the bed is perhaps the most important and expensive item in the room it should never be allowed to look too important, for it is seldom a very lovely piece of furniture! Tailored covers in a simple muted or pastel fabric, a delicate wrought-iron headboard set off with a pretty throw-over bedcover or a washable Terylene quilted cover will all give a luxurious look and at the same time help to make the bed less obvious.

The bedroom has always been acknowledged as the woman's province, so you can have a frankly feminine decor in the bedroom in an otherwise spartanly simple house, but a word of warning: remember that your husband shares the room with you, so if he does not look right in a rosy bower you will have to compromise!

If you want a pretty paper but not too much pattern, try putting it on the wall behind the bed only, and painting the other walls a pastel colour. If you haven't a headboard, remember to make it a washable paper. Before you choose the colour scheme think how it will look, and how you will look against it, first thing in the morning! An acid yellow may look bright and stimulating in the kitchen, but seen first thing on a winter's morning when you have a cold, it is not quite so suitable. Why not try pale lilac, deep green and soft terracotta sparked with white for an unusual scheme, or navy blue, cinnamon and white highlighted with a strong clear pink?

Wardrobes are perhaps the ugliest piece of furniture designed by man, and so the bedroom is the ideal place for built-in cupboards. You can design these yourself, and organise them as you really want. They can be painted or papered to match the rest of the room, and so become unobtrusive. You can even plan the room so well that the cupboards form an alcove for the bed, or place them on either side of a bay window and have a built-in dressing table unit linking them. In a very large room you can even make a separate dressing-room by backing the cupboards on to the head of the bed to make a completely false wall screening off the space required and decorating the backs with wallpaper or paint.

If you live in a rented flat and don't want to actually have cupboards built in you can buy fitted wardrobes built on the modular system (which means that they can be had to fit practically any area) and which you can take away with you when you move. Alternatively you can have the cupboards made so that they can be taken away.

If you are planning to have a handbasin installed or are thinking of renewing an existing one, take a look at some of the vanitory units which are available. These do double duty as dressing table and handbasin, with drawer space at the side, room for a stool underneath and a flat top which comes down over the basin when not in use.

When planning bedroom lighting remember to have a good light to make up by, either on or near the dressing table. You may need supplementary lighting which can be provided by a central light or by wall lights, and you will need two bedside lamps which can be turned off from the bed. If you are having deep cupboards it is nice to have these lit inside too.

Heating in a bedroom is an essential, for there is nothing worse than dressing or undressing in extreme cold. If you are not lucky enough to have central heating choose some form of 'instant' heat such as an electric convector or fan heater or a gas fire, but make sure this is adequately guarded and never place a mirror over a fire, particularly in a bedroom where the hem of a dress or nightdress might catch fire while you look in the mirror.

THE DINING ROOM

THE DINING ROOM should be as near to the kitchen as possible and if you can have a hatchway through with a serving table or sideboard underneath it so much the better. Even more desirable are a set of through-drawers and through-cupboards below the serving counter, which allows you to wash up the silver, plates, etc., put them in the drawer on the kitchen side and have them all ready to be taken out on the dining room side when next needed for the table.

The basic furniture for a dining room is a good table and chairs and it is wise to have a table which is really big enough — either one which extends or one which will seat at least six people. Eighteen to twenty inches is the minimum width for a place setting if you want to measure the top of a table before buying, but remember also to look at the legs and make sure that the appropriate number of chairs will go along the sides. If you are buying matching chairs and table the manufacturer will have seen that chair heights and widths are correct for his particular table. However, if you are buying a table from one place and a set of chairs from another, see that there is at least a four- to six-inch clearance for your knees when you are sitting at the table.

Colour schemes for a dining room can be bright and gay or as restful as you wish and flooring should be practical, particularly where there are several crumb-dropping children! Choose a textured or slightly patterned carpet or one of the easy-to-clean durable floorings or mattings.

The dining table should be well but not harshly lit. A central light on a 'rise and fall' fitting which brings it down lower over the table when you are eating is a good idea, but this does limit the position of the dining table. Wall lights make good supplementary lighting and are best placed on the same wall as the hatch or sideboard, so you can see when you are serving the food.

The dining room can do double duty as a hobbies room, study or spare room if it is large enough and you need extra space. For instance, if there are children with homework to do they can use the dining table or have their own desks permanently situated in the dining room. Wall bookshelves can be at hand, with works of reference which they might need. There may also be space to build cupboards on either side of the chimney breast to hold record player and records, or dressmaking equipment or other hobbies. And if the dining room is to double as a spare room, it can be fitted up with a comfortable studio couch with sofa tables at each end which become bedside tables, and two simple matching chests, one to take visitors' clothes, the other to hold silver and linen.

Heating the dining room can be done in a variety of ways, by a slow burning solid fuel combustion stove (which you can keep in for days on end), by an electric fire, an open fire, a convector heater, a gas fire, etc. If the room is used a lot it is probably wiser to choose a stove or some form of solid fuel fire, but if it is only used for meals some form of 'instant' heat is more practical.

THE HALL

AS SOON AS you open the front door the visitor gets an immediate impression of the whole house and your personal tastes, so the hall should echo the decorations of the rest of the house and at the same time look warm and inviting. In winter this warmth should be a reality, so if you don't have central heating, place an electric convector, oil heater or some other form of heater in the hall (this helps to warm the whole house).

The hall is a place for coming and going, a place for leaving coats and wet umbrellas, somewhere for a last check on appearances before leaving the house. The floor should have a hard-wearing surface or a really good quality carpet, protected from muddy shoes by a good doormat just inside the door. The basic minimum of hall furniture should be a hall table of some sort with a drawer for clothes brushes, etc., a mirror, an overhead general light which can be easily switched on and off from just inside the door. An umbrella stand with a drip tray is another useful thing to have. Coats and hats hanging limply from pegs or a rack are not exactly a decorative asset! If you haven't space for a cloak cupboard under the stairs (which, by the way, will need good lighting, as this is the darkest corner in the whole house), have either a built-in or free-standing clothes cupboard. If there really isn't room for this, have a decorative rack for visitors' coats and insist the family keep theirs in their wardrobes!

If you have a telephone in the hall, see there is proper space for it together with a place for directories, pad and pencil. It is very pleasant to have a proper space-saving built-in bench.

If the stairs can be seen from the front door, the stair carpet should either be the same as the hall carpet or tone well with the hall floor. Similar light fittings to the central hall also help to add a feeling of continuity. If there is a stair window at the top or halfway up the stairs the curtain fabric for this should be thought of in relation to the carpet because, viewed from the front door, this curtain can look almost like an extension to the carpet.

The wall at the side of the stairs is subjected to a great deal of friction, particularly in a house where there are children, so if there is a dado, paint this with a washable gloss paint, otherwise it is advisable to have washable painted walls or a washable wallpaper. Ordinary wallpaper can be given a special cellulose coating which is put on with a brush and makes the surface dirt-repellent and washable.

The walls of a hall can be plain and used to show off a collection of paintings, two of which can be hung in the hall and the others 'stepped' up the staircase wall. This allows for a textured or discreetly patterned carpet. Alternatively the walls can be papered in a style in keeping with the house, and the floor coverings kept simple. If the hall looks like a long narrow corridor, a pretty curved arch can be built about halfway along and painted a contrasting colour. This breaks the apparent distance and gives a 'picture' effect to the rest of the hall. Another way of breaking up a large hall is by painting all the doors different colours, but this should only be attempted where there is plenty of space and the walls should be painted a neutral shade or white.

THE KITCHEN

Kitchen Planning:

A. For a long narrow kitchen
B. For a kitchen with doors at both ends
C. For a small square kitchen

Kitchen Planning and Decorating:

The kitchen is undoubtedly the most important and most used room in the house. A small kitchen in a town flat can become just as friendly and just as much a hub for the whole household as a large country kitchen.

If you are going into a completely new house you will have the advantages of modern kitchen equipment backed by modern kitchen planning, but if you have to convert an existing kitchen you will have to face the fact that it will be a fairly costly business even if you buy the most inexpensive units or even build them yourself. The golden rule when converting is to do all the structural alterations first, and plan the ideal kitchen from the start; buy the essentials first and add the rest of the pieces as you can afford them. It is no good, however, adding equipment piecemeal without completely overhauling the kitchen at the beginning and coping with moving sinks, boilers, dealing with water systems, etc.

The easiest way to replan a kitchen is on paper! Draw a plan by marking a large sheet of paper accurately into half-inch squares, ruling the lines lightly in pencil. Measure the kitchen accurately, and using a scale of half an inch to a foot, make a floor plan on the squared paper, marking windows, doors, etc.

Next decide on the essential equipment you need — which you will be keeping, which you will be renewing, etc., trying to divide the kitchen into areas so that you are able to follow a work sequence with the minimum of effort when cooking. In food preparation the most moves take place between the sink, cooker and work surface, so the most practical sequence is to have the food store (larder and refrigerator) next to a work surface with cupboards above to hold things you need when preparing food (salt, spices, herbs, flour, etc.) then the stove with another surface on the other side and the sink not too far away! Because pans have to be put down beside the cooker it is wise to have these surfaces in a heatproof laminated plastic. (For three simple kitchen layouts, see diagram.) Ideally the cooker should be a split-level one with a hob set into the work surface with space for food preparation on either side and an oven placed at *the correct working height for you.* There should also be a large enough work surface to serve up a main meal, and in many cases it is practical to make this a fairly big kitchen table

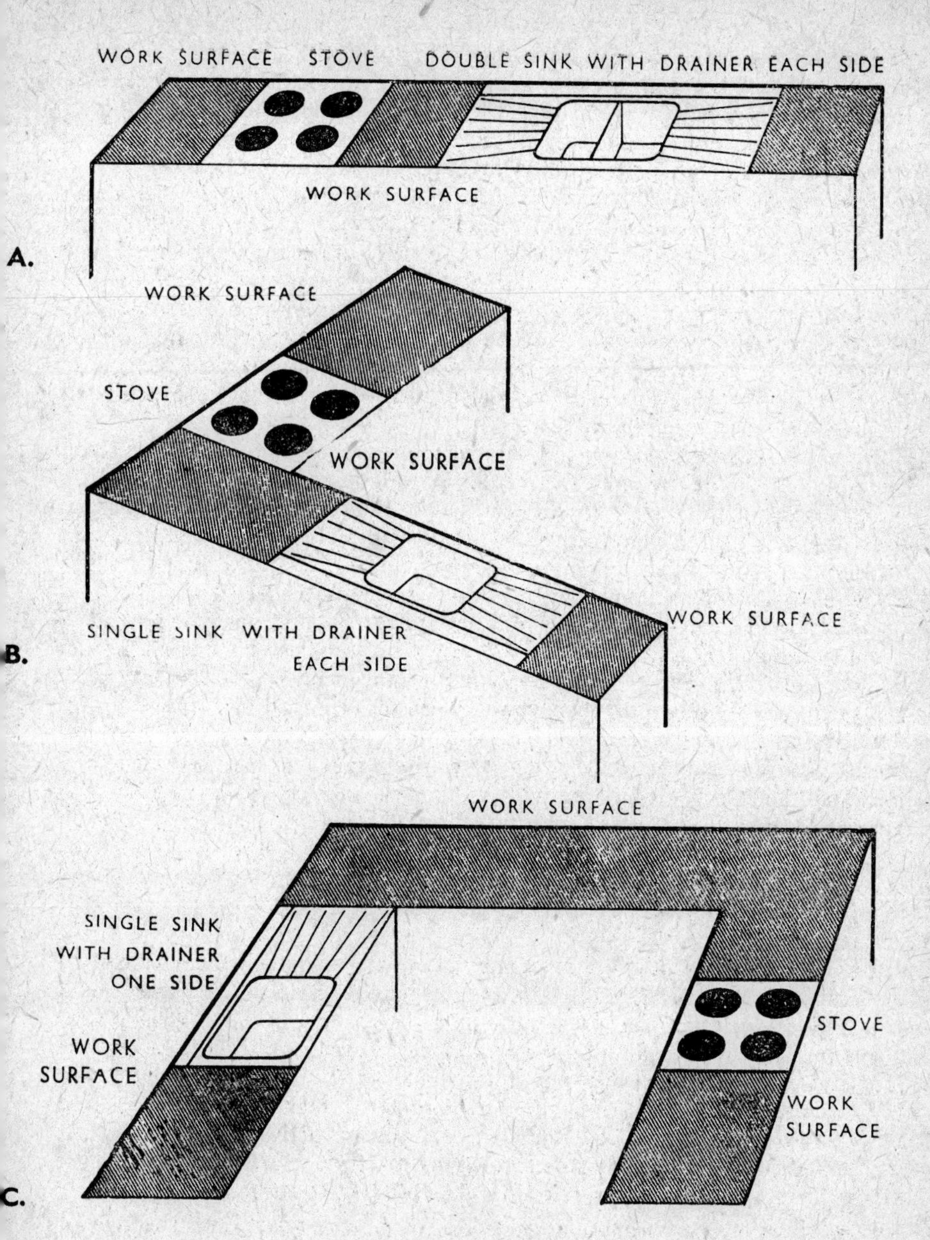

Fig. 1 Kitchen Planning

which can also be used for occasional family meals. This surface should also be as near the dining room as possible to avoid unnecessary walking, and if there is a hatchway through to the dining room there should be an adequate work surface beneath it on the kitchen side. (Ideally, through drawers and cupboards should link the dining room and kitchen.)

Cooking utensils should be stored near to the sink and cooker, either above or below the central work surface, beneath the oven section of a split-level cooker, or in cupboards at the side of the sink. Small implements are best kept in a drawer beneath the main food-preparation surface or hanging on pegboard behind. Storage or place for a chopping board should also be provided as knives should not be used directly on a laminated plastic surface. Place for refuse should be as near to the sink as possible, either in the form of a built-in waste disposal or a bin in an adequately ventilated cupboard directly beneath the sink.

Once you have decided on the sequence you are going to follow and you have looked at kitchen units and made up your mind which ones you want (more about these later) you will need to get their exact measurements and draw them in ground plan to the same scale as the kitchen, cut out, together with plan-to-scale of the cooker, boiler, refrigerator, etc., and try them for size on your squared kitchen plan. You will probably have to compromise on the perfect ideal and have a different unit from the one you intended, or move the cooker a little to the right or left, or you may find you have to fill a few inches. This can be done by asking for a unit with an overhanging work top to the required length, then you can use the space so formed as storage for trays, as drying space for tea towels on a pull-out rack, or you may have room to store a trolley or the fridge or washing machine beneath. Generally speaking the number of household appliances increases in the home with the years, and whether you intend to get a dishwashing machine or washing machine immediately or not, they will need to be fairly near or next to the sink. When planning ahead it is often worth leaving a space beside the sink for later inclusion, while carrying the work surface along as previously described.

If the kitchen is large enough it is marvellous to be able to make a completely separate laundry or 'utility' section. It needs to be near the back door if you are going to hang the washing out in the garden, but at the same time needs to be near the plumbing as some types of washing machine have to be plumbed in. It is sometimes possible to achieve this by installing the sink in an island unit which divides the kitchen in two, making an area for food preparation on one side and an area for laundry activities on the other. If the kitchen is too small to take a washing machine you may be able to use the bathroom as a laundry *(see* THE BATHROOM, *page 22)*.

In a house with few cupboards it is often necessary to have storage for brooms, mops and other cleaning equipment in the kitchen. Much the most practical is a tall broom cupboard situated as near to the door to the rest of the house as possible, with adequate hanging space, and a smaller cupboard above to hold polishes, etc.

Decorating the Kitchen:

You have to spend a great deal of time in the kitchen, so it should be bright and cheerful, at the same time practical and not too jazzy, yet should never appear too clinical. First choose the colour for your units, remembering that they will be with you for a long time! You can have them all the same colour, or have some different coloured doors, or the drawers can be done in one colour and the doors another. Pale grey doors with lemon yellow drawers, light blue drawers with dark blue doors, white drawers with natural wood doors, all pale grey with just one scarlet door — the colour schemes are endless! Next, choose the colour for the work tops, and remember that a gay pattern looks exciting in a pattern swatch, but you quickly get tired of it when you look at it day in, day out, on your units. Also it can cause eyestrain if it is too hectic a design! It is best to choose one of the slightly textured-effect laminates, or one with a shadow check, or a plain colour (but plain white and plain black are not very practical as they show every mark) in a shade to look well with the unit drawers and doors. Next choose your floorings, and the same thing applies to the kitchen floor as it does to the unit tops: too jazzy a floor quickly becomes boring, and too plain a floor shows every mark. A marbled effect floor, or a two-colour check effect with tiles or a slightly harlequin floor with small irregular splashes of colour are the most successful.

The wall colours and the curtain or blind colours are best left till last, for these are the things you will be renewing more often. Walls can be painted, papered with washable paper, panelled with tongued and grooved boarding, tiled, faced with laminated plastic, covered with a self-adhesive plastic or a vinyl wall covering, etc. Whatever you decide to do, it is most sensible to have some form of easily washable surface as a splash-back to the food preparation units, sink and cooker. Tiles or a sheet of laminated plastic or a width of self-adhesive plastic are among the things you can use for this.

Furnishing the Kitchen:

UNITS: It is possible to get units in almost any colour, with various tops and in a wide range of prices. Generally speaking the choice lies between metal and wood — the metal is usually finished with enamel; the wood can be varnished, or waxed to give a natural wood look, painted or sprayed with a special polyester finish in various colours. Usually the tops are of laminated plastic for work surfaces, and you can order one long top with a series of units beneath to give an unbroken line. Sinks and drainers are of stainless steel, enamel, porcelain (with perhaps teak drainers) or fibreglass. The base units are either 21 in. or 18 in. deep, and can have all sorts of fittings including built-in sliding vegetable racks, revolving shelves in corner units, baize-lined cutlery drawers, swing-out pedal bins, adjustable shelves for baking tins, built-in bread bins, bottle storage, built-in plate racks, and one firm even makes an ironing board which stows neatly away under the laminated plastic top of the unit and swings out easily when needed. There are also base units of the peninsular type which can divide a large kitchen, with cupboards above supported by a special rail, to make a separate dining or breakfast area. You will need to select your units to suit your kitchen and the particular needs of your family.

COOKERS: Solid fuel cookers which usually heat the water as well, are wonderfully comforting in the winter and ensure a warm kitchen at all times. They are very economical to run as they do two or three jobs at the same time, and once you have understood their workings, they are very easy to control. There are several ovens of different temperatures and there is always plenty of cooking space. They are particularly suitable for a large country house kitchen where there is a big family. In hot weather they can be a little stifling, so it is nice to be able to have some form of supplementary gas or electric cooker which can be used in the summer.

GAS COOKERS: These are becoming more automatic all the time! The 'traditional' free-standing type of gas cooker now has a pilot light so the burners light automatically, many are fitted with an automatic timing device so the meals can switch themselves on at the right time while you are out. High-level grills and barbecue spits are built into some cookers, and special space-saving ovens have a shelf on the inside of the door for easy basting. Gas cookers can be split-level, and one cooker has a spacious waist-level oven with interior lights and a glass door so that you can see what's cooking. Fitments include a built-in *rôtisserie* and a roasting thermometer which 'buzzes' when the joint is cooked! The counter-top hotplate is fitted with centre-simmer burners and a thermostatically controlled burner (For *gas cooker maintenance*, *see* GAS, *page 114*.).

ELECTRIC COOKERS: There is a wide choice of electric cookers on the market. Many have automatic timers, *rôtisserie* grills and inner glass doors, special lift-up hobs for easy cleaning. Some have simmerstats with a special quick response, and it is possible to cook at two different speeds on the top of the stove. Many electric cookers are available as split-level, with waist high ovens, some with glass doors and automatic shelf-raising and lowering, and a cooking top to let into the work surface. One star electric cooker has a slide-away cooking top, two ovens above the cooking top with glass doors, controls at eye level, and a grill and *rôtisserie,* and pan storage beneath. *(For care of electric cookers, see* ELECTRICITY, *page 101.)*

OTHER AIDS TO COOKERY: Apart from the cooker, kitchen implements are becoming more automatic. Food mixers take much of the drudgery out of food preparation. A large one will mix, beat, whisk and knead with the attachments which are supplied with it. You can add others as necessary and these include a liquidiser, mincer, potato peeler, slicer and shredder, can opener, bean slicer and pea huller, juice extractor, sausage filler, colander and sieve, and a coffee mill. Food mixers can be free-standing, or you can have them built in to the work top used for food preparation. Both types are ideal for a large family or for someone who does a lot of cooking, but for a smaller family the hand-sized ones are very helpful and practical.

Another important item which can be built into the food preparation work surface is the kitchen scale, and the weight is read on a dial inserted into the work top.

VENTILATING THE KITCHEN: When you are cooking, steam and fumes are a constant problem. Adequate heating and open windows do help to reduce condensation, but most kitchens need some auxiliary form of ventilation. A kitchen canopy fitted over the cooker extracts steam and cooking smells, but to ventilate the whole kitchen you need some form of electric extractor fan *(see* VENTILATION, *page 131).*

WASTE DISPOSAL: If you live in a flat at the top of a block and it's a long trip to the dustbin, or the dustman only calls at the house once a week, you may already have, or want to have, a built-in waste disposal unit. These machines take up no floor-space and occupy little more room than the normal trap under the sink — in fact they become an integral part of the sink unit. From the top of the sink the waste disposal unit looks slightly larger than the normal sink waste. Shells, peel, fat and grease, left-overs of all kinds including small bones, are scraped in, the cold water allowed to run and the electricity switched on. All the rubbish is ground to a pulp and flushed away automatically, leaving the machine itself quite clean.

REFRIGERATORS: There are three basic types of refrigerator available:
1. The absorption type, which is silent in operation, can be either gas or electric and does not reach such a low temperature as the other two kinds, so frozen food cannot be stored in it for too long. Small compact refrigerators are often of this type, including ones which work on bottled gas, so even if you live in a caravan or a boat without electricity or mains gas you can still keep your food fresh.
2. The compressor type which does make a noise as it switches itself on and which can reach a colder temperature. This type runs on electricity and

sometimes has its own built-in deep-freeze cabinet at the top which can store frozen food.

3. The last type also works on the compressor system on electricity and is solely a deep freeze. This is ideal if you have a large garden with gluts of fruit and vegetables during the summer, because you can bring them from the garden, clean, trim and freeze them, and keep for months in your deep freeze, and you can also freeze meat, chickens, fish, etc.

Nowadays most refrigerators are fitted with very practical accessories such as door-racks for eggs and bottles, compartments for butter, special crisper drawers for salads, etc. They are sold by size as well as by type, so you will need to decide the right capacity for your family. It is best to calculate one cubic foot per person and one extra (i.e., a family of three need 3.5 to 4 cu. ft. capacity) and it is often wise when buying a refrigerator to think ahead and buy one slightly bigger than you need at the moment.

Not all fridges have a clinical look now. Some are sophisticated black with champagne coloured linings, some are bright scarlet, and you can-even have one with a simulation-wood exterior which looks exactly like a cocktail cabinet and is intended to go in the living room! Many of the plain white refrigerators have an extra coloured worktop.

WASHING MACHINES: There are three different ways of washing in a machine: by tumbling method which revolves the clothes in a drum and is most efficient for cleaning heavily soiled clothes and whites, by agitator which moves the clothes gently and does not tangle them, and the turbulator system which gets good washing results fast. Then there are four basic types of machine:

1. A washing machine with automatic wringer.
2. A twin-tub machine which has a tub for washing and a tub for spin drying (clothes have to be moved from one tub to the other).
3. A semi-automatic machine which washes and part-dries in the same compartment.
4. A fully-automatic machine which you set to a particular washing programme to suit the fabric to be washed and which heats, washes, rinses and spin dries.

Some machines have to be filled with hot water, others heat their own water and some even boil the water. Automatic machines nearly always have to be plumbed in for the best results and most of the other machines are easily movable on castors and are connected to the water with hose pipes. There is one luxury automatic washing machine which washes, rinses and dries all in the same compartment.

DISH WASHERS: Dish washers are now available in a variety of types and sizes. Some are free-standing, and are attached to the taps with a flexible hose and usually stand on the draining board, others can be plumbed in next to the sink and are usually loaded from the top, others sit under a work-surface and are front-loaded. They wash, rinse, in some cases polish, with a special liquid which filters in at the rinsing stage, and heat dry.

THE LIVING OR LIVING-DINING ROOM

THE LIVING ROOM or sitting room is becoming a much more comfortable place these days. It is warmer, cosier and above all it is used by the family instead of being shut up and only opened when visitors call! The living room should be prettily decorated and furnished in whatever style you prefer, but it should not be too elegant and so full of fragile pieces of furniture and ornaments that you are not able to *live* in it!

It will probably be the room where you watch television, so see there are some comfortable chairs or a settee opposite the television set and far enough away to avoid eye strain. There should be a light situated behind and slightly to one side of the set which should be left on when you are all viewing. The chairs for you and your husband should be chosen separately with yourselves in mind, and they should not be bought till you have both tried them and decided they suit you perfectly.

The floor of the living room takes hard wear, so have the best carpet you can afford or one of the permanent floorings softened with rugs. If you have a carpet, remember to protect the area in front of the fire, and in front of the chairs used to watch television, with an extra rug, as these are the places which get most wear from the feet.

Your living room should be warm, so if it is fairly large, and you don't have central heating but rely on an open fire, see there is some form of background heating during the very cold winter months.

Lighting should not be too harsh; there should be several lamps for working and reading and a standard lamp to provide portable light, and wall lights. Usually an overhead light is too glaring in a living room.

As the living-dining room plays such an important part these days, particularly in smaller houses and flats, it is best to decide first of all whether you want to treat it as one big room or cut it up into two different areas. If the room is fairly small it is probably better to treat the whole room as a sitting room, with a sideboard along one wall and a folding or drop-leaf dining table. If, however, the room is fairly large, or better still L-shaped, you will be able to divide it into areas very successfully.

Even if you do divide into areas, you should aim to keep some feeling of continuity between the two halves. It is best to have the same curtains at each end, and perhaps the same wallpaper or paint on the long wall which is common to the two areas. The shorter wall in the dining end can be papered with a more obviously dining-room paper if you like. The floor coverings can contrast, although blending or toning colours look more pleasant. Wood, lino, vinyl or thermoplastic floorings look well and are more practical in the dining end, with a fitted carpet in the living section.

A room divider is often a useful way of breaking the two areas. You can use a sideboard facing inwards to the eating section, and if it does not have a presentable back you can paper it or place the settee in front of it in the living section. You can have open shelves on struts above, filled with books, ornaments and plants to give more of a screen. It is possible to buy special room dividers, or to make one, specially for this purpose. Some have sliding glass doors on both sides. You can also screen off the eating section with filmy curtains, heavy curtains, folding doors, horizontal or vertical venetian blinds.

Heating this sort of room may present a problem, as any open fire will certainly be in the sitting-room section. Provide supplementary heating in the form of electric convector or fan heaters, gas fire, radiators, etc., in the dining end to keep the family warm at meal times.

The dining table will need to be lit with a good light on a rise and fall fitting, and two wall lights above the sideboard will help to make food serving easier. The lights in the rest of the room can be more subdued, but choose the fittings in relation to each other, for they are all in the same room! The same comment applies to the furniture — it is best not to mix styles and woods too much when you have one living-dining room even if it is separated into two distinct areas.

THE NURSERY AND PLAYROOM

THE MOST IMPORTANT thing to remember when planning a room for a child is that it must grow with the child. The floor should be warm and durable, the walls washable, the furniture strongly made and, if it is to be painted, make sure that the paint is a safe lead-free one. There should be adequate centre and wall lighting for young children (table lamps come later when hands no longer grab everything in sight) and heating of a completely *safe* kind. If you do not have central heating, the very best type of heater for a child's room is one of the electric infra-red type fixed high upon the wall well out of reach (remember that children stand on chairs to touch forbidden objects) or alternatively one of the small heaters which blows out hot air in winter, cool air in summer, which can also be fixed high on the wall. *NEVER, NEVER* heat a child's room with an oil heater, and only have a gas fire if it is adequately guarded and you are sure that the child can't turn on the gas tap (special safety taps can be fitted).

If the room has to double as a playroom try to arrange it so that the playing and sleeping areas are kept separate. Have the same flooring throughout (cork, lino or lino tiles or one of the vinyls) with a washable rug beside the cot or bed; the chest of drawers and a small wardrobe with adjustable hanging length can make up the sleeping section. Low shelves or a cupboard or toy box for the toys, a low adjustable table (which also grows with the child) and matching chairs make up the playing section, and if it is possible paint the wall or a part of it with blackboard paint so that the child can try his hand at drawing. For older children, a felt panel on the wall is a great success to use as a notice board or to pin favourite pictures on.

Children like clear bright colours around them and bold designs, but if you choose too obviously 'nursery' fabrics and wallpapers, the child quickly outgrows them. Walls are best painted with washable paint, with perhaps one wall papered with a washable paper, or one which has been specially treated to give it a washable dirt-repellent surface (this can be done by applying a transparent adhesive plastic or brushing on a special liquid), or you can use a gay adhesive plastic. Look for designs which are bold, simple and colourful rather than 'whimsy'.

At the windows it is worth investing in a special 'dimmer' Venetian blind which encourages the child to sleep on light summer evenings. *(For other window ideas see* CURTAINS, *page 64.)*

Apart from the furniture already mentioned, a bed is needed when the child reaches about three years of age. If there is more than one child, or there are likely to be frequent young visitors, bunk beds are well worth buying. They are great space savers, children vie with one another to sleep in the top bunk and they can be taken apart to make adult-sized twin beds. Alternatively there are special beds which grow with the child, shortie beds, or one with arms which can be unscrewed once he is older. While thinking about children's beds remember that it is a medical fact that too soft a mattress is not good for young spines, so make sure that you buy a firm one — a hair-filled one is ideal but many of the washable foam or plastic-filled ones are good, and accidents will not ruin them. Remember also that a child does not need a pillow until he is about three years old and even then it's just as well to have a 'safe' one so the child can't suffocate.

DO-IT-YOURSELF DECORATING CHARTS

Guide to Buying Wallpaper:

To find out how much wallpaper to buy to paper a room, measure the height of the space to be papered, and then measure round the walls, including doors, windows, etc. The number of pieces of wallpaper required can be worked out from this guide, but quantities quoted are for English wallpapers — Continental papers are a different width.

MEASURE-MENT ROUND THE WALLS	HEIGHT OF SPACE TO BE PAPERED					
	3′10″ to 4′5″	4′6″ to 5′3″	5′4″ to 6′4″	6′5″ to 8′1″	8′2″ to 11′0″	11′1″ to 16′9″
	NUMBER OF PIECES (ROLLS) NEEDED					
28′	3	3	4	4	6	7
31′6″	3	3	4	5	6	8
35′	3	4	4	5	7	9
38′6″	4	4	5	6	7	10
42′	4	4	5	6	7	11
45′6″	4	5	6	7	8	12
49′	4	5	6	7	9	13
52′6″	5	5	6	7	9	14
56′	5	6	7	7	10	15
59′6″	5	6	7	8	11	16
63′	6	6	7	8	11	17
66′6″	6	7	7	9	12	17
70′	6	7	7	9	13	18
73′6″	6	7	8	10	13	19
77′	7	7	8	10	14	20
80′6″	7	7	9	11	15	21
84′	7	7	9	11	15	22
87′6″	7	8	9	12	16	23
91′	7	8	10	12	17	24
94′6″	7	8	10	13	17	25
98′	7	9	11	13	17	26
101′6″	8	9	11	14	18	27
105′	8	9	11	14	18	28

Guide to Buying Paint:

For painted walls in living rooms, bedrooms, etc., use either distemper or emulsion paint. To obtain the best results, the wall should be lined with lining paper first. For woodwork, use a hard gloss finishing paint, or for a matt surface an eggshell finish paint. For a really tough finish, for kitchens and bathrooms, use an enamel paint. When estimating quantities, measure the surfaces to be covered and add up in square feet or square yards. The quantities given on the chart are only approximate, as the amount of paint used depends on the quality of the surface to be covered.

TYPE OF PAINT	AMOUNT OF PAINT		
	1 pint	1 quart	1 gallon
Glos and enamel	10 sq. yards	20 sq. yards	80 sq. yards
Emulsion	10–12 sq. yards	20–22 sq. yards	80–84 sq. yards
Primer	70 sq. feet	140 sq. feet	560 sq. feet
Distemper	7 lb. tin covers approximately 30 sq. yards		

GETTING DOWN TO IT!

YOUR COLOUR SCHEME has now been finally decided. You are ready to order paint and paper. You can make sure of ordering the correct quantities by measuring your walls as accurately, and also by employing the two preceding charts.

Also before you begin you must make sure that you have the necessary tools *(see* TOOLS, *page 86)* and apart from these you will need an ample supply of dust sheets and old newspapers. Paint-brushes and scrapers are not expensive, but if the thought of buying steps, trestles, etc., fills you with apprehension, especially if you are not going to do a great deal of decorating or have limited storage space, it is possible to hire some of the equipment from decorating or do-it-yourself shops in certain towns, or some builders and builders' merchants will lend it to you.

Before you can decorate a room it must be prepared properly! It is absolutely no use at all slapping paint on a badly cracked or dirty surface, the cracks quickly show through and dirt mixes in with the new paint. The preparation is the long laborious part of home decorating, but it is well worth the trouble when you see the professional-looking results.

First remove as much furniture as possible to give working space, and stack the rest in the centre of the room. Cover it with newspapers and then dust sheets. Take up carpets and rugs. Remove linoleum or other floor coverings if practicable; if not, cover with paper or sacking. Take down pelmets, curtains, electric light shades, pictures, etc. Remove any removable fittings such as door knobs, bolts, finger plates, etc. Cover electric plug sockets. Remove any old nails, hooks, etc. Then thoroughly dust the room, including ceiling, walls, mouldings, skirtings, etc. This can be done with a vacuum cleaner or a soft brush. (If the ceiling only is being done, pin dust sheets to the picture rail to keep the walls clean.) At this stage, attend to any repairs and alterations necessary — for example the removal of a picture rail, the changing of a light position. If you are stripping off the old wallpaper, soak existing paper with water or a special proprietary stripper, using a distemper brush, and leave for a while to absorb, then loosen and strip off with a scraper. If the existing wallpaper is in good condition and you intend to paint over the top, repair any loose pieces by coating well with paste and pressing back into position. If you are planning to re-paper, always strip off the old paper. Make good any cracks in walls or plaster by cutting out, dampening well with water and refilling with plaster or a proprietary filler (suitable for small area). Any large holes should be made good in two stages, the first part of the filling being allowed to set before the final plaster is added. When the new plaster is thoroughly dry it should be rubbed down to a smooth surface, and again all dust should be removed. Any woodwork should be made good if necessary, bad damage should be repaired by cutting out the affected part and replacing with new wood; small breaks, holes and dents can be filled with plastic wood or filler. *(For more details on* FILLING, *see pages 132—134.)*

Now wash all the woodwork and walls if they are already painted, using soap and water, or a special paint cleanser and warm water, starting at the bottom to avoid runs. The parts of the room which are likely to be greasy should have special attention (door edges, window frames, etc.). After washing, all traces of soap or cleanser must be removed, so rinse with clean warm water, taking care with all crevices and mouldings.

If the paint is in a poor condition it may have to be removed altogether. This can usually be done with a proprietary brand of stripper which should be applied fairly liberally, left on for the amount of time suggested by the makers. Take care not to splash any surrounding surfaces which you do not want stripped! The old paint can then be removed with a scraper and if necessary a second application made to obstinate patches. It may need rubbing down afterwards with sandpaper. In the case of very difficult to move paint, you may have to burn it off with a blow lamp. This can be a dangerous weapon, so make quite sure you know how to use it before starting work with it. It should be held between 6–7 inches away from woodwork and a sheet of metal used to protect glass from the lamp, taking care to use the end of the flame rather than the middle. The woodwork will need sandpapering after burning-off as certain beads of paint tend to stick to the wood. There is also on the market an electric paint stripper which is quite safe to use.

After the old paint has been removed by either method, the surfaces should be wiped clean with turpentine substitute. After removing paint from woodwork, any knots must be treated with a special knotting before repainting.

If the paintwork was in fairly good condition after washing down, the first undercoat can be applied after 'keying' with glass paper. For most painting jobs one undercoat is necessary, but two coats may be needed where you are changing from a very dark colour to a very light one. If you have stripped off all the old paint, the woodwork will need priming before you can apply an undercoat. If two undercoats are being applied, rub the first coat down with glass paper and remove all dust before putting on the second. When the undercoat is dry put on the first layer of topcoat, allow to dry and then, if necessary, 'key' lightly, dust down and apply another coat.

The order of decorating is as follows: first the ceiling, then the woodwork (doors, wainscoting, window frames) and then papering of walls. If the walls are being painted with distemper or emulsion you can undercoat the woodwork, then give the walls two coats of paint and then give the woodwork its final topcoat.

N.B. Most of these remarks apply for the conventional type of paint. If you are using one of the thixotropic or jelly paints which are non-drip you need only apply one or at the most two coats. If you are applying two coats of this type of paint you should still 'key' with glass paper in between coats.

The Right Paint for the Right Job – Ceilings, Walls, Woodwork:

Before actually getting down to painting or papering it is wise to know the various types of paint, and where you can or can't use them.

DISTEMPER is often used for ceilings and walls (particularly in a new house). It goes on over old distemper after washing down, over wallpaper (though several coats may have to be used if it has a bold design) or directly on to plaster or brickwork. It does *not* go on over paint of any kind, gloss, matt or emulsion, so a painted surface will either have to be washed completely clean or relined with lining paper *before* distemper can be applied.

EMULSION PAINT gives a matt surface, is washable and is used for walls and ceilings. It goes on over old emulsion, over gloss, matt and eggshell paints after well washing down and 'keying' with glass paper, over wallpaper in good condition, direct on to plaster or brickwork. It does not go on over old distemper (walls which have been distempered will have to be washed clean before applying emulsion).

GLOSS, MATT, FLAT AND EGGSHELL PAINTS are usually used for the woodwork, but they can be used for walls and ceilings where a particularly good washable surface is needed. They go on over themselves and each other after washing with sugar soap and 'keying', over emulsion (which should only be washed as it acts as an undercoat), over wallpaper, direct on wood or metal, *after* a primer and undercoat. Do *not* attempt to put on over distemper, but wash off first.

Painting a Door:

One of the hardest jobs in painting is a door, especially a much panelled one. First paint the moulding surrounding each panel, and then the panel itself in the order shown, starting with the top panels. Next paint the inside stile between the panels starting at the top, then paint the cross rails, starting at the top again, and finally the two outside edges starting with the hinge side. After the door is finished, paint the architrave *(see Fig. 2)*.

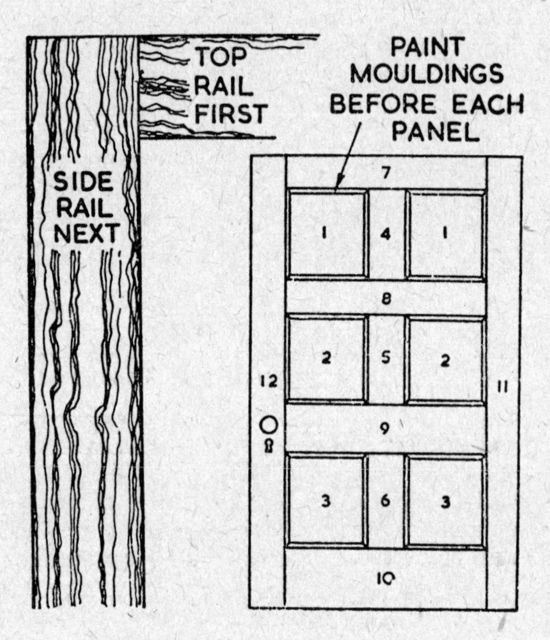

Fig. 2 Painting a Door

Cleaning Paint Brushes:

Take care of your brushes and they will repay you with long service. Overnight (if you need them to complete the job next day) they can be kept soft by being placed in a jar with enough water to cover the bristles. Once the job is completed, clean them immediately. Press the bristles flat on a piece of newspaper and scrape from the ferrule downwards with a putty knife to remove surplus paint. Wipe the brush with newspaper, then swish it around in some turps substitute. Wipe off as much of the turps as possible with newspaper and wash the brush with warm soapy water. Wipe, and place near a stove to dry, but not too near! When the bristles have thoroughly dried out, clean and oil the metal band, wrap the brush in greaseproof paper and put away.

Papering a Ceiling:

This job should be done before papering the walls, and the method used is similar to the one described for papering walls, but it is more difficult because you are not able to use the force of gravity to help get the paper smooth and straight. It is always better to have two people to paper a ceiling, one to hold the folds of paper and the other to position it and brush it smoothly on to the ceiling.

Work across the shortest width of the ceiling and rig up a scaffold either with two pairs of steps and a plank or a succession of tables, so you don't have to dismount halfway through. Paste and then fold the papeı in several folds so you have a pile of folded paper which can be easily balanced on one hand. Mark a line on the ceiling a little less than the width of the paper from the wall against which the first length will be hung. Use this as a guide line while one person positions and brushes the paper in position and the other supports and unfolds it. If you do have to paper a ceiling solo, support the folded paper on another roll held in the left hand while you brush into position with the right *(see Fig. 3)*.

Fig. 3 Ceiling Paper held on Roll

There are some aids to ceiling papering now available, including a paper support which clips on to the steps. If you are thinking of doing a lot of decorating it is well worth asking your local decorating shop about them.

Papering a Wall:

Papering, like all other branches of home decorating, needs the right tools, so before beginning check with the list *(see* CARPENTRY *page 86)* and make sure you have all you need.

Most wallpaper is sold in rolls, called 'pieces' of approximately $11\frac{1}{2}$ yards long and 21 inches wide after trimming. Some Continental wallpapers differ in width and length. There are selvedges at each side of the paper, and these should be trimmed before attempting to hang. Your supplier will trim them for you before you bring the rolls home. Alternatively you can buy a special home trimmer or use decorating shears. To have the paper pre-trimmed rather defeats the purpose of the selvedge. because marked along it at regular intervals are lines showing where to join the paper so that the pattern matches correctly. If you are buying a plain paper or one with a small pattern it does not matter, but you could get into difficulties with a large design.

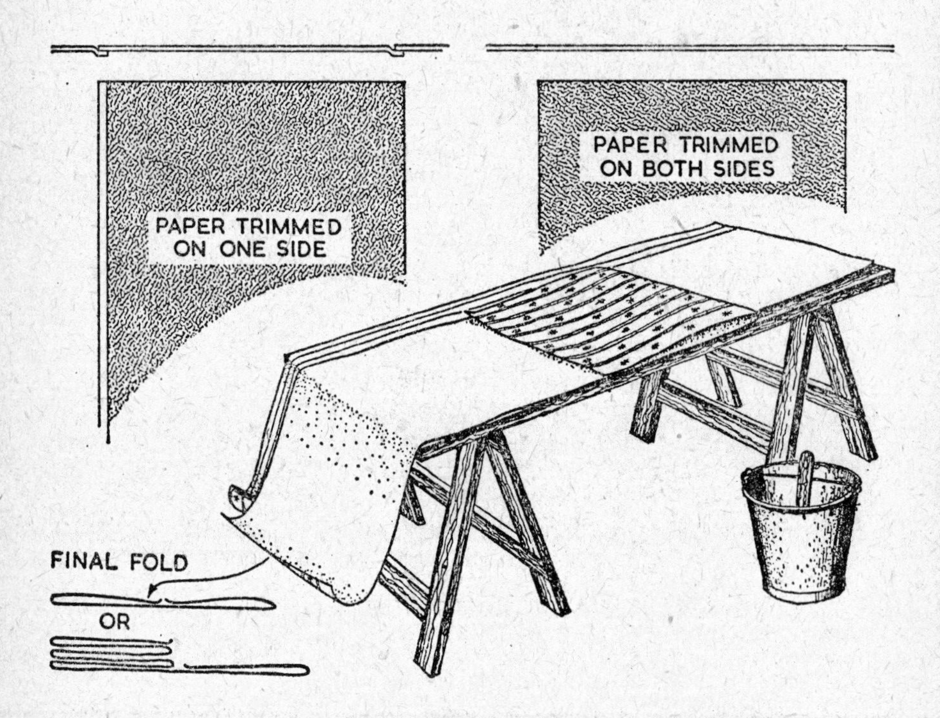

Fig. 4 Preparing Paper

Before you start cutting the paper, look at all the rolls of paper and make sure that they are all colour matched. Sometimes half the rolls may have come from a different printing and be a slightly different shade. It is better to discover this before you start the papering and not when you have the room half finished!

Walls must be just as well prepared for paperhanging as they are for painting, so proceed as previously described and then rub down lightly with glass paper before applying a coat of size. If you are papering the walls of a new house, make sure they are thoroughly dry. Many builders suggest distempering and waiting six months before papering. In case of a 'high spot' of lime in the new plaster give the whole wall a coat of vinegar size (1 pint vinegar to 1 quart water) to neutralise any active lime in the plaster.

Prepare the cellulose adhesive as directed. Work on a large table, trestle table or paste board, near the window, but allow space so you can get round all sides. Unroll the paper, drawing over the edge of the table so it uncurls. Cut the first length slightly longer than the height of the wall and lay this face up on the table. Unroll the paper for the second length, but before cutting place the left edge of the second length along the right edge of the first to make sure the pattern is matched and adjust accordingly before cutting, remembering to leave a little for trimming waste. Cut several more in the same manner. Apply paste down the centre back of the first length, brushing outwards to each edge in herringbone fashion, taking great care not to miss the outside edge. After pasting, fold the length by gently folding the two ends inwards to the centre, taking care not to crease the folded end. If the wall is rather a high one, and the table is not long enough to take the complete length of paper, it may be folded as you paste *(see Fig. 4)*.

It is usual to start hanging paper on the right-hand side of the main window, working round towards the door, but if you are using a strongly patterned paper it is wiser to hang the first strip over the main feature in the room, usually the fireplace, so that the design will be evenly balanced. Mark the wall accurately for the first strip, otherwise you may find all the paper looking as though it is 'sliding' off the wall! To get a straight line use a plumb line which has been run through chalk or charcoal. Fix to picture rail or ceiling and press against the wall so that a chalk or charcoal line is left. Take the first piece of paper, mount the steps and unfold the top half of the paper, and using the guide line slide the paper into position with the palms of the hands. Smooth the paper down the centre with one stroke of the paper-hanger's brush and then to right and left. Do this halfway down the wall, making sure it is still level with the guide line, then unfold the bottom half of the paper following the same procedure. If you do find the paper straying to left or right lift it quickly and cleanly up for a foot or two and then re-smooth it. If it won't come off easily you haven't used enough paste. Press the paper against the picture rail (or ceiling) and skirting with a pair of scissors and then trim. Afterwards brush down all over, making sure that all air bubbles are brushed out, and then remove any paste accidentally left on paintwork or paper with a sponge. Continue with the next length of wallpaper, making sure the edges 'butt' together properly. When each length has been up about 15 minutes, roll the edges with a seam roller, but do not press too hard. When you reach a corner, measure the width required and cut the paper down the length allowing an extra $\frac{1}{4}$ inch for turning, hang the usual way and use the bristles of the paperhanger's brush to tap the paper neatly into the angle. Start the next piece right in the corner. If you reach an obstacle such as a light switch, hang the paper in the usual way till it is reached, then make diagonal slashes in the paper, press down and trim off the excess pieces, but leave final trims until paper has dried out, and then use a razor blade to make final trim *(see Fig. 5)*. This method can be used to cope with other obstructions, such as pipes, window frames, etc.

Fig. 5 Papering round a Light Switch

It is possible to get ready-pasted wallpaper, which simply passes through a special water trough and can then be hung directly, but the number of ready-pasted papers available is limited at the moment.

N.B. With very expensive hand-printed papers, manufacturers recommend that a special paste be used because of the danger of the colours running. Be guided by the manufacturer on this point.

HEATING

A COMFORTABLE home means a warm home. The most beautifully furnished and decorated rooms are useless if you freeze in them from November to April!

It is impossible to say which is the best heating method, which is the cheapest, which the easiest, because each house has a different problem, each family different needs. Heating in Britain is particularly complex, because there are four fuels (electricity, solid fuel, gas and oil) all reasonably competitive. Some people want a central unit which will cook, heat their water, and even supply heating throughout the house; others want a simple clean form of heating in each room at the flick of a switch; others want a constant temperature day and night throughout the winter months. It is easier to decide when you are building or going into a new house, but an existing house, only inadequately heated, presents many problems. Is it better to do away with existing heating and have complete central heating installed? Or would it be wiser to bring in more local heat in the form of strategically placed individual heaters, and so on?

Basically speaking, there are two different ways of heating a house. By central heating, where the whole house is warmed from a central source, and local heating, where separate appliances are used in each room. You can also use a mixture of both types!

CENTRAL HEATING

The warmest house is the one which is centrally heated and there are various systems to choose from, but before you even begin to think of systems, think about heat loss. There is no point in spending a great deal of money installing and running central heating if all the warmth is escaping. In a new house insulation is often already built in, but if you have an older house at least insulate the top floor ceilings *(see* INSULATION, *page 118)*. Central heating is a highly technical subject and as the needs of each house are different it is essential that a reliable builder or firm of heating engineers be consulted. Installing central heating is something which can seldom be tackled by the amateur!

The most widely used central heating system is the one which employs water as the medium for carrying heat round the building through pipes and radiators. The water is heated at a central point either by solid fuel, gas or oil-fired boiler or by electricity, at the same time providing hot water for baths, etc. The water can circulate naturally or be driven by a pump through small pipes (called the small-bore system). The type of fuel you choose will depend on your particular needs, your storage facilities, existing plumbing arrangements, etc., but any of these systems are suitable for putting into an existing house or into a new one.

Gaining popularity in Britain is the system whereby air is heated at a central point and circulated through ducts and outlet grilles. The air is heated by gas, solid fuel, oil or electricity. Generally speaking this method cannot be put into existing property, but is built in with the house, the heating unit being situated beneath the centre of the house and the warm air blown through a trunk system embedded in the walls of the house.

Another method is under-floor central heating, which consists of electric heating coils or ordinary hot water pipes embedded in a concrete screed underneath the permanent floor. This is often installed in a new house, but it is difficult to install in existing property, because it means taking up the floors, embedding the coils or pipes in the sub-floor and re-laying the floor. The advantage with this system is that there is no mess or bother at all and the degree of heat is controlled by a thermostatic control switch on the wall. The one drawback is if the system goes wrong, either part or the whole of the floor must be taken up for repair.

The fuels most commonly used for domestic central heating are solid fuel (coke, anthracite, etc.) domestic fuel oil, kerosene, gas and electricity. None of these can be considered to be the *best* fuel as they all have their advantages and disadvantages. It will largely depend on the type of system you choose, your locality, storage space, etc.

When having central heating installed it is always wise to have some form of thermostatic control and time clock so that the heat can be controlled more finely, made more automatic and at the same time much more economical to run. There is even a form of 'anticipator' which measures the temperature outside the building and controls the internal thermostats.

Electricity

This is not strictly a fuel but a power, which can be used in many ways for heating purposes. It is clean and convenient and readily available in most houses and needs no chimney, but it is undoubtedly the most expensive method of heating. You can take advantage of the cheap night tariff which is specially good for under-floor heating and electric night storage heaters.

There is a new type of electrical central heating which is particularly suitable for installing in existing houses. Skirting or wall heaters of the correct size for the room are installed in the right place by the heating contractor and connected to a ring main circuit (in two-storey houses there is a circuit for downstairs and one for upstairs) with its own time clocks and thermostats. These switch the heaters on and off according to the time you select. Thus the house can be pre-heated before you get up in the morning, yet heat has not been wasted during the night. Each room can be set to a different temperature according to your needs or even completely switched off.

Gas:

The price of gas is subject to slight variation in different parts, but it is generally more expensive than oil. It requires no storage space and as long as the gas is already on tap it can be easily installed. Gas-fired boilers cost less than oil to install, but slightly more to run. They need regular servicing, although not so often as oil, and have to have a chimney and exhaust outlet. Gas burns without leaving soot or ash.

Oil:

There are two kinds of fuel oil available, a light domestic fuel oil which burns only when atomised, and for that reason is used in large houses where a large output of heat is needed. Kerosene is a lighter oil, known by a number of trade names, and can be utilised in smaller boilers, so it is widely used in average-size houses. Both types of oil give running costs slightly higher than solid fuel, and have the advantage that no stoking is necessary. The oil is fed into the boiler from the main storage tank (usually situated outside the house) which is filled up from a tanker when necessary — about two or three times a year is the average. Because of the finely-engineered components necessary in an oil-burning appliance, and the need for storage tanks, the initial costs involved are higher, but it is sometimes possible to convert an existing solid fuel boiler to oil. Oil-fired boilers need regular servicing, and have to have a chimney.

Solid Fuel:

This is a fairly cheap method of heating, but requires storage space, needs a chimney and involves labour in boiler stoking. (It is possible to have a gravity feed type of boiler which needs filling only once a day.) Boilers using this type of fuel cannot be so closely controlled as those using refined fuels and have the disadvantage of needing ash removal with consequent dirt and dust.

LOCAL HEATING

Local heating is provided by separate appliances in each room. You can use electricity, gas, solid fuel or oil to supply this local heat, and it can be either convected heat, which warms the whole room as the hot air is blown out of the heater and cold air sucked in, or radiant heat which is a direct heat and warms the person sitting directly in front of it. Some appliances provide both convected and radiant heat in varying proportions at the same time.

Electric Heaters

These need no flue and can be thermostatically controlled. They can be of convector or radiant type or a mixture of both. Among the types of heater available are high-temperature radiant heaters (including infra-red heaters) and convectors, both of which can be either inset or free-standing. There are also oil-filled radiators which run off electricity, skirting heaters, fan heaters and electric storage heaters which use up electricity during the night at a low cost and let out a constant degree of heat during day and night. Regular servicing is necessary with all electrical appliances.

Gas Appliances

Usually require a flue, although some small gas fires can be used without one. Gas high temperature radiators can be free-standing or inset. Gas convector heaters can be free-standing. Gas fires can now be controlled to give out enormous heat, medium heat or the bare minimum. There is even a glass-fronted fire which keeps heating costs down while magnifying the warmth it gives out. Regular servicing of gas appliances is necessary.

Paraffin or Oil Heaters

These need no flue, are free-standing and usually completely portable. These types of heaters usually supply a background heat in a room where there is already a main form of heating, or they can be used to keep a room warm during the daytime or at night when a high temperature is not required. Care should be taken to see that they always stand level, that they are not placed in a draught or where they can be knocked over, nor should they be left in a confined space like a cupboard or loft. They should never be moved or filled while they are alight and children should never be left in a room alone with them or allowed to touch them. Regular servicing is essential and before buying one of this type of heater make sure it has passed the British Standards Institution Test.

Solid Fuel

Appliances, all of which have flues, can be fitted with a control to adjust the rate of burning. Among the types in use are open fires, overnight fires, fires with back boilers which heat water at the same time, and slow-burning combustion stoves. This last type heats both by high temperature radiation (when the doors are open) and by convection. Generally speaking unless the room is very small the first two appliances need some other form of background heat in the room during cold weather, otherwise your front is toasting while your back is freezing!

NOTE: For more information on the types of heating mentioned in both sections, the various fuel costs and installation costs, you can ask each separate industry, who will provide full details and literature on the subject. Decide what type of heating you need to make *your* home warm and cosy, and then discuss the matter with your builder or heating engineer.

LIGHTING

SUCCESSFUL LIGHTING contributes enormously to the creation of a serene welcoming atmosphere in the home. It makes life not only safer and more convenient but sets the mood appropriate to each room. Good lighting is the magic touch which brings the colours and textures of your furnishings to life and it is something to use generously since the running costs are not high.

The Porch:

Choose a weatherproof fitting which sheds a good light over the front doorstep. An illuminated doorbell is useful, and make sure that your house number or name is also clearly visible.

The Hall:

The hall light probably does double duty and lights your stairs as well, so it should have a two-way switch from the front door and the landing. A relentlessly glaring light does not, however, make for a welcoming appearance to your hall, so choose an attractive light-diffusing shade and if necessary place a fitting on the staircase wall carefully positioned so that tall people won't knock against it on their way up or down. Stairs are a danger spot in any house, so do make sure that yours are really well lit. Another black spot is the familiar cupboard-under-the-stairs, which is usually a gloryhole full of brushes and brooms and old dress-boxes, but this becomes a less hazardous place if it is lit with an automatic light fitted to the doorjamb which switches itself on when the door is opened. Stairs down to the cellar are usually very steep, so lights at the top and bottom of these steps may well be necessary.

Sitting Room:

Here it is possible to exercise one's ingenuity in creating a flexible scheme capable of variation to suit the family's needs. Central lights alone are not attractive, since if they are to be of any use they have to be glaringly strong, which makes them tiring to the eyes. Wall lights make attractive background lighting but are an extravagance in the sense that they should only be used with low-wattage bulbs which will only illuminate the wall! They are the most complicated fitting to install, as a channel must be cut in the wall to conceal the wiring, which is then plastered over. One of the simplest and most effective lighting schemes is based on a number of fairly large table lamps with simple drum-shape shades, with standard lamps as useful additions for portable lights. More specialised fittings add interest to the room. If you have alcoves or a corner china cupboard these can be lit with small concealed strip lights. Curtains can be dramatised with a pelmet fitting which is often pierced with a decorative design through which the light gleams softly. Shelf units can be fitted with strip lighting to show off special ornaments. Pictures can be spotlit or lit from above with a small pelmet-type fitting and a collection of indoor plants can look most attractive if they are carefully spot-lit.

Dining Room:

The best light for this part of the house is a rise-and-fall fitting over the table, with background light such as wall fittings. The rise-and-fall fitting gives sparkle to your glass and china and makes for a pleasantly intimate atmosphere for entertaining. Make sure, though, that the light is shielded from your guests' eyes. The sideboard or serving table should also be adequately lit.

Kitchen:

The kitchen is the workroom of the house and it is essential that this should be efficiently lit. But it is also the hub of the house, where a great deal of the life of the family goes on, so a clinical look should be avoided. The best non-glare shadow free lighting is from fluorescent fittings and a good centrally-placed fitting will ensure this. Working surfaces and danger spots such as the stove may require additional lighting. If wall-hung cupboards project over your working surfaces, fit them with strip lighting hidden behind a narrow pelmet on the front edges. A light in the larder is a necessity and this can either be an automatic one which switches on when the door opens or a foot switch which is useful if your hands are full.

Bedrooms:

A restful look is obviously what you will want to aim for here. If the room is large your minimum lighting should be a central fitting plus lamps for reading in bed. For this, the lamp should be at eye level or above, so that a tall table lamp or a wall fitting is the best solution. Lights placed on low bedside tables or hooked over the bedhead are not suitable.

For dressing-table lighting the aim should be to light one's face, not the mirror! An overhead light casts deep shadows over one's face, so use panels of fluorescent strip lighting at either side of the glass or twin lamps with half-shades which swivel round to shed a bright light when you are making-up.

Two-way switches from door and bedside are an obvious convenience.

Bathroom:

Safety is again of first importance in the bathroom. Switches should not be touched with wet hands and wherever possible pull-cord fittings should be used. A well-lit mirror is a great help for shaving purposes, and here again fluorescent strip panel lights are ideal.

Nursery:

A good overall light is the main essential here, with wall lamps if extra light is needed. A low-wattage night light, if needed, must be well out of the child's reach and should be completely screened from his view, since the bright light of even a small lamp can be harmful to a baby's eyes in an otherwise darkened room.

Garage:

Three lights are most satisfactory here: one over the door which can be switched on from outside; one inside placed over the bonnet of the car; and a hand lamp connected to a plug point which is useful for inspections of the engine. If you have a work bench in the garage another light may be necessary. A fluorescent fitting would be most suitable here.

Garden:

Even in a very small garden floodlights can produce some delightful effects if they are carefully placed. Pick out pretty shrubs, a garden ornament or pond, but make certain that all apparatus of this kind is properly installed and earthed.

General Points:

When buying lamps choose only those marked with the electricity voltage of your locality.

A 100-watt lamp is the correct size for table lamps and pendant ceiling fittings in smaller rooms. Standard lamps usually take 150-watt bulbs. 40 or 60 watt is the best size for wall-bracket fittings, but if the shades are small and the other lighting in the room is good 25-watt bulbs may be sufficient.

Clear lamps are not suitable for domestic use except where you want to create hard shadows and a bright sparkle — with a chandelier fitting, for example. Pearl lamps are the best buy as they give a softer, but not lesser amount of light than clear lamps.

Internally silica-coated lamps give soft, diffused light. For a flattering warm light, buy a pink-tinted type.

Coiled-coil filament lamps are a little more expensive than single-coil lamps but they give up to 20% more light for the same amount of current.

Reflector spotlight lamps can be let into the ceilings for spotlight use. They are available in 75 and 100-watt size.

For use on either side of mirrors, use single cap tubular lamps in 40 to 60 wattages. Double-cap tubular lamps are suitable for use in alcoves or china cupboards where they are unseen. They are available in clear or frosted finish in 30 or 60-watt sizes.

Candle lamps are for use with candelabra-type ceiling or wall fittings. So long as they are used well above eye-level they can be used without shades.

They can be bought in either a clear or frosted finish, in plain or 'twisted' shapes in 25, 40 or 60-watt sizes.

Architectural tubular lamps are intended for use with mirrors, shelf units, curtain pelmets. No shades are needed for them.

Fluorescent lamps have an internal fluorescent coating and it is this that regulates the amount and colour of the light. Many tones are now available, ranging from a colder 'north' light to a warm 'daylight' type. These lamps are cool and so are suitable for use in restricted spaces.

FITTINGS. When choosing your fittings, bear in mind that proportion and style are the important factors. Simple shades and lamp bases will combine happily with all types of interior decoration. If standard or table lamps, they should stand firmly. Shades should give as much light as possible without glare, and for standard and table lamps they should have a wide opening at top and bottom. Whatever colour the exterior, a white lining is best, to give the maximum amount of reflected light. In general, fabric shades are chosen for the softer, diffused light they give, which makes them more suitable for background use than direct lighting. All shades should be easily detachable for cleaning.

Safety Precautions

1. Never allow wiring to become frayed. When it does show signs of wear, replace it entirely — don't rely on temporary patches with insulating tape.
2. Never leave an open socket 'live' where there are children about.
3. Never try to mend a fuse before switching off at the main, and always keep torch, fuse wire and a small insulated screwdriver to hand near the fusebox.

FLOORS AND FLOORINGS

THERE ARE MORE than fifty different types of permanent and semi-permanent floorings available, which can roughly be divided into seven groups: hard floorings (stone, terrazzo, marble, ceramic tiles, etc.), wood, cork, linoleum (including lino tiles), vinyl, thermoplastic and rubber. Some of these are suitable for the do-it-yourselfer to lay and others are not. If you are in doubt about laying a particular type of floor yourself, let the manufacturer be your guide, and if he suggests a professional on the job take his advice. As flooring is such a permanent item in the life of a home it is often worthwhile paying a little extra at the start, for once it is incorrectly laid it can cost a great deal to put right.

The first things to consider before choosing are: the type of wear and tear the floor surface will get: kitchens, living rooms and halls get much heavier traffic than the rest of the rooms: halls (in wet weather), kitchens and bathrooms have to resist a certain amount of damp: and kitchens have to contend with grease as well. If you have a family of several children, look for floorings which are easy to keep clean and are fairly quiet underfoot. When selecting, remember that a large area is cheaper to lay than several small ones so it is often more economical to lay the same surface throughout the ground (or upper) floor of a house at the same time, creating decorative unity. Another thing which will govern your choice is the age and type of house in which you live — some floorings are not suitable if there is an insufficient damp-proof course and heavy flooring cannot always be put upstairs in an old house because of the extra weight the walls have to bear.

Permanent Floorings

These include stone, terrazzo, marble, ceramic in a variety of types. Their great advantage is that they are virtually indestructible. It is now possible to choose almost any colour to go with any type of decoration; they blend well with the architecture of an old house and look marvellously modern in a new one. They are easy to keep clean, usually just require to be washed with soap and water and buffed occasionally, but glowing red quarry tiles do need an occasional polish. Most of these types of flooring are particularly good with underfloor central heating, which in its turn makes them more practical as a flooring.

Nearly all this group are supplied in square tiles or slabs measuring from 4–6 in. square for ceramic tiles, to 12–18 in. square for marble, terrazzo, or granolithic slabs, and often have to be professionally laid as they are usually bedded in cement on a dry concrete base, and pointing is normally necessary.

Semi-permanent Floorings

CORK: As this is the outer bark of a tree it has a pleasant 'living' look, comes mainly in browns and greens, although there are now a few coloured corks available. It is laid in pleasant fairly large square tiles, is warm to the touch and because of its resilience it is soft and noiseless underfoot. It is very hard-wearing, non-slip and can be used with underfloor central heating if not too hot (keep below 85°). These properties make it particularly suitable for living rooms, nurseries, bedrooms, in fact for every room in the house except the kitchen, as grease and staining liquids can penetrate the sealer and corrode the cork.

Cork flooring can be laid on almost any sub-floor providing it is level. Concrete can be levelled with a latex underlay, wood can be levelled with hardboard or plywood. The cork is then fixed by means of an adhesive. Once sanded and swept it is best given a resinous seal which won't chip like a plastic one, and then only needs regular buffing and re-polishing.

There are also cork tiles available impregnated with vinyl, which have immensely hard-wearing qualities and have a grease and stainproof finish. They are more expensive than ordinary cork, but can be used in all rooms including the kitchen and do not need sealing, just washing and occasional buffing.

Cork tiles can be laid by the amateur or by a professional contractor.

LINOLEUM (AND TILES): Linoleum has really come into its own during the last few years, and because it can literally be laid anywhere in the house it is now being produced in a fantastic number of colours, marbled effects, patterns and qualities. It is exceptionally hard-wearing, easy to care for and reasonably warm and quiet underfoot. And you can even 'inlay' your own patterns.

Linoleum is sold by the yard in 6-ft. widths or in 9-or 12-in. tiles. It is easy to cut and shape to the floor area, but see the sub-floor is level and free from damp.

As seven thicknesses are available, your choice will depend on the wear which the linoleum will get. Choose $\frac{1}{8}$ inch thickness for halls, living rooms and kitchens which get the heaviest wear, and lower gauges for bedrooms, bathrooms and occasional rooms.

Sheet lino can be laid by the amateur, provided the existing floor is in good condition. If it is wood, a felt underlay will have to be used to prevent floor-boards eventually showing through. If the floor is very uneven a hardboard floor must first be laid and then the linoleum laid on top. If you have problems of damp, uneven concrete, or wood floors in a very bad condition, do not try and lay linoleum yourself, but get expert advice.

Lino tiles are easy to lay and are simply stuck down with adhesive to a clean level floor. There is one brand available which is already impregnated with adhesive. The tiles are simply dipped into hot water for a few seconds and then pressed on to the prepared floor. One of the advantages with these tiles is that a few can be replaced when one area gets a little worn. Linoleum is easy to look after, it needs occasional polishing or it can be sealed. It should not be allowed to get too wet. Use only a damp sponge-mop or cloth with mild soap or soapless detergent when washing, then rinse and mop dry.

RUBBER: Rubber is hygienic, waterproof, warm and wears well. It now comes in a wide range of colours and can be decorated with inlaid stripes and other small designs, which makes it suitable for all rooms of the house except the kitchen (as grease can cause rubber to perish).

Rubber flooring backed with foam rubber is now available for extra quietness and springiness, and it is particularly suitable for the floors of flats or children's rooms.

Rubber is available in sheet form, which should be laid professionally, and tiles which can be laid by a competent do-it-yourselfer. These come in a variety of sizes from 6–18 in. square. In either case it needs a dry, level, rigid sub-floor as rubber moulds itself to the sub-floor and any unevenness will quickly wear through.

There are also vulcanised rubber tiles available which are even more hard-wearing than rubber, can be used with under-floor central heating and can be used in kitchens as they are not affected by grease.

Once a rubber floor is laid it needs washing occasionally with tepid water and soap (never detergent) and a polish with water or plastic wax emulsion polish. Many manufacturers supply the one they recommend when they supply the floor.

THERMOPLASTIC: This is closely related to vinyl and is in fact a plastic on an asphalt base. It is available in tile form only, and in a wide range of colours; these are not really pure because of the asphalt base, but many of the subtle colours are very good indeed.

Thermoplastic tends to be affected by hot fat, so it is not really suitable for kitchens. If you do put it in the kitchen, make sure you wipe up any spilt fat quickly. For a similar reason never use spirit-based polishes. Thermoplastic tiles can be laid by the do-it-yourselfer and need a similar sub-floor to vinyl. To clean, wash and then polish with liquid wax.

VINYL: Vinyl is a plastic material which can be bought in tiles or sheet form. It is durable, resilient, flexible, easy to lay (especially in the sheet form) and comes in a wide range of good colours and good patterns. One make looks like self-coloured mosaic, and is actually vinyl chips embedded in vinyl. Pure vinyl is rather expensive but the purer the vinyl the purer and more subtle the colour can be (white is really white, for instance, and the range of greeny-greys and subtle bronzes is amazing).

Because it is so tough, it is much thinner than other flooring, but don't let this deter you. The tiles are usually 9 or 12 in. square, and are laid on a smooth dry sub-floor, and in the case of a wood sub-floor, over a covering of felt paper to counteract seasonal movement. Some of the sheet vinyls already have a cord backing to counteract damp. They come in 6 ft. widths and are simply unrolled and cut to room shape with a good pair of scissors. Vinyl flooring is suitable for every room in the house, and because of its thinness, some makes are suitable for stairs as well. All the upkeep needed is a wash and buff when dirty, and an occasional polishing with liquid wax emulsion.

Also under the vinyl 'umbrella' are vinyl and cork (discussed in cork section)., PVC surfaced felts which are quiet, warm, non-slip and stain resistant. These are suitable for children's rooms, bedrooms, bathrooms and some are suitable for stairs. These come in sheet form for do-it-yourself laying.

Vinyl-asbestos tiles which come in a good range of colours and marbled effects are easy to lay at home and suitable for all rooms.

WOOD: This is one of the most used of all floorings, and because of its natural qualities it looks and feels warm, is very resilient and hard wearing. It can be used in any room in the house except for the bathroom and kitchen where, because of the damp, it might develop dry rot. (Some bathroom and kitchen floors are of wood and these should be covered with any of the other suitable floorings mentioned in this section.)

The majority of floors in old and new houses are of wood — often a softwood which is intended to have carpets or other semi-permanent types of flooring laid on top as softwood does not stand up to continual traffic.

If you want the glow of natural polished wood and you have existing hardwood floors in good condition, these can be sanded, either by a contractor, or you can hire a sander and do the job yourself, and then polished or sealed.

If you want a completely new wooden floor laid, you will have a tremendous choice, for there are over fifty types of wood flooring available in different colours with different graining, different degrees of hardness. Some come in strips, some in planks, and some in blocks which can be laid in a variety of patterns.

There are many wood floors available which can be laid by the do-it-yourself enthusiast, mostly confined to prefabricated blocks, which come ready finished and only need waxing, and are very easy to lay. There is even one type which, when laid in interlocking sections over felt paper, can be rolled up and taken away if you move house.

Once laid or sanded, the wood floor only needs occasional polishing to keep it in good condition, or it can be sealed with synthetic resin or plastic dressing which only needs to be swept.

CARPETS

CARPETS ARE an expensive item in the furnishing budget, but generally speaking you get exactly the quality you pay for! The very best quality wool carpet will last for a long time, and inexpensive synthetic fibre tufted carpet will probably only last about five years. The more wear the carpet will be getting the more you must pay for it! For sitting rooms, living rooms, hall and stairs buy the very best quality you can afford. Bedrooms and less frequently used rooms can take inexpensive tufted carpets quite happily.

In decoration one of the most important things to learn is when to use pattern. As a general rule it is wise not to have a hectic design on the thing bought to last longest as it ties you to colour schemes for years to come.

So if you are sinking your capital into your carpets, don't choose heavily patterned ones. Use pattern in the wallpapers or curtain fabrics and choose a plain, two-tone or textured effect carpet which looks right in almost any setting. You can be more adventurous in the hall and stairs as you don't get so tired of a design there as you do in living rooms, but keep to a fairly simple pattern.

When thinking of colour (and carpets come in the most beautiful range of colours these days) remember that the floor is often the most-noticed area in a room, so don't choose something so hectic that it 'comes up and hits you in the eye' each time you open the door! And remember, particularly if you have a small flat or house, that often the doors are left open and the carpets in each room merge together. For this reason a similar carpet used throughout the ground floor and continued up the stairs can make a small house look more spacious. If you do choose a different colour for each room, make sure that they blend rather than scream at each other!

Laying Carpets:

Whatever type of carpet you choose, remember that its life is practically doubled with a good underfelt which acts as a cushion between the carpet and the floor, reducing the friction on the surface. Wool and haircord fitted carpets should be professionally laid, with the pile running from the door into the room. Stair carpets should be laid with the pile brushing down the stairs and should have stair rods or clips to keep heels away from the risers and reduce wear — always remember to buy extra length with stair carpeting, because it needs to be moved occasionally a few inches up or down to prevent wear on one place all the time. A new carpet tends to fluff at first, so it should not be vacuum-cleaned till it has settled; sweep with a carpet sweeper or brush for a while (which encourages the loose fluff to mat back into the carpet). To preserve the life of a carpet, shampoo about once a year without making it too wet. If you have a square, turn it round twice a year. If it is fitted, make sure that heavy furniture is on castors so that the legs don't 'eat' into the pile and move the furniture round occasionally. Clean up spills and remove stains as soon as they happen, and protect places which get most wear (the strip in front of the seating area for watching TV, the piece in front of the fire, and the doorway leading in from the kitchen) with an extra piece of carpet or a rug.

Cord Carpeting:

Cord carpeting is produced in Britain and on the Continent. It is less expensive than most wool carpeting, has a firm looped pile which is not very thick, and is very hard wearing. Because of the method of weaving it only comes in plain colours or with slight textures and stripes and is usually sold by the linear yard (27 or 36 in. wide) which makes it ideal for seaming into wall-to-wall carpeting.

Rugs:

Rugs add colour and a soft luxurious look to a wood, linoleum, ceramic or any other type of hard floor. Apart from their decorative uses, they can prevent wear on certain sections of the floor.

Rugs are available in all sizes, shapes, types and colours. In wool, nylon, acrilan, other synthetic fibres, blends and mixtures, as well as in a natural form (such as sheepskin and cowhide) converted into a rug, and you can even make rugs yourself, either from already marked-out canvas and ready-cut wool, or by cutting your own wool and making your own design. The synthetic fibre rugs are washable, which makes them particularly suitable for use in bedrooms and nurseries. You can even get woven plastic rugs which are hardwearing, scrubbable, particularly good in kitchens, passages and children's rooms. One point to watch when putting rugs on highly polished floors: make sure you have not polished underneath the rug, otherwise accidents can happen. As a double safety precaution, you can buy rugs with non-skid backs or you can back them yourself with hessian or some other coarsely woven fabric.

Synthetic Fibre Carpets:

These now come in an ever-growing list with an ever-increasing range. They are usually produced on the tufted principle, which means that they are woven into a jute backing, the pile is either cut or left looped, and then the whole back of the carpet is impregnated with latex rubber to make it strong, softer to walk on and to prevent tufts coming out. (A few all-wool carpets are also produced this way.) They are made of nylon, acrilan, rayon or blends of wool and synthetics or blends of two types of synthetics, in fact the range is endless. When these types of carpets were first produced, they were in plain colours only, then mixtures of two or three colours were introduced. Now they come in stripes, small designs and in numerous textured effects. Colours are good as synthetic fibres dye very well. Most of the tufted types of carpet come in a range of sizes from 27 in. wide to 15 ft. and almost any length. They are very easy to lay at home with just a pair of scissors to cut them to the right shape, and because of the latex backing there are no problems of fraying. One firm produces carpet tiles for home laying. These carpets can be shampooed at home, but the pile is not so resilient as an all-wool one, although they wear very well. Because of this, it is better to use them in bedrooms, bathrooms and occasional rooms.

Vegetable Fibre Matting:

Sisal mattings are dyed in good colours and are very hard-wearing. Some have rubber backing which makes them a good substitute for a carpet. They are available with small designs, checks and stripes and a two-tone texture effect. They are harder to clean than the more traditional type (which also has had a face lift and come out in good designs and colours) which allows the dirt to go through, and can be taken up, shaken, cleaned underneath and put back. They are immensely hard-wearing, but strong sunlight does tend to fade the bright colours and they are hard on the feet (and knees of small children)!

Rush matting or sea grass matting is thick, has a pleasant greeny-beige colour and smells deliciously of the fresh countryside. It gives good service for the price, and is suitable in modern living rooms or dining rooms and sunrooms. It does tend to dry out and become brittle. Dirt goes straight through so that it needs to be kept clear of furniture (which rubs too much anyway) so that it can be lifted up for cleaning underneath.

Wool Carpets:

The British carpet industry produces six basic types of wool carpet: Axminster, which comes in several qualities and prices according to the closeness of weave and length of pile. All the wool is in the pile and none hidden in the back, so it can be recognised by examining the underside. Wilton is more closely woven and is usually more expensive. The wool is threaded through into the back of the carpet as well, giving almost a built-in cushion. Brussels carpets are woven in the same way but the surface is looped instead of being cut. Tapestry Brussels has the same looped surface but does not have the extra wool threaded through to the back. Tapestry velvet is woven in the same way but has a cut pile, and with a chenille carpet the pile is made first and then woven into the heavy back. These various types can be bought as BODY CARPET — that is by the yard in either 27 or 36 in. widths for seaming into wall-to-wall carpeting or using for stairs and hall. As BROADLOOM, which is in the piece either 7 ft. 6 in., 9 ft., 10 ft. 6 in. and 12 ft. wide and almost any length. As CARPET SQUARES which are not necessarily square and can measure from about 7 ft. square to one 15 ft. by 12 ft. These are usually intended for a room with polished wood or other hard surface surround.

Apart from these British carpets there are also the famous Indian, Persian and Chinese carpets in various qualities and types.

CURTAINS

CURTAINS are as important to a room as accessories to an outfit! If they are well-made and well-lined they can make inexpensive furniture look much more luxurious and an inexpensive fabric look more expensive.

Curtains should never be skimpy, but should hang in plentiful folds during the daytime and when drawn across the window there should be generous fullness. When making curtains always allow one and a half times the width of the window and if possible two widths. This is particularly important with filmy curtains which should be very full. It is always better to have plenty of an inexpensive fabric than not enough of a costly one.

Length of curtains depends on the room and the type of window, but in living rooms, dining rooms and bedrooms floor-length curtains usually look much better than sill-length. Long curtains add a sense of proportion to a room, they make small windows look larger, they can give a feeling of unity when there are several windows of different sizes in one room and they keep out draughts much more effectively. If short curtains have to be used they can hang just to touch the sill or about four inches below to keep out draughts. Always allow about a six-inch hem when making up because of shrinkage.

Large 'picture windows' of the type seen in modern houses and tall sash windows of the type found in some old houses need important curtains to balance the actual window size and for a really luxurious look they can be carried past the window to give the impression of a complete 'wall' of folded fabric.

Generally speaking curtains in living-rooms and bedrooms should be lined as this makes them hang really well, improves the look of the fabric, makes it look more expensive, prevents fading and makes the room more cosy in winter.

There are many types of curtain fabric available in a wide range of designs, colours and textures and there are many styles of curtain to choose from. Your choice will be governed by the type of windows you have, the type of decorations and furnishings and the use of the room, but there are one or two basic rules to follow: large fabric designs are more suitable for large windows, while small designs, narrow stripes and plain fabric are more suitable for smaller windows; hectic 'contemporary' designs are better in kitchens, playrooms, etc.; ultra modern designs look best in a modern home with simple furnishings, chintzes and cretonnes look right in the country and more sophisticated fabrics suit a town home. Before finally deciding look at the fabric in both day and electric light as you will be seeing it in both, and see a few yards of the fabric draped and folded, as this is how you will see it when it is made up into curtains.

Curtain Fittings:

Curtains may be hung in many ways; with rings from rods, with cord (stitched to the top of the curtain) on a wooden pole, from spiral wires, from metal or plastic curtain track (which is often hidden behind a wooden pelmet or frilled valance) or on an aluminium or nylon groove let into the ceiling. The type of fitting will determine the type of heading you make for the top of the curtain. Curtains on rings can have a stiff heading with the rings sewn an inch or two below the top which will hide the pole when the curtains are drawn, or the rings can be made a decorative feature of the curtain. This is more usual when the pole is of brass or painted wrought iron with decorative ends. The top of the curtain can be scalloped, pinch pleated etc. One type of curtain can be made in two layers on a rod half way up the window and at the top of the window — this style is known as 'café curtains'.

Curtains to be fixed to the more usual 'railway' type of track, including the groove type, are headed with Rufflette tape, into which brass, nylon or plastic hooks are slotted at regular intervals and then fixed into tiny rings at the bottom of the rollers which run along the track. A wider version of this tape, with special pronged hooks, gives the impression of 'pinch pleating'. Curtains to be hung on spiral wire only need a hem wide enough to take the wire.

Inexpensive Curtain Ideas:

If your budget is really tight and you cannot afford the fabric of your dreams, it is sometimes possible to find a fabric which was not really intended for curtains at all, yet which looks wonderful when well made up and hung at the windows.

Hessian for example comes in really lovely colours, is not too expensive, is wide and is heavy enough to hang well. It must be lined, though, because it does tend to fade in bright sunlight. An inexpensive felt can also be an economy because of its width (some felts are 84 inches wide) and this does not need lining. Gingham is still one of the cheapest furnishing fabrics and comes in some very good colours. If you can't find the shade you want, take a look in the dress fabric department but remember dress gingham is usually only 36 inches wide so you will need more than you would of a wider furnishing gingham.

Plain dress fabrics can also sometimes be used for curtains if they are heavy enough, and particularly at sale time a bargain in a wool mixture fabric can often make very luxurious curtains. It is often in a colour which has not sold well because of its unsuitability for clothes, yet it makes a wonderful furnishing colour.

Some shops stock silk *voile,* an imported fabric made from the rough silk which remains after the best has been taken for silk dress fabric. It comes in good colours (but must be lined as it fades, and allow a generous hem because of shrinkage.)

If you are no good with a needle and the extra expense of having curtains made up professionally is going to ruin your budget, look for ready-made curtains in local shops. These can now be bought ready-made in several standard sizes and in cotton, damask, fibreglass fabrics, nets, etc., for a very reasonable price.

BEDROOMS like pretty curtains in a plain or patterned fabric to blend with the general decorative scheme. The style of curtain will also depend on the feeling of the room, but it is often possible to have really prettily trimmed, draped or bowed curtains in a frankly feminine bedroom. The fabric can be cotton, glazed chintz, taffeta, satin, lightweight velvet, *broderie anglaise,* etc. If the bedroom is overlooked or extra reflected light is needed, net curtains can also be used. These can be made in a variety of styles, shirred, frilled, crossed and held with ribbon or left plain and trimmed with a deep flounce. You can use white or pastel coloured net, muslin, organdie, voile, chiffon, nylon, terylene, most of which can be plain, flocked, spotted or embroidered.

CHILDREN'S ROOMS are best curtained in gay washable fabrics, lined with a dark colour-fast lining to prevent the summer sun waking the children too early in the morning. Don't always look for so-called nursery fabrics as the child quickly outgrows a fabric patterned with fairies or bunnies! Look among the gay striped or diamond patterned cottons and linens, checked gingham, spotted cottons and plain chintzes, or choose a more sophisticated design which will be suitable as the child grows older.

KITCHENS AND BATHROOMS need easily washable curtains, and because of frequent washing and ironing it is best to keep them to a simple style, unlined and in sturdy unshrinkable fabric (in any case leave a good hem). Use gay printed cottons, checked gingham linen, towelling, nylon, fibreglass or a drapable plastic. Hang on nylon or plastic track hidden behind a painted wood pelmet or frilled valance.

LIVING-ROOMS should have the best curtain fabric you can afford in a style which suits the rest of the furnishings. The curtains in a living room are best lined with a good quality lining in a colour to tone. The main fabric could be colour-fast and the lining fade resistant (particularly in rooms which face south). Fabrics can be cotton, linen, silk, satin, taffeta, damask, velvet, tweed, cretonne, etc., and the curtains can be made up in a variety of styles and trimmed in a number of ways or left plain. If the window is very large and gives a great deal of glare, an all-over transparent curtain can be hung to cover the glass.

FURNITURE

General Advice on Buying Furniture:

Whether you decide to furnish your home with priceless antiques, reproduction furniture, modern 'Scandinavian influence' pieces, or a pleasing hotch-potch gleaned from local junk shops, there are several basic rules to follow before finally parting with your money. Firstly, furniture must be well-designed, pleasant to look at and at the same time functional. Secondly, consider whether you will still be happy with it in ten years' time, and that you are not being misled by the glamorous setting in which it is presented, or in the case of new furniture, by its up to the minute fashion gimmick. Thirdly, think of the room for which you need it — its general decoration scheme and above all its size. Nothing is more heartbreaking than to buy a large piece of furniture and spend the rest of your life dodging round it trying to avoid bruises! Also, it's very embarrassing having to send something back because it won't go through the doorway! To avoid these mishaps, always carry room measurements with you when buying, and if you doubt whether a certain piece of furniture will fit, measure the room size out to scale on squared paper and cut out furniture shapes to scale too, and then make sure they will go in comfortably.

Furniture is an expensive item in today's setting-up-home budget, and however clever you are at spotting bargains, it will still cost in the region of £400–£500 to furnish an average three-bedroomed house. (This is allowing for certain second-hand buys and some home-made items. To furnish completely with brand-new furniture would cost about £700–£1,000 or more.)

As furniture costs such a lot, make sure you are getting value for money, and when buying pieces which are going to get a great deal of family wear and tear, see they are strongly built.

Economies can be made, but it is essential not to try to save money on beds and bedding, which should be of the very best quality that you can afford; upholstered furniture which should be comfortable, sturdy yet not too heavy, and the dining table, which should stand firmly and be large enough (or extend) to seat all the family comfortably, plus guests.

Buying New Furniture:

There is so much good new furniture in the stores these days, all pleasantly presented. It is possible to get anything from long, low furniture inspired by the Japanese, to a complete reproduction antique dining room!

Most furniture is sold by brand names these days, and this in itself is a form of customer protection, and the best manufacturers put their furniture through severe tests for quality, strength and finish before launching it on the market. Before buying, pay a visit to several stores and have a good look at what's available. Also look at women's magazines which specialise in decoration and furnishing, and write to the manufacturers they recommend in decoration and furnishing, and write for catalogues to the manufacturers they recommend on their editorial pages. Compare prices, designs, finishes, etc., and decide how much you have to spend for each room and which basic pieces you will need to start with.

Decide only to buy what you need for comfortable living, not what anybody else tells you you should have. Why buy a complete suite of furniture when you don't really need it? It is only made up in this way for the convenience of the manufacturer, so don't be talked into buying what you don't want. No reputable shop will make you have the whole suite if you only want one piece (unless it is a sale bargain or something else of that sort).

When you have made up your mind, go to a good shop where the salesmen are trained to help you. Take a second or third look at the furniture of your choice bearing in mind the following points:

1. Look for simplicity of design.
2. Look for comfort in an easy chair. Sit in it, test ease of getting in and out, as well as comfort.
3. Make sure the piece you are buying is functional — a bookcase with shelves too narrow to take your books is a useless buy.
4. Test cabinet furniture (dressing tables, wardrobes, dining tables, etc.) for rigidity. Look at the drawers to see if they run smoothly, open cupboard doors to see if they open and close properly and if they hang well. Study hinges, handles and the back of chests and wardrobes.
5. Look for movability. After all, chairs have to be moved and you have to clean under chests and beds.
6. Cleanability is important too — some of the table and sideboard tops are treated with a special stain and heat resistant surface which is well worth the extra money. Some furniture has a laminated plastic finish which is particularly useful in children's rooms, bedrooms and dressing rooms. Some upholstered furniture has a silicone-treated surface which keeps clean longer.

Most of today's furniture is veneered, as solid wood would be very expensive and also very heavy, though this depends on the woods chosen, but some manufacturers do still make solid wood pieces which are definitely the best buy for hard-wearing qualities. If choosing veneered furniture, look for as natural-looking a finish as possible. It should be fairly matt, and do avoid the heavy treacly dark brown finish like the plague! If possible, when choosing dining tables, headboards and wardrobes, have ones with slightly rounded edges as the veneer is less likely to chipo (If you do have an accident and chip the veneer it *can* be repaired, *see* RENOVATING FURNITURE *page 72* section.)

Finally, don't buy in a hurry, take as long as you like to make up your mind. After all you will have to live with the furniture you have chosen.

Buying Old Furniture:

Old furniture can largely be divided into two categories, 'antique' which is always more than a hundred years old (this term has now come to mean more often than not an easily recognisable piece by one of the great masters such as Sheraton, Chippendale or Hepplewhite, or of some such popular period as Queen Anne, Jacobean or Regency) and 'secondhand' which usually means junk shop and auction room finds, less than a hundred years old.

Before shopping it is certainly wise to acquire a little knowledge of the various periods and types of antique and old furniture, so that you can make up your mind which styles you particularly like and will want to live with. Most libraries have some good books on the history of furniture or they will get them in for you and these will give you an outline on which to work. A trip to a local museum or 'stately home' will often provide some mouth-watering examples of really fine furniture, and some local education authorities include a history of furniture in their evening class curriculum.

Whatever old furniture you are considering buying, always look for woodworm before you buy. This can be detected by the little holes which appear close together, generally in one area of the furniture. They look exactly as though a small nail had been repeatedly hammered into the wood and withdrawn. In severe cases there will be wood dust on the floor under the furniture and a general 'crumbly' look. A small amount of worm need not deter you from buying, particularly if you are able to knock the price well down because of it! It can be treated at home *(see* HOUSEHOLD PESTS, *page 116)* but do not bring it into the house before you have treated it, otherwise it may contaminate other furniture. Woodworm also loves wooden floors, so do not stand an infected piece on your floor until you are sure there is no longer any worm on it. If possible keep it in a garage on a concrete floor until you have finished the treatment.

Other pitfalls to watch for, particularly with high-priced antique furniture, are restoration marks. Naturally a piece of furniture which has been in existence for several hundred years cannot always be in perfect condition, but it was the practice some time ago amongst unscrupulous dealers to take one genuine piece and make two from it! The moral is obvious — try to buy from a well-known dealer, or at a high-class auction where the history of the furniture is fully catalogued (unless you are really getting a 'snip' and at the price it really won't matter if the furniture is 100 per cent genuine or not). Second-hand finds are usually picked up in a junk shop, local street market, auction or sale rooms, where several pieces may be lumped together in one 'lot' and you will have to take the other things as well as the coveted pieces; or through advertisements in local papers and shop windows. Sometimes even a jumble sale provides a treasure. Half the fun of buying this type of furniture is that you never quite know where or when you are going to find what you want, so there is always an excuse to go peering into dusty second-hand shop windows, to linger at the market stall or make an expedition to the auction room.

It must be pointed out, however, that although many people think there is a chance of finding a really priceless antique in the dusty depths of a junk shop, it is very rare for this to happen. In the main it is the comfortable, solid, well-loved pieces which are found this way, forgotten from the twenties and 'thirties. These are often well-made, sturdy and dependable and with a little refurbishing they can take on a new lease of life. It is often their weight which is against them, but castors can be fitted to make moving easier *(see* RENOVATING FURNITURE *page 72)*.

Before finally parting with your money, consider whether you really are getting a bargain — often something which looks a real find in the shop becomes a white elephant when you get it home. With upholstered furniture especially, look at the underneath and at the springs, think how much it will cost to re-spring and re-cover (be honest and ask yourself if you can really tackle this job). A suite picked up for £5 is not really a bargain if it will cost over £50 to renovate! Apart from upholstery, canework is another expensive item to repair, so are broken brass beadings and mouldings.

Bad scratches, dents and stains can be removed *(see* RENOVATING FURNITURE, *page 72)* but don't pay high prices for pieces which are badly damaged. They are only a good buy if you pick them up for a few shillings and give them a new lease of life with paint.

Another point worth consideration is how to get the furniture home! If there are no delivery facilities it may cost an extra pound or two to get it delivered, so this must be added to the cost of your bargain.

Making Furniture:

It would be very satisfying to be able to look round your home and say that you had made the majority of the furniture yourself. But where do you begin if you are a complete novice? It is possible to attend classes to learn the art of furniture-making where, just like dressmaking classes, you make something while you are learning, with every stage supervised by an expert.

If you have no access to classes, you can start by building furniture from some of the ready-to-assemble kits which are now on the market. Start with an easy piece like a simple bookcase, and work up from there. Or if you want to make an occasional table, stool or very simple chair you can buy ready-made wood or metal legs in several shapes and sizes. These are fitted to suitably shaped wooden tops by means of screws which fit into the screw-plate at the top of the leg. When you have done this, the wood will have to be finished — either polished, varnished, painted or covered with adhesive plastic. When you feel ready to tackle something a little more complicated, you could try a tray, a padded-topped stool or a bedside cabinet. Before you start you will need certain basic tools *(see* TOOLS, *page 86)*.

Another fairly simple job for the handyman is the making of a built-in cupboard and bookshelves for the living room from wood-veneered chipboard. This is sold pre-cut in an immense number of different sizes and the shelves and cupboards are mounted on lightweight aluminium struts which are screwed to the wall. The manufacturers of the board supply full making instructions.

Painting Furniture:

Before furniture can be painted, all old polish and varnish or old paint must be removed, dents must be smoothed out, broken pieces repaired. Because once the furniture is covered with immaculate new paint, all the faults show through! It is well worth the extra time spent in preparation.

Remove all trimmings such as handles, keyhole surrounds, knobs, etc. first. Then strip off all the old polish or paint with a proprietary stripper. You can apply this with a stiff brush and then rub off. To remove obstinate varnish use a stiff brush. A scraper will help to get rid of old paint. Use a painter's shavehook on mouldings and scrape out the corners with a knife. If the furniture has delicate carvings use *acetone* or *carbon tetrachloride* brushed on with a small soft brush (a toothbrush will do).

When the surface is perfectly clean from paint, polish or varnish, wash down with soap and water, otherwise the remains of the stripper in the wood will cause new paint to flake. Allow to dry thoroughly and then repair any cracks and splits with cellulose plaster filler, smoothed well into the crack, and wipe any extra away with a damp sponge. Mend broken corners with this filler, moulded into shape like putty, build it up a little at a time and leave it to harden in between.

Next sand down all surfaces with the glass paper wrapped round a cork sanding block. This gives extra firmness and also protects your fingernails! Dust down and seal all knots with two coats of special primer, then apply one coat of primer. Allow this to dry thoroughly (at least 24 hours) before sanding lightly with very fine glasspaper. If you are painting whitewood furniture it is sometimes necessary to give two coats of primer, as this is generally made from soft deal which soaks up a great deal. If painting furniture which includes a mirror, it is wise to mask the edge of the glass before painting. This can be stripped off when the paint is thoroughly dry, leave a paint-free surface. Dust down and apply a coat of undercoat, also leaving this to dry thoroughly before sanding, dusting and giving the final topcoat. This should go on quite smoothly, so do not overload the brush, and work with a flexible wrist. When finished, check for splashes and drips, and smooth these out carefully. Clean all trimmings (which you previously removed) whilst the topcoat is drying, and replace. If they are brass it is wise to lacquer them and allow them to dry thoroughly before replacing.

When painting furniture with drawers, these should be removed, primed and painted as described above, and replaced when the job is complete. Be careful not to get extra blobs of paint underneath the drawers or at the corner where the drawer fits the shell, otherwise the drawer may not fit properly once all is painted. If the drawer does not run smoothly, rub with sandpaper and then apply a little soap or wax to the runners.

Decoration Ideas:

Half the fun of painting furniture is the fact that you can turn a duckling into a swan! You can paint the furniture to tone with the walls of your room (particularly suitable in a bedroom) so that it does not assume too great importance, or you can go really gay and lacquer it bright red and decorate it with a black design. Before starting on the painting, it is well worth while to visit your local museum in search of ideas to see how furniture used to be lacquered and painted.

If you do want a decorated effect, first paint as described above with the plain colour of your choice, and if you're no artist, try using transfers to supply the design. Another way of getting contrast is to paint the shell of the furniture, and decorate the drawer fronts with self-adhesive plastic in a suitable design — or vice versa. Or drawer fronts can even be faced with linoleum off-cuts, and this is certainly a practical way of making the flat-topped surface of a chest into a sturdy desk. Felt or fabric can also be used in conjunction with paint to give a very pretty effect, but this does tend to get grubby with time.

Renovating and Mending Furniture:

If a piece of furniture is badly damaged it is not really possible for the amateur to carry out major repairs, and unless you happen to be a gifted carpenter it is wise, in the case of a valuable piece of furniture, to call in a professional cabinet maker. It is possible in some towns to join a day or evening class where you can repair and renovate furniture under professional supervision, and this is well worth while, as you learn a great deal as well as ending up with a perfect piece of furniture for very little cost.

Quite a lot of minor renovating can be done at home. Painting, for instance, can give a new lease of life to the most battered piece *(see* PAINTING FURNITURE, *page 71)* but often you need not go to such great lengths to make it usable. In any case, it is often a great pity to cover beautifully grained wood with a coat of paint.

CASTORS: Castors are another thing which can be repaired at home (they need oiling annually and failure to do this often causes the breakage in the first place). The screw type is repaired by removing the castor and old screw, plugging the hole with a wooden plug and then screwing in the new castor. Do not use a drill, but start the hole for the screw with a bradawl, then screw in the castor.

The cup type of castor supports the end of the leg in a metal cup which is screwed into the leg. Sometimes the screws simply need renewing, but quite often the leg becomes cracked and it is impossible to insert new screws. Saw the leg off at the top of the castor and make a new base for it of similar shape and size, drill a hole in the centre and glue in a dowel and leave till the glue has set hard. Bore a hole in the leg to take the other end of the dowel and fix in place with glue. Leave until thoroughly dry and firm and then screw back the castor cup on the repaired foot.

The latest castors are made of nylon or plastic and in some cases are completely silent and transparent, with a variety of fittings for different types of furniture. Sometimes it is as well to remove all the old castors and replace them with some of the new type.

DENTS: You can remove dents by soaking a small wad of cotton wool in water. Place this over the dent and gently press down with the point of a hot clothes iron (be careful not to burn the surrounding woodwork in the process), the steam in the cotton wool causes the dent to 'steam out'. For a small dent you can use a wad of blotting paper just as effectively.

FRAMES: Chair frames sometimes come loose, especially on dining chairs when the sitter has the bad habit of balancing on the two back legs. You can strengthen the chair by fitting a triangular piece of wood into the corners of the frame where legs and seat join. Fix with glue or screws. Well-made chairs often already have these strengtheners, and they need occasional tightening.

Renovating upholstered furniture is another job which can often be tackled at home *(see* UPHOLSTERY, *page 74)*.

HANDLES: Often a piece of furniture is completely transformed by a new set of handles and it is now possible to buy almost any type. Choose them to suit the furniture — A Queen Anne chest would look stupid with modern plastic knobs, yet a decorative brass handle can sometimes add distinction to a modern piece of painted 'white wood'. Remove old handles carefully and if the new handles are smaller plug the old holes with plastic wood before fixing new handles. Stain or paint any bare parts to match the rest of the drawer or door.

JOINTS: Sideboards and wardrobes may come loose at the joints. You can deal with this by fixing angle plates to the plinths and other crucial joints on the structure. Ill-fitting doors are another fault, and usually happen when the hinges give way (like castors, these need occasional lubrication). New hinges are quite easy to fix *(see* DOORS, *page 95)*.

RUNG OR LEG: Perhaps the most common furniture repair job is a simple break in the leg or rung of a chair, table or stool. When the break is near the floor, you can often repair it by dowelling. Mate the two pieces together, use a thin piece of wood as a splint to get a firm grip on both parts and clamp the leg firmly to a table or bench. Mark the centre of the leg and drill a $\frac{3}{8}$-inch hole up through the break to take a dowel. Glue lightly into the hole and cut off flush with the end of the leg. Leave in splints until the glue hardens. For breaks further up the leg it is impossible to drill the two parts simultaneously. Drill separately and joint together with dowelling.

SCRATCH MARKS: You can disguise scratch marks by thoroughly cleansing the furniture with soap and water or equal parts of water and vinegar and allow to dry, then apply linseed oil to the affected part. Do not leave this on too long or it will darken the wood too much. Wipe it off after a few moments and then give the whole surface a polish with a good wax polish. Dark brown boot polish is also a good cover-up for light scratches. If small sections of veneer have flaked off, clean the break and replace the piece with liquid glue or liquid wood. The latter is only suitable for small repairs as it does not 'breathe' like wood. In the case of an old break, remove all traces of former glue with soap and water and wait until thoroughly dry. Then proceed as described above. Apply pressure while the glue is setting and remove any surplus glue carefully before it has hardened. Finish by giving the whole surface a polish, but take care not to catch the corner of the duster in the repair.

Upholstery and Upholstering Repairs:

Upholstery can be as simple or as difficult as you choose! There are several different methods of upholstering a piece of furniture and the one you decide upon will depend on the type and use of the furniture, whether it is a new piece you have made and are intending to upholster, or an old piece which needs re-upholstering.

The simplest method is padding a seat with a solid base and then covering with fabric (window seats, ottomans, piano stool, set). A second method is the use of canvas webbing stretched across a wooden frame to support padding and stuffing (dining chairs, upholstered stools, etc.). For larger seats and where more 'give' is needed, coil springs on a canvas or mesh centre can be stretched across the frame; alternatively strips of elasticised webbing or a type of cylindrical elasticised cording can be used (dining chairs with larger seats, some lightweight easy chairs, etc.). For larger pieces of furniture with sprung backs, arms and seats, the more traditional spiral or helical springs are used (settees, studio couches, the 'club' type of armchair, etc., *see Fig. 6*). Upholstering may also be done with synthetic materials such as foam rubber or foam plastic, and these are the most suitable for beginners to use when tackling an easy job such as the upholstering of a simple wooden chair, bench, window seat, etc. In addition to the methods mentioned above, you can use rushes, seagrass or cane for the seats of stools or small chairs.

Before you can begin to upholster or re-upholster you will need a few simple tools, which are not expensive but are essential *(see* TOOLS, *page 86)*.

RESEATING AN ARMCHAIR: This is one of the most common types of upholstery job you may have to tackle, for it is often possible to buy a second-hand chair quite reasonably because the seat has become hollow. Very often the job is not nearly as extensive as it looks, for the springs in a chair seat are held in position with twine, and sometimes this twine rots and breaks, causing the springs to become misshapen. Turn the chair upside down and remove the dust cover of hessian which you will find protecting the underside of the chair. If the dust cover is in good condition, remove it carefully by taking out the tacks all round with a tack remover or screwdriver. If the only damage is the rotting of the twine, manipulate the springs back into position through the divisions formed by the crossed strips of webbing (the pattern can be seen by the ones remaining in position). When the springs are replaced they should be secured in position by stitching over the end rings through the webbing with upholsterer's twine threaded on a curved needle. Four stitches should be made at equal distance apart to secure each spring and the twine firmly tied before cutting. Turn the chair upright again to check that the seat is in the correct position and then turn back and either replace the old hessian dust cover or tack a new piece into position, turning the edges under before securing to the frame.

Sometimes, once the dust cover is removed, you find the repairs needed may be a little more extensive and you may have to replace the webbing. Support the upside-down chair on a packing case or other suitable support to make the right working level. Before removing any of the springs or webbing, make a rough sketch so you will get some idea of the replacing of both springs and webbing. Even if it seems once the chair is open that only one or two strips of webbing need repairing, it is better to replace all the webbing. Otherwise the new webbing being so much stronger will cause the old to break, and the chair will soon need repairing again. Remove all the old tacks and webbing carefully and then, with all the springs, webbing and hessian removed, clean out the cavity with a vacuum cleaner. If the padding has become displaced, reshape it from inside the cavity and re-line with a piece of tightly woven hessian. The next job is replacing the springs which are positioned according to the sketch made before you took the seat to pieces. Stitch and tie the inner ends of the spring to the new hessian, taking care not to pierce through the covering of the seat when you are sewing. Stitch and tie each spring in four places as previously described. Next replace

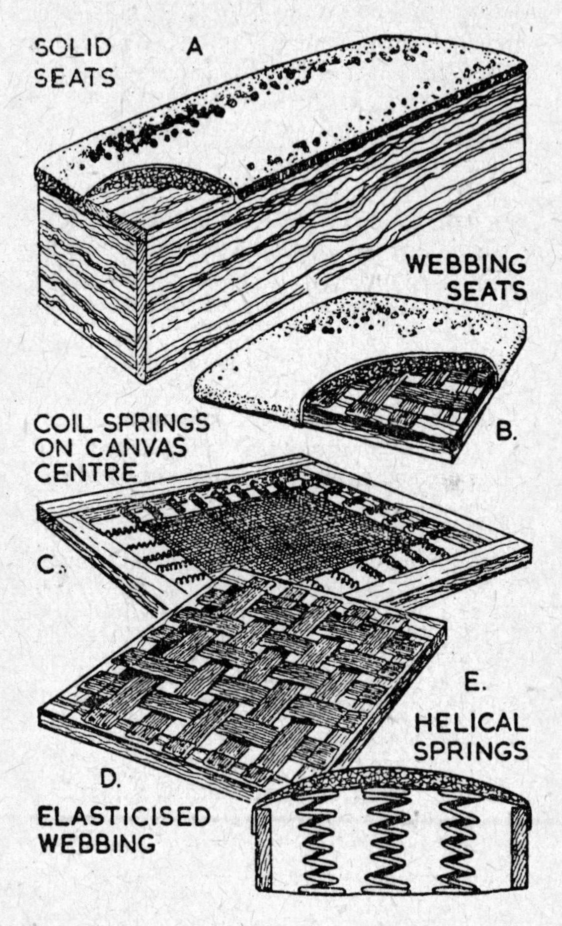

Fig. 6 Methods of Upholstering

the strips of webbing with new of exactly the same width. Do not cut each length, but use directly from the roll. First place the webbing flat on the wooden edge of the seat *(see A, Fig. 7)*. Tack with two tacks *(see B)*, leaving a small amount over for turning and staggering the tacks slightly, fold over the end of the webbing and secure with three more tacks *(see C)*, driven home firmly but not so hard that they cut into the webbing. Unroll across the frame, stretch *(see D)*, and fix to the opposite end of the frame, tacking into position in the same sequence as described above. Fix all the rest of the strips of webbing going in the same direction, before starting on the cross strips which are threaded through lattice fashion *(see E)*. Then fix the springs

Fig. 7 Reseating a Chair

in position as previously described, stitching and tying into position and finally replacing the dust cover.

If the fabric is in good repair and only needs cleaning, vacuum thoroughly and then shampoo with a good upholstery shampoo, working up a good lather and remembering not to saturate the chair. If the chair is in good condition and clean and yet the colour is all wrong with your furnishing schemes you can buy a type of spray-on dye in an aerosol canister which quickly and easily covers the chairs in a new vibrant colour. This can also be used to give faded upholstery a new lease of life if you spray with a similar but slightly deeper colour. Like all dyes it is possible to dye a light fabric a darker shade but it is not possible to dye a darker fabric a lighter shade.

The chair may need a set of loose covers, which you can make or have made, but if you are no good with a needle or simply haven't any time it is possible to buy loose covers for chairs in three pieces (four if there's a cushion) which will fit practically any armchair. They fix on in a very simple way with transparent headed screw-in pins and the sides and back are kept in position with elastic. They are quite reasonably priced and come in a range of plain or patterned fabrics.

How to Hit the Nail on the Head

HOUSEHOLD REPAIRS

HOME MAINTENANCE

IF YOU HAVE just the beginnings of an interest and know-how of do-it-yourself, it is worth tackling at least some of your routine home maintenance. Apart from the satisfaction and pride in your own efforts, you will save a considerable amount of money on labour costs.

On the other hand, try not to let your enthusiasm run away with you to such an extent that you take on jobs too difficult for you, waste time and money, and then have to call in a professional. In general, it is both safer and wiser to call in the qualified people when anything needs doing with gas or electricity, when you suspect serious outbreaks of dry rot or woodworm, or when there appears to be something seriously amiss with the roof or the plumbing.

The familiar saying says: 'A stitch in time saves nine' — and this is especially true of home maintenance. Regular checking inside and outside the home always pays dividends, and this chapter will list the main danger points and

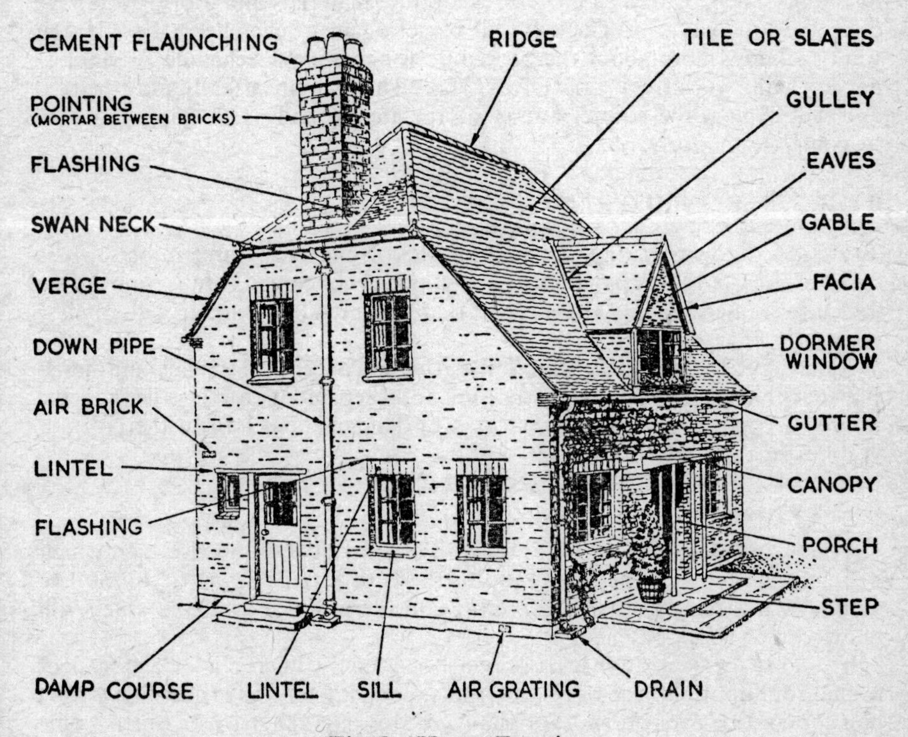

Fig. 8 House Exterior

show you how to deal with them *(see Fig. 8)* and help you locate the various areas where trouble may occur. It will also help you to know the correct terms when ordering materials or briefing your builder.

Remember that efficient home maintenance means that you are constantly adding to its value — depreciation will set in rapidly if you neglect it and then you will get an unpleasant shock when you try to sell! If you can organise your budget, it is worth setting aside a set amount each month for maintenance. Although costs may be quite small for several years, a sudden severe wintry spell or even normal wear and tear could lead to an unexpectedly heavy bill.

Check that you are fully insured. It is normally part of the agreement that you should be covered for fire if you are buying a house on mortgage. But it is better to take out a comprehensive all-risks policy which will cover you against such things as flood, frozen pipes and burglary in addition to fire. And have you insured the contents of your house?

Do keep all bills relating to work carried out on the house by professionals or odd job men, as well as bills for decorating materials and tools if you have done the jobs yourself. They can all be set against Schedule A Tax. If you want to know more about the procedure for making a Schedule A Maintenance Claim, ask at your local Tax Office. The staff are usually most helpful and will explain the complications of the tax as well as showing you how to complete the forms.

BURGLAR PROOFING

WITH BURGLARIES taking place at the rate of one every three minutes, it is wiser to be safe than sorry where your home is concerned. Make your home difficult to enter and the chances are that the intending burglar will go elsewhere.

Remember these basic precautions: Always cancel tradesmen's and newspaper deliveries when going away; do not keep money or jewellery in the house — deposit it at your bank; lock up ladders; and inform the police if you notice anything suspicious.

Locks on Doors:

Your front door should be fitted with a good quality mortise lock which will withstand any of the recognised methods of forcing an entry. If you live alone or in a remote area, it is worth considering a door chain which will allow you to check on callers.

If you use the back door when leaving the house, you need a lock equivalent to the front door. Otherwise, if you always lock it from the inside, fit a strong bolt top and bottom plus a door chain, because the majority of callers come to the back door.

A wise extra precaution would be to fit locks to the ground floor inside doors, locking from the hall side. This will restrict a burglar's movements, and double the chances of catching him.

Do not forget the garage, garden shed or other outbuildings. These should be fitted with efficient padlocks and the keys kept in a safe place inside the house.

Safety Catches on Windows:

Check all window locks or catches. There is a variety of reliable locking bolts, catches and screws available for steel casement windows and fanlights; wooden casement windows and fanlights; and sliding sash windows. These locks prevent the burglar from entering without breaking sufficient glass to admit his whole body — an obvious deterrent. A standard fastener is no protection — the thief has only to break a small area of glass and insert his hand in order to open the window.

Additional Safeguards:

If in doubt about the best way of safeguarding property, consult the police, your ironmonger or builder's merchant, or a reputable maker of security locks. Insurance companies are always interested in the security of premises they cover, and many companies are prepared to give advice.

CARPENTRY

General:

If you are fortunate enough to have a room or shed in which to work, then you are a long way towards producing a successful job. Do-it-yourself projects need space — to move, for storage, to drop everything for five hours or even days without having to clean up behind you. By this it is not suggested that you should be untidy in your workshop! But it is sometimes inconvenient to have to tidy up as you would if your workroom was the kitchen and therefore needed by other members of the family.

For those who have a limited amount of space in which to work, there are now plenty of pieces of furniture which come 'in packets', and the only tools needed to put them together are screwdriver, chisel, saw, hammer and glue. There is also a new construction system from which you can build furniture to your own design. *(see* MAKING FURNITURE, *page 70)*.

Before you start any job, sit down and plan. If possible, make a sketch of what you hope it will look like when finished!

Every job needs the right materials if it is going to look anything at all. For example, a small shelf which is going to hold one or two small items of glassware should not be made from 1-in. boards — it will not only look ugly but it is a waste of good boards. On your plan, work out which joints you are going to use and note which wall fixings are required, if any. When you have completed and checked your plans, make a cutting list and a list of other materials needed. Take them to your do-it-yourself shop and, before you actually buy the materials, get an idea of how much everything is going to cost.

When making a cupboard to fit into a corner, check that the corner is square and, if it is not, make the necessary adjustment when building the cupboard or you might find that you are unable to shut the doors properly. Whatever you make, ensure that you can get it out of your workroom or shed!

The following ideas can be adapted to fit your own particular needs: If you have a chimney breast (with the fireplace taken away and the opening boxed in) plus one or two alcoves, you can build a dressing table and wardrobes across the frontage. Make the main structure in 2×1 in. battens and hardboard; smaller door frames in 1×1 in. battens faced with hardboard; large doors in 2×1 in. battens faced with hardboard; shelf supports in 1×1 in. battens; and wardrobe rails in 1 in. hardwood dowel. If the space is available, make the wardrobes 22 or 23 in. hardwood dowel. If the space is available, make the wardrobes 22 or 23 in. deep so that clothes hang perfectly straight. If you have no time to make dressing-table drawers — or find them rather difficult to make — you can buy a pair of whitewood chests and link them with hardboard to make a dressing-table top.

Disguise an ugly waste pipe under the handbasin in the bathroom by boxing in the space beneath as a cupboard. If you have the space, extend the top about 6 in. on either side of the basin and cover with laminated plastic. Add a matching splashback.

Open stairs can be panelled flush with hardboard, one piece fixed on either side of the rails. Fit a bay window with a window seat made of 2×1 battens and hardboard, and finish with latex foam cushion. You can buy latex foam quite cheaply from surplus stores and make it up into any shape by glueing the pieces together.

Sink units can also be built with 2×1 in. battens and hardboard. Two points to remember: The waste pipe has to enter the back at a given point so do not board the back up; and be sure to give enough clearance for the basin part of the sink which will drop quite low in the framework.

These are just a few suggested home carpentry jobs. Take a look round *your* house — the possibilities are endless.

Make Your Own Bench:

If you have not got a workroom or shed, the table top work bench shown in *Fig. 9* can be adapted to suit your particular needs.

For those who have a workroom or shed, there is a bench (*see Fig. 10*) which can also be adapted to suit individual needs. The four legs are made

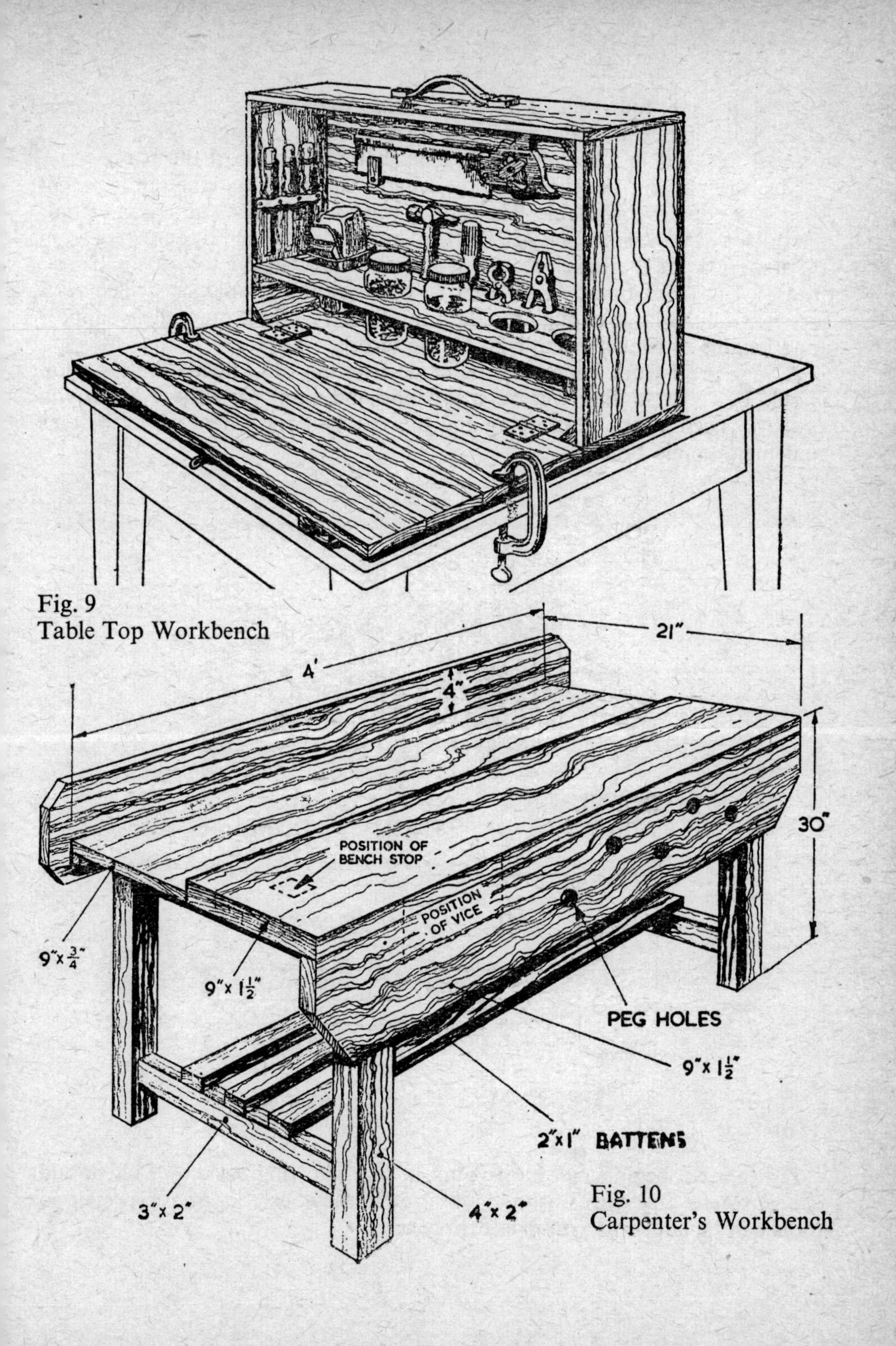

Fig. 9
Table Top Workbench

Fig. 10
Carpenter's Workbench

of 2×4 in. pine; four rails of 3×2 in. (2 rails to each pair of legs); 3 lengths of 2×1 in. batten nailed to rails to form a shelf; 3 lengths of 9×1½ in.; 1 length of 9×¾ in.; 1 length of 2×1 in. batten to support the back.

Measure and cut the timber to the lengths shown in the diagram or to fit the space you have available. The rail/leg joint is a mortise and tenon, details of which can be seen in *Fig. 11*. The top and back are fixed by screwing from the underside of the bench frame. No screws through the top of the bench, please! The front board is screwed to the legs and should be drilled with a series of holes large enough to take 1 in. dowels — these are to help support long lengths of timber being held by the vice.

A very good work bench can be made from an old kitchen table — you should be able to find one in a second-hand shop for little cost. It will probably need a little reinforcing and this can be done with 2×1 in. battens and metal angle brackets.

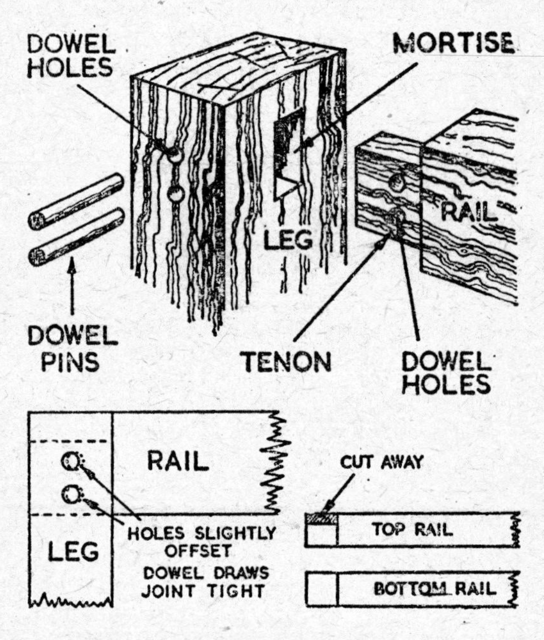

Fig. 11 Mortise and Tenon Joint

Tools:

If you are a beginner in do-it-yourself, the following basic tool kit should enable you to cope with most odd jobs around the house. The more specialised tools can be added as you gain experience:

Tenon saw
Handsaw
Hacksaws (large and small)
Claw hammer
Warrington hammer
Wooden mallet
Side-cutting pliers (large and small)
2 in. steel jack plane
Smoothing plane
Screwdrivers (assorted, including electrician's and Phillips)
Chisels ($\frac{1}{8}$ in., $\frac{1}{4}$ in., $\frac{1}{2}$ in., $\frac{3}{4}$ in., 1 in.)
Brace and bits of various sizes including countersink
Hand drill with drills of various sizes (including countersink)
Square
Rules (folding and steel tape)
Pincers
Wrench or grips
Files (wood and metal)
Clamps
Soldering iron
Marking gauge
Vice (steel)
Centre punch
Nail punch
Oilstone
Oil can
Glues

General tools for use when decorating:

Putty knife
Trowels (small and medium)
Floats (metal and wood)
Scrapers
Paperhanger's brush and shears
Plumb bob and line
Distemper brushes
Ladder and steps
Buckets
Paste board

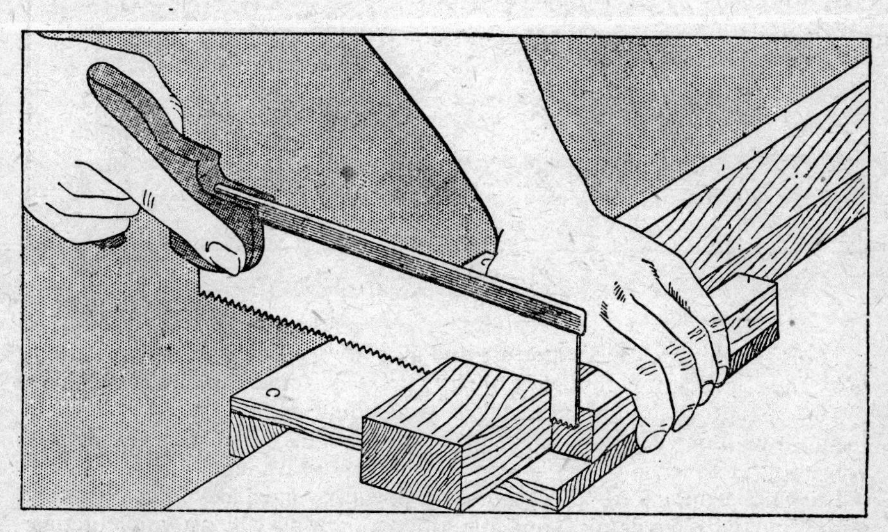

Fig. 12 Use of Mitre Box, Correct Holding of Tenon Saw

You should also have a mitre box and a bench hook. The mitre box enables you to mitre beadings, picture frames, etc., accurately (*see Fig. 12, page 87,* for the correct way of holding a tenon saw when using a mitre box). The bench hook will protect your bench top (*see Fig. 13*).

A bench stop is another useful piece of equipment. It is fitted into the bench top and lies perfectly flat when not in use (*see Fig. 14*).

Always keep a constant supply of nails (all types and sizes), screws, nuts, bolts, washers, panel pins and wall plugs. There is nothing so infuriating as having to break off a job for the want of a screw!

Fig. 13 Use of Bench Hook

Tools should be cleaned after use and all cutting edges kept sharp. Chisels, saws and similar tools should be slightly greased — there is then less chance of rust spots forming on the metal. If you should find any rust spots, clean them off with fine emery paper and then grease. You might also like to store your tools in a special rustproof paper which is now available.

It is false economy to buy cheap tools. Spend as much as you can possibly afford and, with regular care and attention, good tools will last you a lifetime and never let you down.

Safety note: Keep sharp tools out of reach of children. When using a chisel, keep your free hand BEHIND the cutting direction.

If you can afford a power tool with its variety of attachments, a lot of hard work can be taken out of many jobs around the house. Even so, it is wise to have the brace or hand drill as alternatives — power tools occasionally go wrong. If you are not going to use the drill a great deal, then it is not really worth buying dozens of attachments. As a start, you could have wire brushes, a sanding disc, and a rabbeter-cum-rip saw. Add other attachments as you gain experience and tackle more ambitious projects.

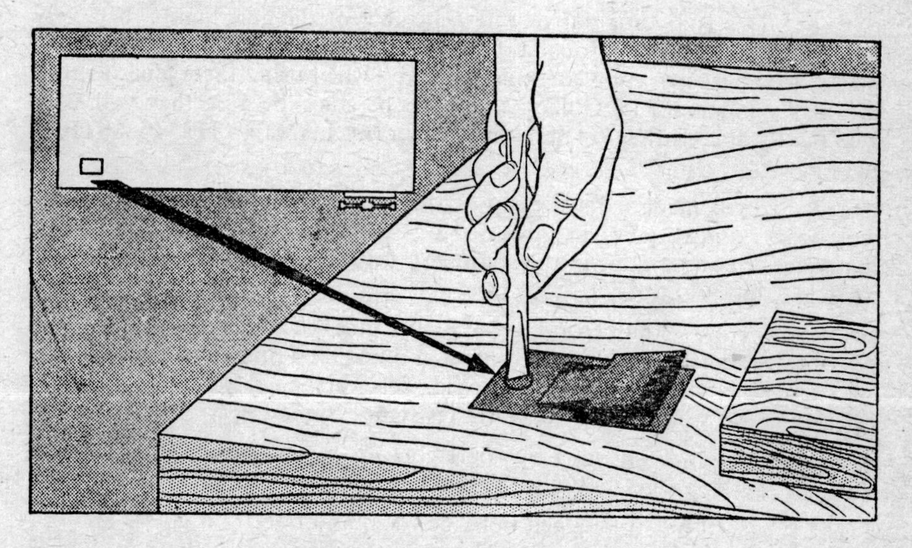

Fig. 14 Use of Bench Stop

Glues:

Why use this or that glue? This frequently asked question is answered in the following list of the various types of glue and the materials they can be used upon:

CASEIN: This is an animal glue made from skimmed and dried milk and it is used mainly in joinery work and in the making of flush doors. It will stick wood and linoleum and some plastics, and takes about six hours to set. Its resistance to water is good.

EMULSION: There are quite a number of emulsions used as glues but the one known to most people is polyvinyl acetate or, to give it its common name, PVA. It has a wide range of uses from bookbinding to woodwork. It is suitable for use on tiles and cement, and its setting time is about four hours. Its resistance to water is moderate.

EPOXY: Because of its high cost, epoxy is used on special jobs where no other glue could cope. It sticks metal to metal, china and glass, and plaster. Takes about twelve hours to set, but it is absolutely waterproof. Epoxy glues are two-part glues so always follow the manufacturers' instructions in use.

GELATINE: This is an animal glue which is very good for use on wood and can also be used on linoleum. Its water resistance is very low and it sets in about four hours. Gelatine glues can be used in either hot or cold form.

IMPACT: This is a comparatively new member of the glue family. It is very good for use on non-porous surfaces and is ideal for bonding laminated plastic to table tops, etc. Care must be taken when using these glues as they are highly inflammable. Guide surfaces to be stuck because they will stick very tightly directly they are brought together (*see* LAMINATED PLASTICS, *page 92*).

LATEX: This is made from the sap of the rubber tree. It is not suitable for woodwork joints, and is mainly used on sackings, carpet edges and other materials. It is used a lot in the stationery trade. Latex sets quickly and has a fair resistance to water.

SOLVENT: This is another rather specialist glue known to most people as polystyrene cement and Perspex cement and it is used on all types of plastics. Its sticking action is rather like a weld. Sets very quickly indeed, but it is rarely used on wood joints. Its water resistance is good.

SYNTHETIC RESIN: This is a two-part glue for use on wood and plastic. It sets glass hard in eight hours so its resistance to water is high.

The two surfaces to be glued must be clean and free from grease and oil, otherwise the surfaces will not stick no matter how much glue you use or what type it is. Choose the right glue for the job — so many glued joints part company after a time solely because the wrong glue has been used, e.g. a gelatine glue is for use on wood, not plastic, whereas a solvent glue is ideal for sticking plastics but useless for sticking wood.

Joints:

Listed below are the joints used in woodwork construction — you can practise making them on old pieces of timber or off-cuts. A point to remember when cutting any joint — always cut a little on the tight side to begin with. You can always cut more away but as a rule you cannot put back.

HALVED JOINT: This is a simple joint for making a framework of almost any description and it is quick to make. Here is an example, using 2×1 in battens. Square the ends of the pieces of wood; then make a line down the centre of the 1 in. edge; now make a line 2 in. from the end. Repeat on the second piece of wood. Following the marks, cut away half of the area marked, leaving the end of the pieces of wood looking rather like the letter L. Bring together, check fitting, and then glue together and set in clamps after making any adjustments necessary. If clamps are not available, hold together with four nails until the glue has set — they can then be pulled out.

MORTISE AND TENON: This is one of the strongest of all woodworking joints. All types of furniture and nearly all doors are made with this joint. For marking out, it is essential that you use a gauge. Set the gauge so that the wood to be joined is split into three equal sections. Next make the tenon rebate and then mark the slot at the outer end. Now mark the other end of the slot and then the tenon's shoulders. This can be seen in *Fig. 11*, *page 86*). Cut the tenon with a tenon saw, leaving the rough surface made by the saw as a key for glueing. Drill out the mortise and then square up with a chisel. The tenon should fit into the mortise with a slight tap from a mallet. If it is too tight, rub down the tenon with a rasp, to keep a rough surface for keying, until it fits. The joint is now ready to be brushed with glue and fixed into position. Any waste wood at the end of the tenon should be cut away after the glue has set.

DOWELLED JOINTS: This is a good way in which to construct a framework for light to medium-weight doors, and also for fixing timber together at odd angles. Always use two dowels — a single dowel joint twists. Mark out the two pieces of wood to be joined and drill the holes to correspond exactly with each other. Brush the holes, dowels and joint faces with glue and, to avoid trapping the glue in dowel holes, cut a notch down the sides of the dowels, thus allowing the glue to escape.

MITRED JOINT: This joint is used mainly in picture-frame making and where beading is added to a door or panel. The mitre is normally at 45 degrees, and can be cut easily with the use of a mitre block. Hold the wood firmly in the block, place the saw in the correct slot, and cut the wood *(see Fig. 12, page 87)*.

In the case of picture frames, drill holes across the mitre so that they can be pinned and glued. Pin and glue decorative beading direct to the chosen surface.

You can strengthen a mitred joint of a picture frame by making one or two saw cuts across the corners and inserting strips of thick veneer in the cuts. These, of course, should be glued and planed smooth after it has set.

ANGLE BRIDLE: This joint is a substitute for the mortise and tenon although not quite so strong — but it is stronger than the halved joint. As for the mortise and tenon, mark the wood into three equal sections. Cut the 'tenon' part of this joint — it has no rebate and is the full width of the wood. The 'mortise' part has an open end. Chisel away the centre section to form a two-prong fork. Glue and join together (not too tightly or the wood may split) and clamp. Before tightening the clamp, check for squareness.

HOUSED JOINT: This is a concealed joint used mainly for book-shelves. On the insides of the side supports mark the thickness of the shelves. If you lay the supports side by side, you can mark both at the same time and ensure accuracy. Cut these grooves to the required depth, falling short at the front by the thickness of the wood being used. Use a tenon saw and chisel for the cutting out — make sure that the saw does not mark the front of the supports. Lay the shelf end to each groove and mark a notch on the shelf to correspond with the groove. Cut these notches on the shelves. Glue together, and if possible keep under pressure until the glue has set. Panel pins can be used to add strength but this should be done with care.

LAPPED JOINT: This simple joint is used at the corners of boxes, drawers, book units and display boxes. The end of one piece of wood simply fits into a rebate cut in the other piece of wood. The rebate is L-shaped, and its depth and thickness are determined by the thickness of the wood to be lapped. To assemble, brush glue on to both pieces of wood and then pin with panel pins, checking at the same time that the joint is square.

CROSS HALVING: This joint is used to join two pieces of wood of the same thickness when they are required to cross each other. Mark the position where the two pieces of wood cross, and from each piece cut a slot which measures half the thickness of the wood by its width. Both pieces should be cut in exactly the same way. With a tenon saw, cut down to your half-way mark and then cut away the waste portion with a chisel. Repeat on the other piece. Test fitting and make any necessary adjustments. Apply glue to both supports, join together and place in a clamp. After the glue has set, clean up the joint with a smoother plane.

Tools needed for these joints are chisels, plane, mallet, square, tenon saw and marking gauge.

Laminated Plastics:

The uses of laminated plastic are so numerous that it would be impossible to list them all. Here are a few examples of how laminated plastic sheets can be used: On working tops in the kitchen; as splashbacks for sinks and cookers; table tops; trays; bathroom fittings; door facings; wall panelling, etc.

To cut laminated plastic, you need a sharp fine-toothed tenon saw. When cutting, the sheet should be well supported or it will crack, and the cutting action should be done with the saw a little off vertical. Cut with the decorative side facing upwards. If you use a circular saw, cut the sheet with the plain side upwards. In general, it is best to cut sheets a little over-size — this will give a small margin for error when you come to stick them down.

If permanent flatness is to be obtained and kept, the surface to which you fix the plastic sheet must be able to support it. Fix a balancer on the underside of the surface. This balancer can be made either from 2×1 in. battens or bonded with a piece of wood with its grain going in the opposite direction.

Before applying impact adhesive, make sure that all surfaces to be bonded are free from dust and grease and are perfectly dry. Apply the adhesive to the back of the plastic sheet and to the top of the surface. Now allow about twenty minutes for the adhesive to dry. During this time the two surfaces must not touch each other.

As there are no second chances to be had in the bonding of the two surfaces make a guide for fitting the plastic sheet. Pin a length of beading at one end and on part of one side of the surface, projecting slightly above it. Alternatively, push drawing pins into the end and side of the surface so that they project above it.

The next step must be done accurately. Lay the plastic sheet up against the guides, allowing only the edge of the plastic to come into contact with the other surface. To keep the plastic sheet from touching the other surface while you locate and square off the edge, flex the sheet upwards. When the sheet edge is in the correct position, release it gradually so that little by little the two surfaces come together. At the same time, press the sheet firmly on to the surface.

There are many sorts of edging materials to use for finishing off. Before fixing, neaten the edges with a plane or file — thus removing the over-size cutting recommended above.

CEILINGS

Cracks:

Definite cracks are the ones to worry about, not the hairline ones. The definite crack should be tested for loose plaster surrounding it. To do this, tap the plaster with the knuckles of your hand — loose plaster gives off a dull sound while firm plaster gives a much higher pitched sound. If the plaster on either side of the crack is solid, the crack should be scraped out slightly with the point of a trowel and filled with one of the many plaster fillers now available. Cracks right through plaster should be scraped out to at least one-sixteenth of an inch. Cut a wider groove in the plaster at the base of the crack, so that the filler has a base to which it can stick. Then brush out any loose dust. This type of crack is usually caused through ceiling laths being so close together that they fail to form a key for the plaster.

A crack with loose plaster round it should not be filled, but the loose plaster should be hacked away until solid plaster is reached. If, when you have taken away the loose plaster, you find that you have a large patch, fill in the normal way with an undercoat and then a topcoat. Undercoat for wood laths is composed of 1 part cement, 2 parts lime, and 8 parts sand; or 1 part gypsum and $1\frac{1}{2}$ or 2 parts sand. Undercoat for plasterboard consists of 1 part gypsum special haired browning plaster and $1\frac{1}{2}$ parts sand.

REPAIRING CRACKS: Wet edges of the old plaster and apply the undercoat. (In the case of a lath and plaster ceiling, make sure that the plaster is pushed between the laths to form a key.) Before the undercoat sets, it should be scratched up so as to form a key for the topcoat — use a piece of pointed stick for scratching the key. Before the topcoat is applied, the undercoat should be thoroughly damped down with a wet brush, otherwise the top will not 'stick'.

If the laths under the hacked away plaster are in a poor condition, they can be made good by first cutting them away altogether and renewing. Alternatively, nail a piece of plasterboard in their place to which an undercoat and topcoat can be applied as described above. A topcoat can be put direct on to plasterboard at about three-sixteenths of an inch thick. There is a board plaster made specifically for this purpose, and it can also be used as a finishing coat.

'Hair' cracks can be filled by brushing over with a watery mixed filler. Alternatively, they can be filled with emulsion paint when decorating.

Plastering:

To the amateur, plastering at first appears to be a difficult job. The difficulty is that of getting the mix to stay on. The main causes of this are: The mix being too coarse or too dry, thus making it hard to apply, so that in turn it falls off; or the mix being too wet so that it slides and runs; or the background or undercoat being so dry that it absorbs all the water in the plaster. In this case it will stick for only an hour or two after application.

The ideal mix should be one that will hold its shape without slumping, and yet on the other hand be wet enough to trowel easily. This state of the mix is partly controlled by the coarseness of the sand — but the amounts of cement, lime or plaster recommended by the manufacturer will make a mix of the right consistency.

Tools:

You will need the following tools for plastering ceilings and walls: Trowel, wood float, hawk to carry plaster, filling knife, small trowel, and bucket and an old distemper brush.

DOORS

Converting an Old Front Door:

An old-style front door can be modernised in various ways. Here are two ideas for you to consider. Before you start, make sure that the joints of the door between the stiles and rails are sound and tight.

1. Remove the door from its frame, and then remove hinges, locks, bolts, knocker and letter-box. Using the main framework as a guide (stiles, top rail, and middle rail), cut a rectangular panel in the top half of the door as near to the frame as possible. Cut two pieces of $\frac{1}{8}$ in. hardboard to cover both sides of the door, cutting a rectangle to match that already cut in the door. Glue and pin the hardboard panels to the door. The hinges should now be re-sited *(see* DOOR HINGES, *page 99)* and also the door stop. This is because in making the door flush with hardboard, $\frac{1}{4}$ in. has been added to its thickness.

A sheet of reeded glass should be fitted into the panel in the following way: Pin quarter round beading round the inside of the panel flush with the front of the door. Lay a thin cushion of putty on the inside edge of the beading and insert glass, pressing it against the putty and so forming a seal. Next, pin quarter round beading, which has been buttered with putty, to the inside of the panel pressing it firmly against the glass. The combined widths of the beading plus the thickness of the glass must make up the total thickness of the door including the hardboard panels.

Decide where your letter-box is to be fixed, cut the necessary opening and fix. A British Standards Institution specification recommends that a letter-box should be not less than $8 \times 1\frac{3}{4}$ in., should have no rough edges, and should be fitted between 2 ft. 6 in. and 4 ft. 9 in. from the ground. Fill all nail holes, smooth edge of door, sandpaper and re-decorate.

2. Fit a long narrow reeded glass window on the lock side of the door, about 9 in. wide $\times$ 66 in. deep, using the outside stile and centre rail as your guides. This is done in the same way as Method 1.

How to Flush a Door:

If the panels in an older type of door begin to shrink and show gaps or panels crack, making it difficult to keep it in good decorative order, the answer is to make it a flush door. Or, if you just want to modernise an old door, make it flush. There are two ways of flushing a door.

Measure the size of the door. You will probably find that it is one of the standard sizes and that you wood shop stocks hardboard panels to fit. Remove the door handles and also the lock, if fitted on the outside of the door, and any beading that may be above the level of the actual door frame. Now measure the width of the door opening between the door stops, and between the stop at the top of the door and the floor. Mark these measurements on the hardboard panels. When marking the depth of the door, make it the thickness of the door stop *less* than the original measurements. This is so that the panels, when fitted to the door, will have the same borders all round. Now bevel all edges of both panels, and sandpaper. Take one panel at a time and temporarily pin to the door in the correct position, and mark where the hole for the door handle spindle is to be drilled. Drill the holes, and the panels can then be glued and pinned to the door *(see Fig. 15)*. Reassemble the door handle and lock. When you are ready to decorate the door, sandpaper the hardboard panels and give them a coat of primer, then proceed in the normal way.

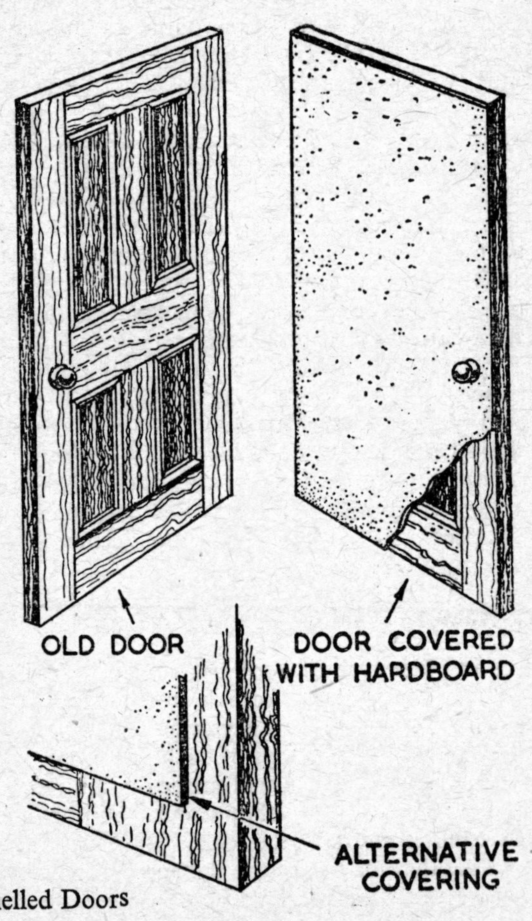

Fig. 15
Covering Panelled Doors

If you want a completely flush door, take measurements and buy appropriate size panels of hardboard from your wood shop. Remove hinges (from door and frame) and door handles and lock. Using the same method as above, mark the position of the hole for the door handle; then glue and pin panels to the door, first removing all beading that might be projecting above the frame level. Re-site the hinges, then remove the door stop beading. This will have to be trimmed by a quarter of an inch so that the door will close — you added an eighth of an inch each side of the door when you fixed the panels. Re-hang the door, and nail back the stop beading in the correct position. Re-fix all bolts, locks, etc., and adjust the lock and keep so that the door shuts smoothly. Re-decorate as for the first method.

Sliding Doors:

Light-weight cupboard doors are usually made of hardboard and they slide in wooden or nylon runners. Providing these runners are kept free of dust, sugar, flour, etc., this type of door should not give any trouble. Dust is best removed with a vacuum cleaner. If there are signs of wear between the doors and wooden runners, cut strips of laminated plastic and stick in the runners. This stops friction and thus reduces wear.

Room doors fitted with sliding gear running in a floor track or channel must be kept free of all dust and dirt. Be sparing with the oil-can as an excess of oil on the working parts of sliding door equipment can cause dirt to collect and clog tracks and wheels. Where the maker states that no oiling is needed, it is because the bearings of this type of gear are packed with grease during manufacture.

There are too many types of sliding door gear to describe here, but your local hardware store should be able to show them to you if you consider turning an ordinary door into a sliding one. If it is possible to fix the overhead track type, you will avoid obstruction and the collection of dust which goes with bottom running gear.

Doors with bottom running gear should be considered if the door you wish to convert is on a light partition wall and will therefore not take the weight of the door fixed on the overhead type of track.

There are several types of pleated sliding doors which can be fixed at home by following the manufacturer's instructions. These doors are made to fit openings 2 ft. 3 in. to 8 ft. wide, by 6 ft. 6 in., 6 ft. 8 in. and 8 ft. high.

Warped Doors:

Well-fitting doors not only look good but they do keep out draughts. A door with a slight warp is very difficult to correct, and it might well be that if the lock was made to fit a little tighter in its keep it would give a good fit between door and frame. If the lock and keep are visible on the outside of the door and frame (rim lock), then the adjustment is fairly simple. Close the door and then push it hard to see if there is any play between keep and lock. If so, the amount of this play should be taken up by setting the keep further into the frame.

If your door is fitted with a mortise lock (only the door knobs or handles are visible), then the adjustment is more difficult. The keep to this type of lock is fitted on the inside of the door frame, and this is moved towards the door stop until it is in a position to hold the door very firmly but without strain. If this adjustment does not close the gap, then try one of the following methods of sealing: Stick self-adhesive plastic foam strip on the inside of the door stop so that it forms a cushion for the door to rest in. This strip should not be stuck to the door. Alternatively, pin sprung copper strip to the inside of the door frame so that the door edge closes against the sprung section of the copper strip. In addition, you may find that the bottom of the door has been cut at some stage or other to go over a carpet, leaving a gap between door and floor. This can be filled by fixing one of the plastic or wooden draught excluders either to the floor or to the bottom of the door — whichever is more convenient.

Modern doors sometimes develop twists due to unseasoned timber being used in their construction. To correct a twist or warp, use one of the following methods — providing that the door is only about ½ inch out of true.

Open the door towards the wall and leave it open at right-angles to the frame, assuming that the warp is at the top. Fix a short length of batten to the floor in front of the door, so that the door will stay in the open position. Then measure the distance between the door and the wall when the door is tight against the batten on the floor. Cut a length of batten to this measurement, adding about one inch. Wedge this piece of batten between the door and wall, using odd pieces of timber to protect their surfaces. The door should be left in this position for three days. It should in that period go back into place.

Another method is to open the door about 12 inches, and then fix a batten to the floor to prevent the door opening any further. Cut a wedge batten as described above, and insert it between the door stop and the door. Once again, use odd pieces of timber to protect the door and frame. The door should be left in this position for three days.

The older type of door has probably had time to dry out and set in position, and no amount of straining as described above will correct a warp — especially if the door is made of hardwood.

It is possible to correct a twist by re-siting the hinges, and this also applies to modern doors which cannot be sprung back into position by one of the methods already described. If the warp is at the top of the door, the bottom hinge should be moved outwards to the extent of the warp, providing that this is not more than a quarter of an inch, and by this same method the top hinge is moved to check a warp on the bottom of the door.

When re-siting a hinge, the existing screw holes should be plugged with strips of wood before the new position of the hinge is marked. When cutting off the tops of the plugs, use a sharp chisel so that a smooth surface is obtained for the re-siting of the hinges.

If any of these adjustments prove successful, you may find that the positions of the keep, lock, bolts, or even all three, also need slight adjustments to keep them in efficient working order.

Re-shaping the door stop is yet another way in which a door can be made to fit. With this method, the opening is made to fit the door. First, close the door and then measure exactly the extent of the warp. Cut a piece of batten to this measurement and, with the door still closed, run this piece of wood, with a pencil held firmly to it, down the door so that the pencil marks out the shape of the warp on the door stop. This shape should now be cut away from the stop using a sharp chisel. *Warning:* Do not attempt to cut away large pieces of wood, cut small amounts.

With warps in flush doors, it is possible that the warp will correct itself if the door is turned upside down. This will involve, however, the re-hanging of the door plus the re-siting of locks and bolts, and 'making good' where hinges, locks, etc., were before.

Door Hinges (Or Butts):

If door hinges are worn and you wish to replace them but cannot undo the screws, try this method. Heat the end of a poker until it is red hot and hot and hold it to the head of each screw. Repeat this two or three times and you will find that you can then undo the screws.

When putting a new hinge on a door, use new screws. Fix hinges to the door first and then to the door frame. Keep the door in position with odd scraps of wood placed between it and the floor.

Rising butts are sold for left-hand and right-hand openings so make sure that you get the correct ones. Take off the old hinges and fill all screw holes tightly with strips of wood. These butts should be fitted so that the door can be lifted on and off with the top of the door just clearing the frame when the door is at right-angles to it. The half of the hinge with the spindle should be fitted to the framework, and the other half to the door. The two pivot sections should not be set tightly into the door and frame but should project into the room. If this is not done, you will be unable to put the door on to the frame or, if you do get it on, the door will bind.

Locks:

In this day and age of burglar-proof locks *(see* BURGLAR PROOFING, *page 82)*, there is very little you can do in the way of repairing locks. The majority are so complicated in design that it needs an expert locksmith to deal with them. The common rim or mortise lock found on many inside doors can be repaired at home. The repair needed is invariably the fitting of a new spring *(see Fig. 16)*. Remove the lock from the door and then remove the facing plate screw, then the plate. Next, remove the old spring from its spindle and insert the new one. Oil and clean, then reassemble and re-fix to the door.

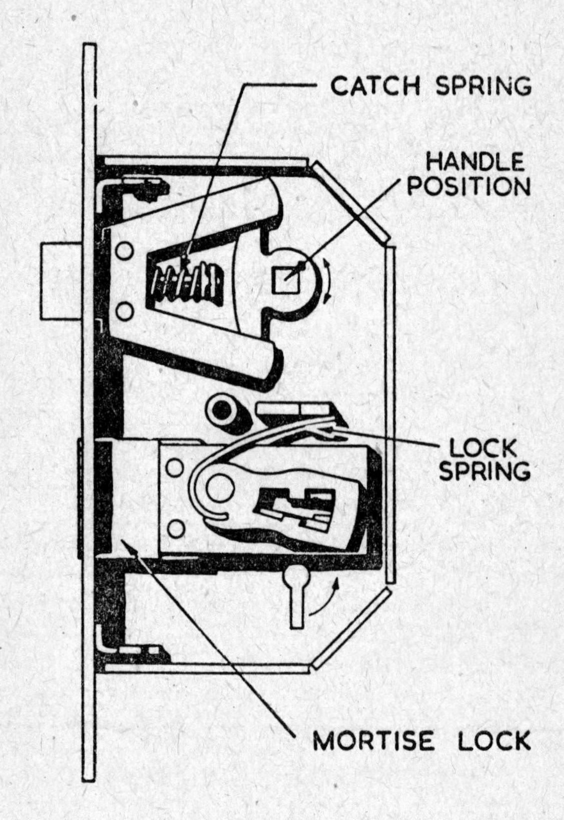

Fig. 16 Simple Lock Mechanism

Woodworm:

This is usually found at the bottom edge of the door, and the holes should be injected with one of the killing fluids available for this purpose *(see* HOUSEHOLD PESTS, *page 116)*.

ELECTRICITY

ELECTRICITY CAN be baffling — and it is both wise and safe to have a little knowledge of the way it works. You should know: how a fuse operates; what appliances you can run from the points in your home; how to keep your appliances at the maximum efficiency level; and what to do if something should go wrong.

If you have any doubt about the efficiency of any of your electrical installations or appliances, and you feel that you have not sufficient experience or know-how to cope with the necessary repairs, do call in a qualified electrician or a representative of your local Electricity Board.

The jobs you can safely do include mending a fuse; replacing a cartridge fuse; connecting up or renewing a plug or lamp holder; keeping the various leads in good order and checking for signs of wear. You can also learn how to read your own meter and so be able to calculate the amount of electricity you are consuming.

General:

The electricity supply enters your home through the Electricity Board's cable. This cable consists of wires — a red or live wire which brings in the supply at 240 volts, and a black or neutral wire which takes it back to the power station. In Great Britain, these colours are used and are a standard guide to circuits — *RED* wire for *live*; *BLACK* for *neutral* and *GREEN* for *earth.*

The Electricity Board's cable runs into the Board's own box with its sealed fuses, and then into the distribution fuse box or boxes — thus dividing the main supply into separate circuits according to the needs of the householder. It is these circuits that are the householder's responsibility. In old houses, you will probably find that cooker, heater, sockets, etc., have separate circuits, while a single circuit will carry several lighting points.

A.C. and D.C.:

A.C. means alternating current. D.C. means direct current. It is not necessary to know the difference between the two forms of power supply but you should know which you have because, in general, appliances marked D.C. cannot be used on an A.C. circuit, and likewise A.C. appliances cannot be used on a D.C. circuit.

There are a few areas in Great Britain which still use the D.C. supply but these are gradually being altered to A.C. When buying appliances, do check that you get the right type.

Cookers:

Keep your cooker clean and free from grease, but before attempting to clean make sure that it is switched off. You will find the job easier if the cooker is still warm — before the splashes have had a chance to harden. It is safer not to meddle if the switches do not work or if the thermostat fails or if a plate refuses to get hot. You should call in an experienced electrician rather than 'see for yourself'.

Faulty Switches:

Switch off at the mains before you begin to investigate a faulty switch. There are three common faults which you can quite easily put right.

If you find the mechanism of the switch broken, it cannot be repaired, so buy a new one, making sure that it is of the same type as the old one. If you do this, you will find that in nine cases out of ten the same fixing holes will do — thus obviating the need for fresh fixings. The leads should be fixed to the new switch in the same terminals as they were in the old. Make sure that all terminal screws are tight before replacing the switch cover.

A second fault in a switch is a loose wire or terminal. This is easily rectified by tightening the grub screw, but you would be well advised to check the reason for the loose wire or terminal. If in doubt, install a new one.

If, when you switch on the light, it flickers or the radio crackles it probably means that the delicate spring contacts which receive the moving part of the the switch have become weak and are failing to grip. Switch off the current and then, using a small pair of strong pliers, press the spring contacts together with steady pressure, checking that the knives (moving part of the switch) fall into the correct position when you switch on. If the spring contacts are too tight, the knives will rest on top of them.

Fires:

All new electric fires must have guards — this is law. If you have an old fire, enquire about having a guard fitted at your local electricity showroom or through the manufacturers.

To get the maximum possible heat from radiant fires, the reflectors must be kept clean and polished. A dirty reflector absorbs heat instead of pushing it out into the room.

Never light spills, paper or cigarettes from the element — you could break it. And remember that a frayed flex could give you a nasty shock.

If the element does burn out, it is fairly simple to replace. Remove the guard; unscrew the old element and lift from the spring supports; insert the new element (of the right voltage and wattage); tighten the terminal units; and then replace the guard. Once again, make sure that the fire is NOT connected to the mains before you start work.

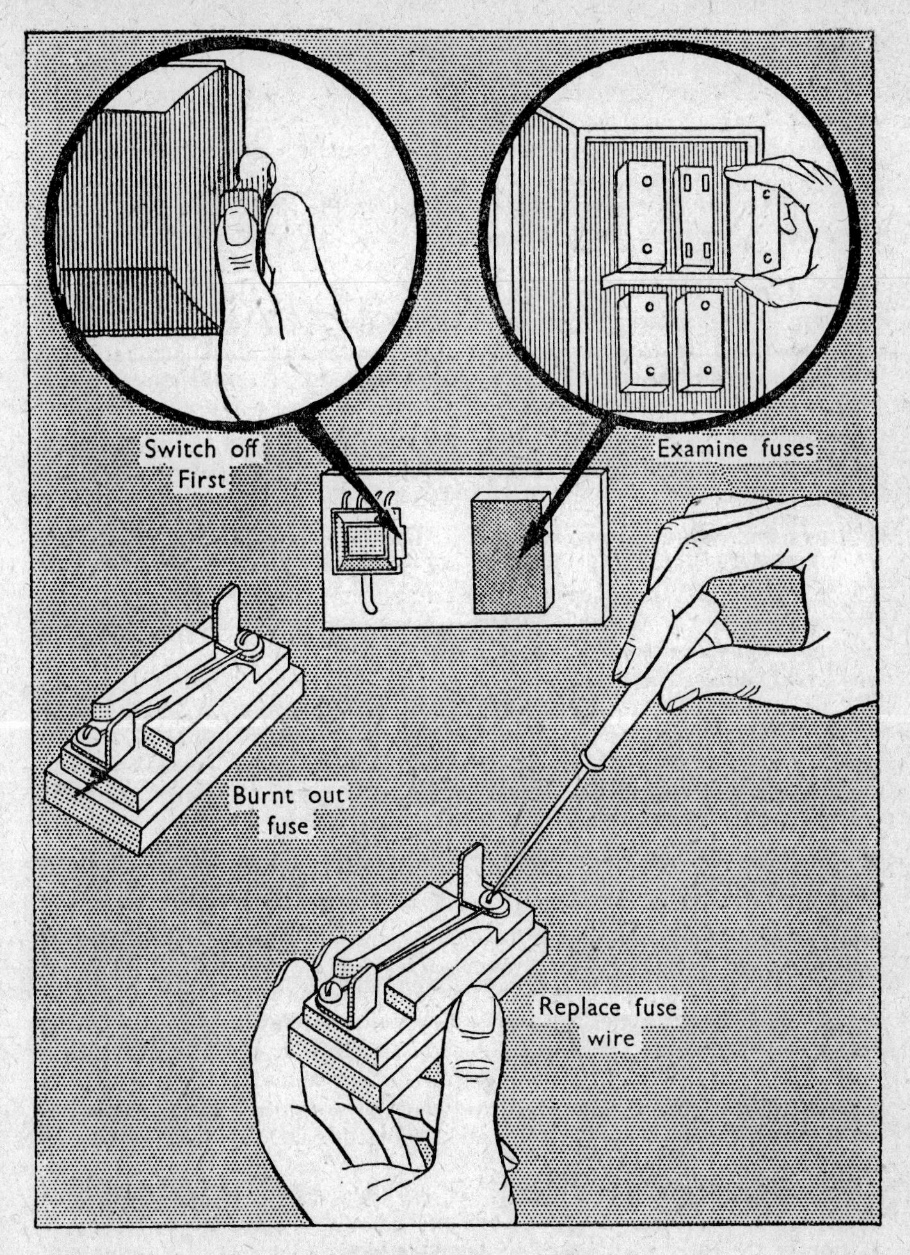

Fig. 17 Repairing a Fuse

Fuses:

These are the 'deliberate mistakes' in your circuits and are designed to melt or break if a particular circuit is overloaded.

Rewireable and cartridge fuses are the two main types. If your home is fitted with the old type of installation, you will find the fuses arranged in rows and they will be of the porcelain type (on the ring circuit there is only one fuse). A cartridge fuse is found inside each standard 13 amp. square pin plug — it is a small cylinder with a metal cap at each end. These fuses are supplied in the following ratings: 2 amp — blue case; 5 amp — grey case; 13 amp — brown case. Some round 3-pin plugs are fused. The live or real pin screws into the base of the plug and carries the fuse. To change, unscrew and screw in the new pin. These fused pins are as follows: 3 amp — blue; 5 amp — red; 7 amp — yellow; 13 amp — white.

When one of your appliances stops working, or the lights go out, it usually means that a fuse has blown. The cause may be due to:

1. Too many appliances being run at the same time all on one circuit.

2. Irons and/or fires being run off the lighting circuit. *THIS PRACTICE IS VERY DANGEROUS AND MUST NOT BE DONE IN ANY CIRCUMSTANCES.* Appliances must be earthed in the proper manner.

3. The wires into a plug or holder have frayed and are shorting out (current passing from red wire to black or direct to earth *(see* PLUGS, SOCKETS *and* LEADS, *page 108)*.

When moving house, label the fuse boxes so that you know which circuits they cover — lighting or power. Make this one of your first jobs — you will then be able to trace a blown fuse more quickly. Spare fuses, fuse wire, small electrician's screwdriver (there are several makes of screwdriver for this job incorporating a device for cutting fuse wire) and a small torch or candles should have a permanent home as near to the fuse box as possible. This will save both time and temper!

To renew or change a fuse, first switch off the electricity supply. Most fuse boxes have an ON/OFF switch built into them but, if your installation is of the older type, switch off at the mains.

Take the fuse from the box and remove the broken wire. Check that there are not any bits left under the screws. Insert the new fuse wire, of the correct rating, first round one screw, then over the bridge and round the other screw *(see Fig. 17, page 103)*. Tighten the screws, cut away any long ends of wire, and check that you have not pulled the wire too tight. Then push the fuse back into the box, close the box, and switch on. DO NOT SWITCH ON BEFORE THE BOX IS SHUT.

If your entire electrical system is not working and you have checked your fuses and found them in order, then there is either a failure at the power station or the Electricity Board's fuses have blown — either at a sub-station or inside your home. Inform the Board who will advise you — there is an emergency service in operation 24 hours a day.

Replacing a cartridge fuse is a much simpler job. Normally the fuse is situated in the top of the plug. To renew it, the plug top should be removed and the fuse will then be seen held in position by two spring clips on the red or live side *(see Fig. 18)*. Lift out the old cartridge fuse and press in the new but make sure that the new fuse is of the correct rating. In the latest type of plug, there is no need to take the top off. The fuse is in its own case which can be levered out, new fuse inserted, and then pushed back into position.

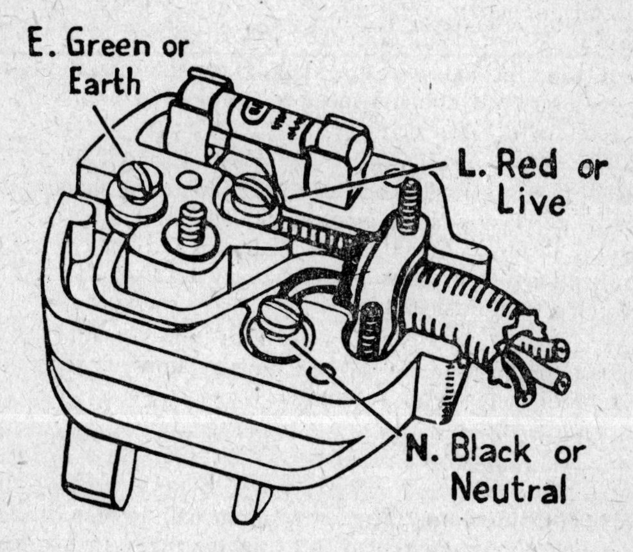

Fig. 18 Cartridge Fuse

A general guide to the load that can be placed on a cartridge fuse is as follows: 2 amp fuse (blue) below 400 watts; 5 amp fuse (grey) between 400 and 1200 watts; 13 amp fuse (brown) between 1200 and 3000 watts.

Irons:

Most irons these days are thermostatically controlled and when the correct heat is reached a small pilot bulb, usually found in the handle, goes out. This bulb can burn out and it is quite a simple job to replace it. Make sure the iron is not plugged into the mains and then unscrew the plate that houses the bulb — it is fixed to the iron handle with a single bolt. The bulb is found at the top of this plate held in position in a spring clip or screwed into a cup. Remove the old bulb and insert the new one, then screw the plate back into position.

Lamps:

There are many different sorts and sizes of the electric lamp but only a few of these of interst for home use *see* LIGHTING, *page 52.*

Clear lamps are made of clear glass and give a hard brilliant light that casts shadows. They are very good for use in cut glass or Perspex fittings because they add a certain glitter. Pearl lamps are made of frosted glass to give a soft light, and are suitable for most kinds of home lighting.

Silica lamps give a softer light than pearl and are ideal for use in open fittings. Mushroom lamps are fairly new. Their great advantage is their smallness without loss of light, and they will fit into the smallest of shades.

Fluorescent tubes provide excellent lighting for the workroom or kitchen. They give an even light and are most economical in use. Spotlights have built-in reflectors which can be angled to direct beams of light on favourite pictures, flower arrangements, etc.

A surprising amount of dust and dirt accumulates in shades and fittings, and even more surprising is the amount of light robbed by the dirt. Avoid this by regular cleaning. Clean shades with the vacuum cleaner; and take down and wash Perspex or glass shades. If they are fixed fittings, make sure that you switch off before cleaning.

Always keep several spare lamps in the house and remember that the best is the cheapest in the long run. When buying lamps, check that you are buying the correct voltage and wattage.

Wiring a Lampholder:

Switch off the mains supply. Cut away about half an inch of the insulated covering on each wire, twist the wires to tighten them, then thread the flex through the top section of the holder. Undo the terminal screws, then fold the ends of the wires back on themselves leaving about a quarter of an inch strip of bare wire which is inserted into the terminals. Tighten the screws and pass the flex round the shoulders of the holder and tighten the top. This action grips the flex in the holder so that it will take the weight of the lampshade.

If you have to renew the flex into the ceiling rose, first switch off, then unscrew the ceiling rose cover. Loosen the terminals holding the old flex in position — noting which they are so that the new flex is connected to them. Cut back the insulated covering, thread the rose cap on to the wire, insert the wire into the terminals and tighten the screws. If the rose is made with shoulders to hold the flex, they should be used so that the weight of the light fitting is not borne entirely by the terminal screws. Screw back the cover, and switch on.

Loading of Electrical Appliances:

Here is a useful list showing the loading in watts of many familiar household appliances:

Appliance	Watts
Blankets	100
Clocks	negligible
Clothes dryers (heated)	3,000
Cookers	6,000 to 12,000
Convectors	2,000
Shavers	8
Fan heaters	2,000
Radiant fires	2,000
Floor polishers	250
Food mixers: + large	200
+ small	40
Hair dryers	450
Immersion heaters	3,000
Irons: ordinary	450
heat controlled	900
steam dry	1,000

Appliance	Watts
Kettles	2,000
Radio	50
Record players	50
Refrigerators: absorption	125
compression	200
Spin dryers	150
Tape recorders	50
Tea makers	750
Television receivers	150
Toasters: ordinary	450
automatic	900
Vacuum cleaners	150
Washing machines: unheated	200
heated	3,000
with spin dryer and heater	3,000
Water heaters: sink	2,000
supplying all taps	3,000

Meter Reading:

You can keep a check on expenditure by learning how to read your own meter *(see Fig. 19)*. The units consumed are calculated by subtracting the last reading taken from the present reading. Read a meter as follows: Ignore the smallest circle of figures which may be in red. The far right-hand circle indicates single units; the next tens; then hundreds; and finally thousands. If the pointer is in between two numbers, the lower figure is taken for the reading.

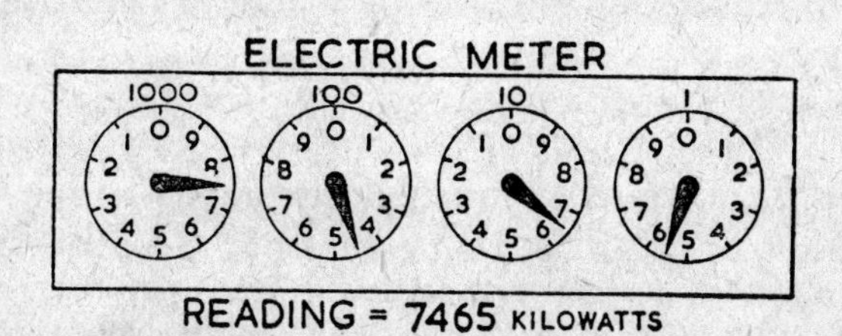

Fig. 19 Electric Meter Reading

Plugs, Sockets and Leads:

A periodic check should be made on all leads, flexes, plugs and socket connections, adaptors, switches and holders — not forgetting the lengths of wire from which overhead light fittings are suspended. Before attempting any repairs, *SWITCH OFF.*

On appliances such as irons and vacuum cleaners, which have a lot of heavy work, plugs should be checked for tightness. Make sure that the wires have not pulled away from their terminals — holding by one strand of wire is not good enough. If you find that the wires have frayed or the insulated covering has broken, cut the wire well back and make fresh connections. If you find when you cut back the coverings that the wires are perished, then renew the whole cable. *Fig. 18, page 105* will help you to wire a standard 3-pin 13 amp plug. This method of re-wiring also applies to conventional round 3-pin plugs. Pins are labelled N-BLACK, L-RED and E-GREEN. The earth or green pin is always the thicker one.

All modern sockets and switched sockets are marked in the same way. If reasonable care is taken and the black wire is put to N, the red wire to L, and the green wire to E, it is possible to change a broken socket or plug without having to call in an electrician.

Radio and Television Sets:

Before you attempt to do any repairs or even look in the back of a radio or TV set, *IT MUST BE DISCONNECTED* from the electricity supply — switching off at the set or socket is not good enough. The plug must be removed from the socket. The reason for this is that most radio and TV sets are connected to the electricity supply with a 2-pin plug. As this plug can be fitted either way round in the socket, it could make the chassis of the set live although it may be switched off. The outside cabinet and controls are insulated against this so the set is quite safe — until you 'have a look' without removing the plug from the socket.

Refrigerators:

The modern refrigerator is so designed that it rarely goes wrong. If it does, it is best to call in your local Electricity Board or a qualified electrician.

You can keep your fridge efficient by defrosting at regular intervals so that the freezing unit does not get festooned with ice. Keep the inside free from dirt (from the bottom of milk bottles, etc.) and always wrap food in polythene bags or place in plastic containers. When the refrigerator is not in use and the current is turned off, always leave the door ajar.

Ring Circuits:

This is the modern method of wiring circuits. Instead of running separate circuits to each point or socket, one length of cable encircles the house starting and ending at the fuse box. From this single cable you run as many points as are needed, each socket being the same size and each plug carrying its own fuse which can be used in any of the sockets on the circuit. The fuses in these plugs are of the cartridge type. The great advantage of the ring circuit is that if you blow one of the fused plugs the rest of the sockets can still be used (*see* REPAIRING A FUSE. *Fig. 17, page 103)*.

The ring circuit is cheaper to install than a series of separate circuits. The plugs and sockets are standard which makes it possible to use appliances at any socket without changing the plug or using an adaptor. It is an ideal system with which to modernise or even to supplement old installations.

Vacuum Cleaners:

There are two main faults that occur in vacuum cleaners: Broken or badly fitting leads, and worn out carbon brushes. Leads and plugs should be checked and made good as described in PLUGS, SOCKETS AND LEADS, *page 108*.

Carbon brushes on an upright cleaner are housed either side of the motor casing and are held in position with a large grub screw. Unscrew, and lift out the old brushes and springs. In the cylinder type cleaner, the end cap has to be removed to gain access to the motor and the carbon brush slots. As in the upright cleaner, these brushes are held in position with grub screws. Make sure that the new brushes are of the right type for your particular cleaner. They vary in size and shape according to the make of the cleaner, and if you insert the wrong type of brush you will damage the motor.

A vacuum cleaner motor usually runs warm, but if it gets very hot and smells, switch off and do not use the cleaner until a qualified electrician has overhauled it.

On upright models, keep the slits at the rear of the motor casing free from dust and fluff — these slits are part of the motor's cooling system. Keep the motor clean and free of carbon dust. With a cylinder machine, the end cap will have to be removed to do this. Cleaning is done with a piece of *dry* cloth.

Do observe the following safety precautions: Before you attempt to do any repair on the machine, you MUST isolate it from the electricity supply — this means pulling the plug out of the wall socket. Do not attempt to stretch carbon brush springs to make up for the worn brush. Do not attempt to join broken leads by twisting them together and covering them with insulating tape. Do not run your cleaner off the lighting circuit.

Voltage:

The supply of electricity is measured in volts and it is gradually being standardised at 240 volts in Great Britain. Your local Electricity Board will inform you of your present voltage. Electric bulbs are made to an exact voltage whereas heaters have a range between 200–210, 220–230, or 230–240. Appliances with motors work on a wider range still — 220–250.

FLOORS

General:

Sanding machines can be hired to enable you to get a smooth flat floor either for laying floor tiles, wood blocks, or parquet flooring, or for preparing the wood before staining and polishing.

If you are unable to hire a sanding machine and you wish to lay lino tiles or something similar, plane the floor as level as you possibly can with a jack plane. Then pin ⅛-in. hardboard panels of the largest manageable size to cover the floor. Lay your new floor on these panels.

When nailing boards to joists, the nails should be twice the thickness of the floorboards. For example, if the board is one inch thick the nail should be two inches long. Hammer in at a slight angle.

Dry Rot in Wooden Floors:

One of the most important things about a wooden floor, particularly a ground floor, is good ventilation *(see* VENTILATION, *page 131)*. Check that air bricks are properly placed, therefore ensuring a complete circulation of air between the boards. It is nearly always in the corners created by misplaced air bricks that the air 'stands still' and dry rot begins. From the outside, it may look as though your air bricks are all right but check that the parting walls have holes to allow the air to pass across the entire floor from air bick to air brick.

Dry rot usually attacks at ground floor level or below. If you suspect dry rot, these are the signs to look for: A damp musty smell; skirting and floorboards curving outwards; the presence of a fine reddish powder; surface cracks across the grain of the wood; or even the appearance of a toadstool or fruit body. Push a bradawl into the suspect wood — if it meets with no resistance, then the wood is almost certain to be infected.

Any sign of dry rot *(or woodworm — see* HOUSEHOLD PESTS, *page 116)* in floorboards should be treated immediately. If it has only affected the floorboards, you have no choice but to rip the boards out and burn them at once. If you cannot afford to do this, you must destroy the board 3 ft. on either side of the trouble spot. Check the joists and, if they are not infected, be safe and paint with creosote or one of the special dry rot fluids. If you can get at the wall, it should be heat treated with a blow lamp to kill all spoors, and then treated with dry rot fluid.

The common causes of dry rot are: Faulty guttering and down pipes; dripping overflow pipes; floors with impermeable floor coverings; clogged air bricks, as described above; and condensation in moist overheated conditions.

When making repairs with new wood, give it two coats of dry rot fluid before putting into place. Immerse the ends of the timber in a pail containing some of the fluid for a few minutes.

Floorboards:

To lift a floorboard, drill a small hole through the board as close to the joist as possible. Insert a pad-saw in the hole and saw the board at a slight

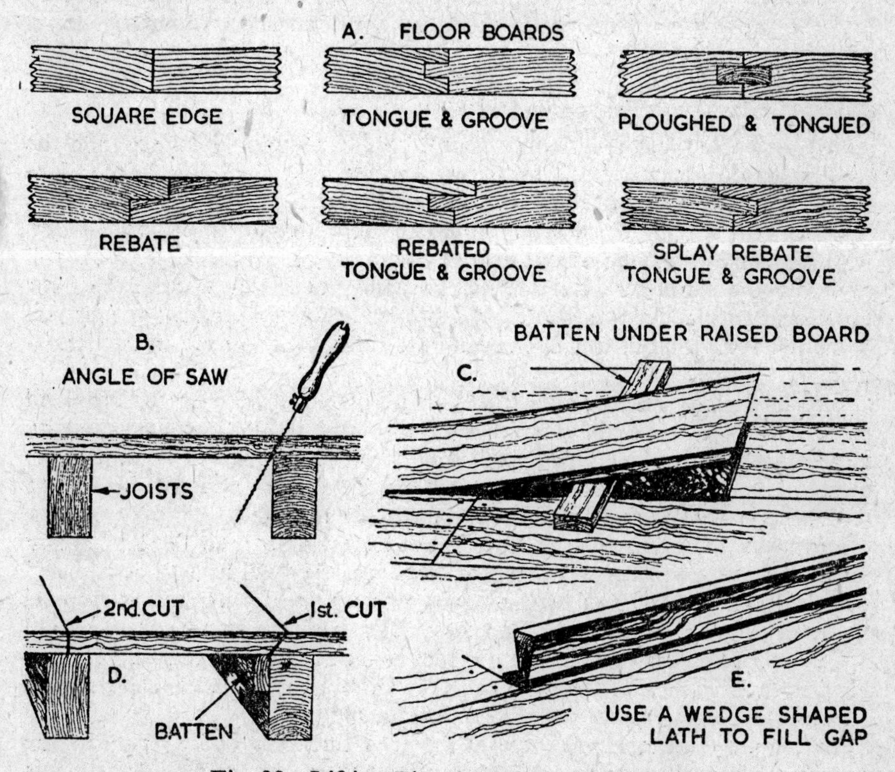

Fig. 20 Lifting Floorboards and Filling Gaps

angle. Before replacing the board, fix a short length of batten to the side of the joist to support the cut board *(see Fig. 20, page 111)*.

If the middle of a floorboard is warped and bows downwards, take the board up and reverse it. Then, instead of nailing it to the joists, screw it with one screw in the centre of the board at every joist. If the board bows upwards, release the nails holding the board to the joists and then screw down as described above.

If the gaps between floorboards are large and cover the whole floor, it would be better to lift all the boards and re-lay them, filling the space left with a new board. Small gaps, or odd large gaps, can be filled by inserting wedge-shaped laths between the boards concerned and then planing off level with the rest of the floor *(see E, Fig. 20)*.

Small gaps can also be filled with papier mâché. Tear newspaper into small pieces and place in an old saucepan; cover with water and heat. When the paper softens, add about 1 oz. size for each pint of pulp. Allow the mixture to boil for five minutes or so and then beat to a smooth pulp. Press the pulp into the gaps with a putty knife or similar tool and allow to harden. Level off with sandpaper.

Tiled or Flagstone Floors in Old Houses:

It is probable that these floors will not have concrete foundations, and the tiles or flagstones will be laid directly on to the earth. There is therefore no insulation and no real base on which to do repairs.

One of the special plastic mixes could be laid on this type of floor — but, with no solid foundation beneath, its durability is questionable. You will also lose the character of the floor. The only remedy is to take the floor up altogether and lay a new one on a proper concrete foundation. This will be quite a long job but it is not beyond the skill of the average home handyman.

Lift the existing flagstones or tiles with a crowbar, using a small hardwood block to give the necessary leverage. If the floor is tiled, you will find on inspection that they are so cracked, split or worn that it will be impossible to use them again except for use in the concrete base. You will be able to re-use flagstones except for those that are badly damaged.

Dig away the earth to a depth of about 4 in. or so and fill 3 in. (these measurements are for quarry tiles; for flagstones they will have to be adjusted according to the thickness of the stone) with a mix of 4 parts coarse gravel to 1 part cement. When making up the mix, it would be an advantage to add a water-proofing ingredient. The old tiles can be used as aggregate but must be measured as part of the mix, and they should be cleaned and broken up so that the pieces are about the size of large marbles.

To help lay the concrete base at an even thickness and to prevent the concrete from cracking when drying, lay battens to form compartments of about 6 × 2 ft. Lay a spirit level along and across the battens to ensure that they are perfectly level — broken slate is ideal as packing to bring the battens up to the correct level. These battens also need support so that they do not move when you lay the concrete mix. Do this either by laying bricks or flagstones on the battens, moving them along as you concrete, or fix them in position by driving pegs into the earth.

The mix should now be laid into the compartments formed by the battens, one or two sections at a time. Level off with a baulk of timber long enough to span two compartments; then with the straight edge resting on the battens, make a zigzag motion across the top of the concrete. This will remove any surplus mix (which can be trowelled off and dropped into the bed of the next section) and produce a level surface. Do not attempt to smooth this surface out — its roughness will act as a key for the next layer of cement. The base must be given plenty of time to harden and no more work should be done on it until then. When hard, the wooden battens (and pegs, if used) should be lifted away and the surface made good with the same mix. Allow these fillings to harden before proceeding with the next stage.

The next step is to lay the cement floor, and this should consist of a strong mix of 3 parts clean sand to 1 part cement with a waterproofing ingredient added. Before laying the mix, check the space left to be filled between the bottom of the skirting board and concrete base, allowing for the thickness of the tile or flagstone to be used.

Using a float, lay the mix to a thickness of about 1 in. This may be slightly more or less depending on the finished floor heights and the thickness of the tiles or flagstones. Inch thick battens, weighted to hold them in position, will help you to keep a level surface. This must be left to harden and dry out before you begin to lay the tiles or flagstones. There are two ways in which they can be laid on the cement floor, but do take notice of the warning in the first method.

1. Tiles or flagstones can be fixed in a bed of bitumen, brushed on to the cement at $\frac{1}{8}$ in. thick. The cement surface must be clean of all dust and *must be absolutely dry*. Time must be given for the cement to dry right out (not just surface dry) — the period of drying could take as much as three months according to the weather and the time of the year. Put the tiles or flagstones in position before the bitumen has time to set. With this method, the bitumen acts as a damp course, but all your efforts will be wasted if the bitumen is applied to the cement before it has properly dried out.
2. Set the tiles or flagstones in a cement adhesive made up of equal parts of clean dry sand and cement and mixed to a consistency of batter. Soak them in water before setting in the mix, and use a spirit level to help you lay them evenly. A watery version of the mix can be poured in the joins between the tiles or flagstones. In the case of tiles, any mix spilt on the tile faces should be removed immediately or it will mark. After two or three days

drying out period, you will probably find that the joins will need a little more filling. Although this is a boring job, it should be done or the joins will collect dust and dirt and the floor will never be clean.

One or two points about cement mixes: Use only dry clean sand or aggregate; see that the cement is fresh and free from lumps; and dry mixing should be done before adding water — do not add too much water, just enough to make a mix like stiff dough.

GAS

REGULAR CLEANING is the best way of keeping your gas appliances in efficient working order. There are a few small maintenance jobs which can be done at home but, for safety reasons, you should ask the advice of your local Gas Board regarding choice and installation of appliances. The Board's fitters also service and overhaul appliances — the cost of a servicing contract is very reasonable.

General:

NEVER look for a gas leak with a naked light. If you smell gas, check first that all taps are turned off and that all pilot jets are alight. If these are all right and the smell persists, you can make the following test.

Turn off all appliances and pilot lights and ensure that the main cock tap is full on. Now watch the meter dials. The test dial is situated above the other four *(see Fig. 21, page 116)*. Mark the position of the pointer and after a few minutes check to see if the pointer has moved. If it remains steady, there is no leakage, but if the smell still persists inform your local Gas Board. There could be a fractured main in the vicinity of your home and gas may be coming through the floors or walls. If the dial has registered gas usage, it denotes a definite leak in your installation. Call in your Gas Board fitter immediately to check and repair.

If you do locate a leak, a temporary repair job can be carried out with putty or a layer of wet soap bound with insulating tape. Then call the Gas Board to come and make a proper repair.

Every so often you should check that your main cock and main taps attached to the water heaters are working properly. *Warning:* After checking, be sure to relight all pilot jets.

Cookers:

Every cooker should be cleaned frequently — and it is an easier task if carried out while the cooker is still warm. Dismantle and clean the burners every month or two, making sure that the jet holes are free from grease, etc. A pipe cleaner is an ideal tool for this job. Check that all taps are working correctly and that the inlet gas jet is quite clean and free from grease and dirt. If the taps on the older type of cooker are difficult to operate, the small brass nut at the rear of each tap should be loosened by not more than a quarter of a turn — a tap must never be so loose that it can be turned on at the slightest touch. If, on the other hand, the tap is loose, then tighten the nut slowly, checking until it is tight.

Most modern cookers are fitted with self-igniting burners. You should ensure that the pilot light jet and the tubes running from it to the various burners are kept clean and free from scraps and grease. If they become clogged, the light from the pilot cannot travel along to the burners. Dirty tubes therefore can be dangerous. For example, if the oven failed to ignite, you could open the door after a few minutes expecting to find it warm and instead discover an oven full of gas. If this should happen, turn off the tap, open all windows and doors (including the oven door!) and allow gas to disperse before relighting.

Gas Fires:

All gas fires must be guarded and the law states that special guarding is necessary on any fire in a room in which young children are left alone. Modern fires are sold with guards fitted, and you should enquire at your local Gas Board showroom about having a guard fitted to an older fire. Another safety rule — do not use rubber tubing.

The reflector on portable fires should be kept clean and polished so that maximum heat is obtained.

Replacing a broken radiant is quite a simple job. In most cases you push it up as far as it will go and then pull the bottom towards the front of the fire and downwards. Reverse this procedure when inserting a new radiant.

Reading a Gas Meter:

If you can read your gas meter *(see Fig. 21, page 116)*, you will be able to check either the consumption of an individual appliance or the week-by-week usage. Quarterly payment meters are fitted with a series of dials — the exact number of dials may vary from three to five. The diagram shows a four-dial window. However many the dials, each is marked with its value. The dials shown, from left to right, indicate 10,000, 1,000, 100 and 10 cubic feet. Consumption is indicated by the position of the needle on each dial, and an example reading is given in the diagram. Deduct the total of the last reading from the new total to determine the consumption between last and present readings.

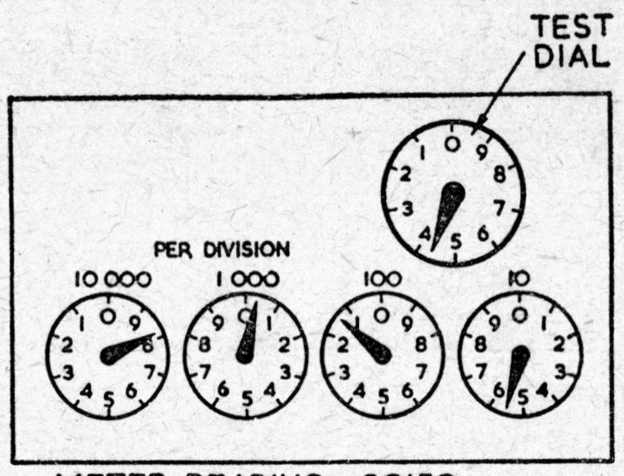

Fig. 21 Gas Meter Reading

Refrigerators:

Apart from keeping the flue and burner free of dirt, there is nothing else that you can do other than regular defrosting. If you allow too much ice to form on the freezing unit, the efficiency of the refrigerator is impaired, and it will cost more to run. Do not cover the grille at the back of the refrigerator when it is in operation.

HOUSEHOLD PESTS

DESPITE MODERN STANDARDS of hygiene, household pests are still a menace and have to be dealt with. It is worth remembering that pests will flourish in household articles which are not given regular attention. Thorough cleaning and inspection is still the greatest preventive.

Fleas:

Human fleas and cat and dog fleas usually infest and breed in bedrooms, on carpets, rugs, or in the baskets or kennels in which pets sleep.

If an animal has fleas, dust DDT into its fur. It will try to lick the powder off so avoid heavy powdering or your pet will make itself ill. Keep its sleeping mat or blanket clean and well shaken — treat with insecticide if necessary.

If there is a serious outbreak of human fleas, fumigate the room concerned by closing all doors and windows; then spread flaked naphthalene on the floor. Leave for 24 hours. Open and air the room, clean carpets and rugs, and scrub the floor with hot water and soda.

Flies, Bluebottles and Blowflies:

Avoid the attentions of these pests by always wrapping waste food before placing it in the dustbin; keeping food covered at all times; and keeping your dustbin disinfected and free from rust. If you are still plagued by flies, etc., use an aerosol fly killer.

Moths:

The clothes moth and house moth grubs are most likely to be found indoors as they feed on animal products such as wool and fur. The clothes moth is small, coloured pale yellow or brown, and folds its wings like a humped tent. The brown or grey house moth folds its wings flat and scissor-wise. They breed in birds' nests — so be on the look out if you have nests near the house.

If you keep rooms thoroughly aired and cleaned, there is less likelihood of moth damage. But keep a check on rooms which are seldom used; if you have central heating; and if you have fitted carpets (many are now moth-proofed during manufacture). Never put winter woollies and blankets away unless they have been dry-cleaned or washed. Furs should be sealed in stout paper packages.

Keep moths at bay by placing protective discs in cupboards and drawers or by spraying carpets, upholstery, blankets, cloths, etc., with a mothproofing spray or aerosol. If an article should become infested, it should be burned immediately.

Rats and Mice:

If you spot rats or mice in or around your home, inform your local authority. Most authorities maintain a free service to deal with these rodents.

Alternatively, you can buy specially prepared poisons from the chemist, or set baited traps. Special care should be taken if you keep poultry or pets. Unwanted food should not be left where it is likely to attract the attention of unwanted rats or mice! And remember that an energetic cat is still the best preventive.

Woodworm:

Woodworm has become Britain's national pest! Every year thousands of private houses, often quite modern ones, have to be treated for attack by the grubs of the common furniture beetle. It pays to look out for the adults' flight holes (about one-sixteenth of an inch in diameter) and bore dust, and thus prevent an infestation building up. Check especially on floorboards where they are laid on joists, stair treads, plywood backs of furniture and radio sets, between the tiles or under the eaves of your loft.

The beetles can come into your home in furniture bought from second-hand shops or at sales, from a neighbour's house, or from the dead branches of nearby trees. If you spot a serious structural outbreak, get professional advice. One firm gives a free survey, followed by a 20-year guarantee against reinfestation after the work has been carried out.

If the outbreak is less serious, you can treat it yourself with special woodworm killing fluid, injector and silicone wax or cream polish. First, remove dust and dirt from the affected piece of furniture; also remove fabric covers, drawers and shelves, where necessary. Treat all surfaces with the fluid, flooding it thoroughly into cracks and crevices. Use the injector (or fountain pen filler or syringe) to introduce the fluid into the flight holes. After 24 hours, use a clean, dry cloth to remove surplus fluid, then polish with the wax or cream. Do not allow the furniture to stand directly on the carpet for several weeks.

Badly infested furniture or individual floorboards should be removed from the house and burned.

In view of the increasing menace of woodworm, many new houses are being built with pre-treated timbers. But woodworm can attack the timbers of houses less than ten years old, so it is worth considering woodworm insurance. This will cover you against an unexpected outlay of anything from £20 to £200. Your home will be surveyed first and, if woodworm is found, it must, of course, be treated before the property is insured. The premium will be reduced by up to 25 per cent, providing the work is carried out by approved specialists, preferably members of The British Wood Preserving Association. You can obtain more information from your insurance broker, estate agent, building society, or from The Woodworm Insurance Co. Ltd., 16 Dover Street, London W. 1.

INSULATION

General:

It is false economy to spend a lot on heating your home if the heat produced is lost by inadequate insulation. In addition, less heat — and therefore less financial outlay — will be required if some form of insulation is installed in your home. Insulation will also help in the prevention of condensation.

Heat is lost through doors, windows, floors, ceilings and roofs.

Doors:

See WARPED DOORS, *page 97*, for draught-proofing by using sealing strips.

Roofs, Ceilings and Walls:

There are many types of insulating materials to choose from. There is the loose fill which can be tipped straight from its bag on to the ceiling between the joists. Insulating board, fibreglass 'blanket' or aluminium foil can also be fitted between or over the joists.

If the roof tiles or slates have not been laid on an underfelt, they let in the cold — and they also let out heat. To prevent this heat loss, nail building paper faced with reflective foil to the rafters, with the foil side facing downwards.

Hardboard and plywood are not thick enough in themselves to give much thermal insulation but they can be used as facings to such insulating materials as fibreglass 'blanket', mineral wool or expanded polystyrene boards. Thin polystyrene boards, if stuck to walls and ceiling, will provide a low density surface which will reduce condensation quite considerably. As it warms up quickly, it is ideal in places where quick heat is required.

See PLUMBING, FROZEN PIPES, *page 122, and* TANKS, *page 125* for information on lagging pipes and tanks.

When working in the loft, do remember not to balance yourself on the joists — have a couple of planks on which to walk.

Windows:

Sash windows can be sealed, at top and bottom, by sticking self-adhesive plastic foam strips on to the frames. Gaps at the sides of sash windows are difficult to fill with one hundred per cent success — adjusting the staff beads so that they fit more tightly would help.

For hinged windows, use the plastic foam or felt-faced strip stuck in position to form a cushion for the window to close on to — thus making a perfect seal. For metal windows, there is also a sprung copper strip which clips to the window and forms a seal when it is in the closed position.

Double glazing of large windows certainly helps to keep the heat in but it is rather expensive. You can cut the cost of double glazing by using a special transparent plastic sheeting. Stretch and pin a sheet over a wooden frame which has been made to fit tightly in the window opening on the inside or outside. This framework is then screwed into position in the window frame, preferably with thumb screws. It can easily be taken down for cleaning, and can be stored away during the summer.

Ball Valve Washers:

The two most common types of ball valves are the Portsmouth and the Croydon. With the Portsmouth, the action is up and down, whereas in the Croydon the action is across *(see Fig. 22)*.

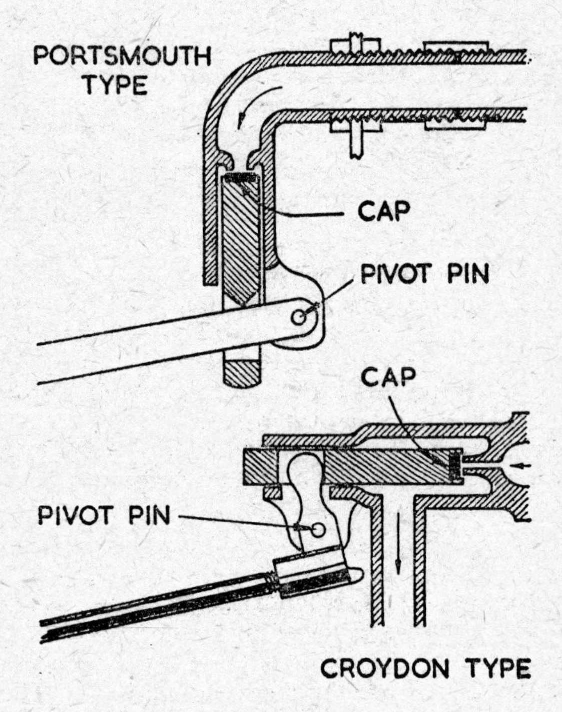

Fig. 22 Ball Valve Washers

To renew a ball valve washer, turn off the water; then use a pair of pliers to remove the pivot pin which will release the lever and allow the plug (which houses the cap or washer) to fall out. Be careful to hold on to the lever and the plug or else they may fall into the cistern or tank. Unscrew the cap, taking care not to damage it because it is rather thin. Remove the old washer, insert the new one, checking that it fits exactly. Reassemble valve and turn on the water. If you have to put in a new split pin, it should be of copper or brass, not steel.

Baths:

The vitreous enamel or porcelain enamel on your bath is really a glass surface which is fixed to the cast iron body under immense heat. This surface will stand up to most wear and tear, but chemical deposits and scum from washing water will mark its surface. In addition, cleaning materials of the wrong kind will leave marks. From your local hardware store, you can buy many good non-abrasive cleaning powders, fluids, creams and gels which will remove most stains. But even these products cannot be expected to cope with years of ill-treatment.

When a gas water heater is situated over the end of the bath, a certain amount of deposit from the heater falls into the bath. If not cleaned off immediately, it will mark. A gel is most suitable for removing this sort of stain.

If you cannot get your bath clean by these methods, you may like to re-enamel it. But this is only a temporary solution. There is no known way in which a bath can be re-enamelled to look like new.

First the bath must be cleaned with a good paste or powder cleaner, paying particular attention to the areas around the taps, overflow and waste hole. If the taps need new washers, this is the time to fit them.

If the enamel has worn away or is chipped, clean with strong soda water to clear away any greasy deposits. Rinse these places thoroughly, and then swab with a rag soaked in white spirit. When dry, wipe with a cloth soaked in methylated spirit. Let this evaporate, and then apply a coat of zinc-chromate primer to all bare metal. Allow to dry. Any necessary filling should be done with a white lead paste filler and rubbed down smooth when dry.

The whole bath should now be sandpapered with a fine paper and then the dust taken up with a 'sticky' decorator's duster. Now wipe the entire bath with a rag soaked in methylated spirit. It is from this point that the job is a success or a failure! You *must not* touch any part of the bath with your hands — the oil deposit from your skin will prevent the paint sticking to the bath.

The undercoat should now be applied, starting with the part of the bath that is farthest away from you. Brush it out well. When this coat has dried hard, lightly rub down with sandpaper, then take off the dust — being careful not to finger the surface with bare hands. The first coat of enamel can now be applied, and again work the side farthest from you first. When this coat of enamel has dried hard, lightly sandpaper and dust off. Now apply a second coat of enamel and let dry hard. To finish the hardening process, fill the bath with cold water (the oxygen in the water does the hardening).

The bath is now ready for normal use, except that from now on a small amount of cold water should be run into the bath before the hot. Hot water tends to soften enamel and make it peel off.

Panelling a Bath:

The position of the bath will determine the amount and the way in which the panelling is fitted. Frequently, a bath is in such a position that one side and end (sometimes both ends) are in full view — complete with all the unsightly pipes!

Frames of 2×1 in. battens, using the simple half joint, can be made to fit the side and end. This framework is fixed to the wall and floor, fitting fairly tightly under the lip of the bath. Alternatively, pieces of 2×1 in. batten can be fixed in. the floor and wall, and the framework fixed to these.

The side and end panels are either cut from $\frac{1}{8}$ in. hardboard or from one of the many coated hardboards or laminated plastics. These panels should be fixed to the frames with chromium plated screws and cups so that they can be easily removed if the plumbing needs attention. Your local ironmonger will be able to supply you with a chromium plated metal corner piece which will cover the join of the panels at the corner.

If your bath is the type with rounded ends, the 2×1 in. framework should extend about 2 in. beyond the end of the bath and a piece of laminated plastic cut to shape and fitted very tightly under the lip of the bath. This is to prevent water from running down inside the 'box'. If water is allowed to seep into the 'box', it could eventually cause the floorboards to rot *(see* FLOORS, *page 110).*

If your bath end is within 2 or 3 ft. of a wall, it is worth considering running the 2×1 framework right to this wall and so making a storage cupboard. This section could be fitted with shelves and sliding doors, and the top — which should be covered with an easy-to-clean laminated plastic or self-adhesive plastic surface — would provide a place for bath salts, talcum powder, etc.

Cracked Basins:

A damaged basin or sink will eventually have to be replaced, but there is a method by which it can be repaired and kept in use. Cover the crack with adhesive cellulose tape, making sure that the basin is properly dry before applying the tape. The tape should then be painted in order to make it waterproof. Cracks can also be filled and chips replaced with epoxy resin compounds.

Frozen Pipes:

'Prevention is better than cure' — this old saying applies especially to the case of frozen pipes. They should be lagged, particularly where they are exposed to the cold, with either one of the many glass fibre bandages; the cheaper treated hair felt; rigid lengths of polystyrene, glass fibre or asbestos composition; or the plastic foam lagging which is made in sections and stuck on or around the pipes.

The bandage type of lagging is wrapped fairly loosely around the pipe, then tightened up, and secured at intervals with string ties. The halves of rigid lagging are placed around the pipes and tied with either tapes or metal clips.

When lagging, make sure that you cover the whole length of the exposed pipe and this includes any taps or stopcocks or difficult corners. It is at these awkward points that ice is likely to form quickly. The tap tops only should be clear of lagging.

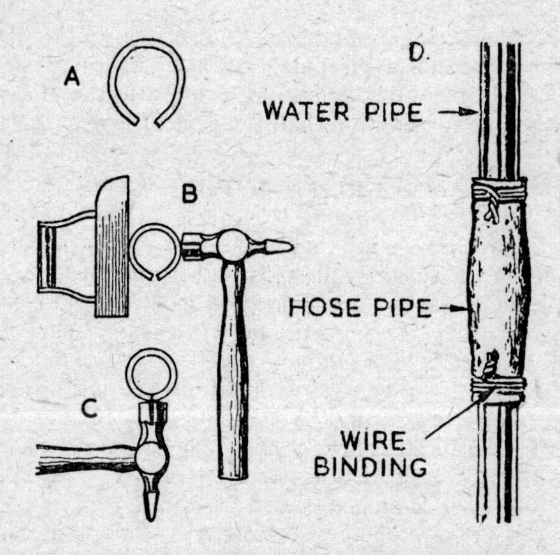

Fig. 23 Temporary Repair of Burst Pipe

If you are unfortunate enough to get frozen up, do not apply direct heat to the pipes concerned. A gentle heat should be applied, and you cannot go far wrong using the old method of applying cloths soaked in hot water to the pipes. Alternatively, use the gentle heat of hot water bottles, a fan heater on half heat, or a hair dryer.

If you do have a burst pipe, first turn off the main stopcock so that the water does not spoil your decorations. The following method will serve as a temporary repair: In the case of lead pipes, tap gently with a light hammer towards the centre of the hole until it closes right up, and then bind very tightly with sticky tape — binding the pipe at least two inches on either side of the burst. The water may now be turned on at half pressure only.

In the case of copper pipes, you will need two hammers — one to act as an anvil (or an old flat iron will do). You will see the split in a copper pipe quite clearly, and this split should be closed by placing one hammer (anvil) on the side of the pipe level with the burst, while hammering the split with the other. Reverse the action and hammer the split from the other side, repeating these actions until the split closes. After you have hammered the split together as tightly as possible, you will notice the pipe is now oval and not round. Now hammer the front of the bulge (or split section) — this action brings the lips of the split very tightly together *(see Fig. 23)*. The pipe should now be bound with sticky tape in the same way as the lead pipe, above.

Another way of repairing a burst is as follows: cut out the section of pipe that is holed and re-connect the pipe with a length of garden hose, using a wire binding at each end of the hose to secure it to the pipe *(see Fig. 23)*. Water should then be turned on at half pressure or lower.

Renewing Tap Washers and Repair of Taps:

Renewing a tap washer is a job that most handymen — and women! — can tackle. The modern tap washer will do for either the hot or cold, but be sure that you get the right size — the washers on most bath taps are larger than those on sinks or basins. The tools needed are a pair of pliers, an adjustable spanner or grip, and a piece of cloth.

First turn off the water supply at the mains or, if it is a hot water tap, turn off the storage supply tap. Turn on the tap to its fullest extent and then unscrew the top. This should only be hand tight but, if you have to use grips on it, place a piece of cloth between the jaws of the grips and the tap top to protect it from being scratched. When the top is unscrewed, it will reveal the nut that holds the tap together. Unscrew it — modern taps have a right thread whereas the older type may have a left hand thread — but be careful not to use too much force, particularly on a hand basin because this could easily crack. When the nut is unscrewed, you will see the 'jumper' *(see Fig. 24)*, and the washer will in all probability be held to the jumper plate with a small nut. In some taps, the jumper is loose and will come out as the tap is unscrewed.

To renew the washer, unscrew the nut being careful not to damage the jumper stem. Take off the old washer and put on the new — the washer should be the same size as the washer plate. Now tighten the nut, refit the jumper into the spindle, and then screw the tap together. Replace the top and turn off the tap, turn on the mains, and the tap is ready to use.

This type of tap is found in most homes — others have the 'Supatap' which has a combined spindle and washer. The whole of this has to be renewed, but it is quite simple to do. The casing is removed, the old spindlewaher removed, and a new one inserted *(see Fig. 24)*. If you still have a leaky tap after renewing the washer, it means that the packing around the spindle is faulty and the stuffing box needs repacking, although sometimes the tightening of the gland nut (hexagon or a milled ring) will stop the leak. If the gland nut is unscrewed, it will reveal the cotton or hemp packing which should be picked out with a piece of wire or a stell knitting needle. Then wind waxed string around the spindle to fill the packing space, and replace the gland nut. A word of warning — if there is too much packing the tap will be difficult to operate. Too little packing will not stop the leak.

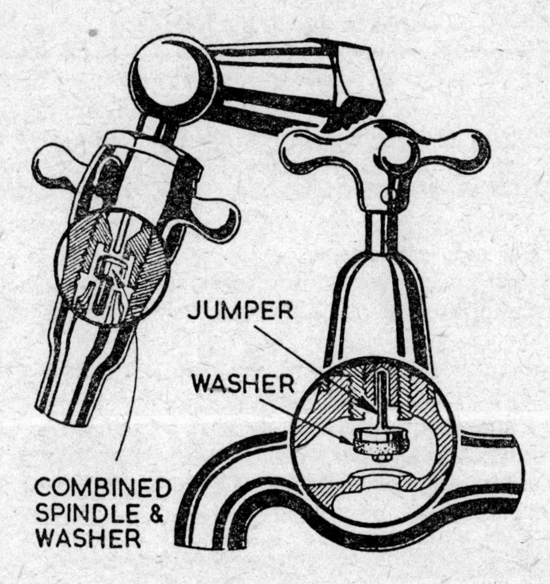

Fig. 24 Tap Washers

Tanks:

The cold water tank should be lagged and this can be done in several ways. The traditional method is to box in the tank, leaving a space between tank and box, and this space is filled with sawdust, wood-wool or one of the many insulating materials now available.

Complete do-it-yourself kits can also be bought and they cover a wide range of tank sizes and shapes. You can also make-up a box from expanded polystyrene sheets. These, by the way, are very easy to 'nail' together.

When considering tank lagging, there is a tendency to think only of the cold tank, but the hot water tank will waste heat and money if not properly lagged. You can use one of the new plastic or nylon tank jackets.

ROOFS

General:

Always keep gutters and pipes clear of dead leaves and debris so that the water can run away quite freely. Cut back any tree branches that overhang on the roof because they could cause damage, particularly in a high wind.

Before attempting to repair the roof, it is as well to find out what has caused the damage or leak. By doing this you will in all probability save yourself another repair job.

Faults can usually be traced to one of the following:

1. Rainwater which finds its way either through the nail holes or over the heads of the slates or tiles. Rain will also penetrate where slates or tiles are broken, loose, or where they have slipped out of position.

2. Torching which has become faulty or even dropped out altogether. Torching is the term applied to the cement joint between the battens or laths on the underside of a tile roof.

3. If on a previous roof repair you have used old slates or tiles, these could now be 'worn out' and letting in water.

4. On a very low pitched roof, if the covering is of a porous nature, you may get rain coming through the slates or tiles and then finding its way to the ceiling below.

5. Leaking where the slates or tiles join such structures as verges or abutments or the lead flashings (where stack and roof meet).

To find out if the roof is watertight, you should inspect it from the inside on a windy and rainy day. Where water penetration is noticed, it should be marked in some way so that at a more convenient time you can carry out the necessary repairs.

General Roof Repairs:

The faults listed above can be repaired as follows:

1. Take out the offending slate or tile and insert the new one. On slate roofs, there is quite a big overlap and this will probably stop you re-nailing the new slate direct to its correct batten. Instead, cut a length of lead about 1 in. wide, long enough to be nailed to the batten and to be longer than the new slate by about 2 in. when in position. Nail this strip to the batten and insert the new slate on top of the lead strip. When the slate is fitted, turn the end of the lead strip back over the end of the slate.

2. Here the repair is obvious. The torching has to be renewed with a mortar mix. *(see* TILED ROOFS, *page 128)*. Before applying the mix, check that all loose pieces of previous torching have been removed. Dampen the tiles before applying the new mix.

3. Repair as for No. 1.

4. The only real solution for this condition is to have a new roof. A temporary repair would be to give the roof two coats of one of the liquid bitumens that are made for waterproofing. This is applied with a wide paint brush or household soft brush.

5. Leaks occur at the junction of the roof and chimney stack. The flashings are made of lead and after years this wears out. There is now on the market a neat roll of do-it-yourself zinc sheeting which is rust-proof and easy to work. It comes in a sheet measuring 36×12 in. and costs very little. Using the old flashing as a pattern, cut a new one from the zinc sheeting. When the old flashing is removed, note its fixing into the brickwork and the overlap required under the slates or tiles so that the new flashing can be fixed in the right position. Before fixing, new flashing, check that the soakers are in good condition. Renew any brickwork or concrete that you may have had to remove in the process and repoint the brickwork. When repairing roofs, match the new slate or tile in colour with the old so that you avoid a patchwork effect.

Roof Construction:

Before tackling repairs, it would be as well to understand a little of the construction of a tiled or slate roof. The boards of slate roofs are laid over the rafters, and on these boards a layer of felt is spread followed by slate laths or battens. It is to these laths or battens that the slates are actually fixed.

Tiled roofs are rather more complicated than slate roofs because of the different shapes of tile. The two main types are plain tiles, and single lap tiles (pantiles or Roman tiles). The more popular of these is the plain tile which has two holes for fixing and a lap which hooks it to the roof batten. The pantile or Roman tile is made of clay and is shaped. Each tile is held to the roofing lath by one nail.

Cedar Shingle:

This is another type of modern roofing. To keep in good order, it should be treated with a clear wood preservative five years after fixing, and then every seven years afterwards. Valley gutters on this type of roof should be made of lead (because the shingles may contain acid which could prove harmful to any other materials used) and coated with bitumen.

Chimney Stacks:

Pointing should be watched for signs of crumbling. Re-point as soon as possible. The pots themselves should be inspected periodically, giving special attention to their concrete beds which should be renewed at any sign of crumbling. Also make sure that the roof flashing into the chimney brickwork is in good order — chimney stacks stand a lot of buffeting from wind and rain.

Concrete Tiles:

These tiles are found on modern houses and are guaranteed to last fifty years. The only necessary care and attention needed is the replacement of tiles that may have slipped.

Flat Roofs:

These are usually surfaced with bituminous felt and should be checked every five years, if possible by an expert, for signs of drying out. There is a certain amount of oil in felt that dries out in time.

You should make sure that the water is able to run away quite freely. Leaks in the joins can be sealed with a special waterproofing sealing tape which is self-adhesive, and the roof itself can be treated with one of the many liquid bitumen seals that can be brushed on. These seals come in black and colours — but colours cost more.

Thatch:

The thatched roof is still very popular in the country as it keeps the house cool in summer and warm in winter. The thatch should be covered with wire netting so as to keep out vermin which can cause damage to the roof. For repairs, it is essential that a trained thatcher should be employed. If you do not know of one locally, you can write to the Rural Industries Bureau, 35 Camp Road, London, S.W.19, who will be able to help you.

Tiled Roofs:

Tiled roofs are a little more difficult to repair than slate with the possible exception of those built of plain tiles. These are quite easy to replace; the nib of each tile fits over the batten and if the tile needs to be pinned to the batten, use copper nails. If the tiles are in good order, you can stop rain penetrating by torching the underneath of the tiles with a weak mortar mix of 1 part hydrated powder lime (non-hydraulic) to 6 parts sand, to which is added ½ part cement after wet mixing.

Some single lap tiles (pantile or Roman tile) are secured separately to the roof battens with one 2 in. × 10 gauge copper, aluminium alloy or galvanised nail with a broad head. Other single lap tiles are fitted with nibs that fit over the roof battens.

If it is difficult to push up a new tile or to remove an old one, insert a wooden wedge between the adjacent tiles. This will relieve the pressure and you will be able to nail or slot the tile in position.

To remove a slate which has been nailed, use a ripper tool (*see Fig. 25*). As you will see, this has a hooked blade which is inserted between the slates and hooked on to the nail. A sharp pull downwards will cut the nail, allowing the slate to be removed.

Keep tiled roofs free from moss — which causes tiles to become porous — by spraying with a toxic wash. After 24 hours remove any moss growths, then repeat the wash. This should then be carried out once a year. Be careful not to let the wash fall on flower beds!

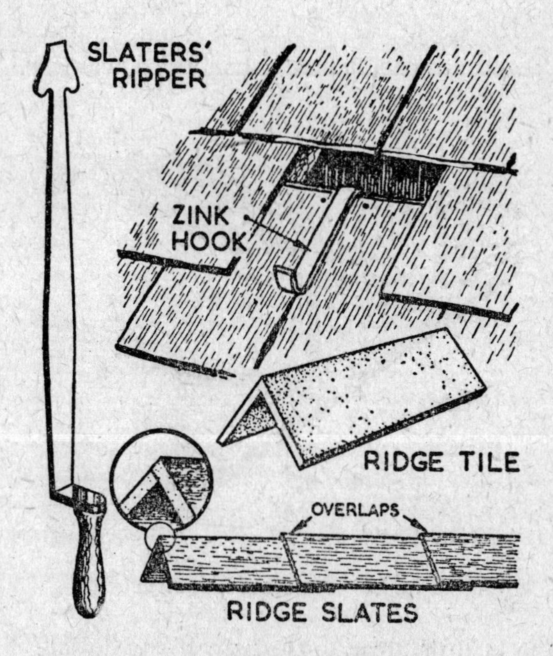

Fig. 25 Repairs to Roofs

Before attempting any roof repairs, check that you have a ladder long enough to reach the roof. You will also need a roof ladder on which to stand while carrying out repairs. If you cannot borrow one, try making it. You need a length of $10 \times \frac{3}{4}$ in. or 1 in. planking to which a piece of 4×2, 18 in. long, is nailed at one end (this is to hook over the ridge of the roof). On the same side, nail a 15 in. length of 2×1 every 2 ft. 6 in. — these battens help to distribute your weight evenly on the roof joists. On the opposite side, nail 10 in. lengths of 2×1 every foot — these act in the same way as the rungs on a ladder.

STAIRS

There is no need to put up with creaking stairs. Creaks are caused by the movement of the stair tread against the riser. This happens because the triangular wooden blocks stuck between the tread and riser have broken away from either the tread or the riser, or have broken away altogether.

Mending Creaking Stairs:

It is quite a simple job to glue these blocks or new ones back into position, but if the stair tread has warped (which makes it difficult to fit blocks to take the weight of people using the stairs), a small metal angle iron can be screwed

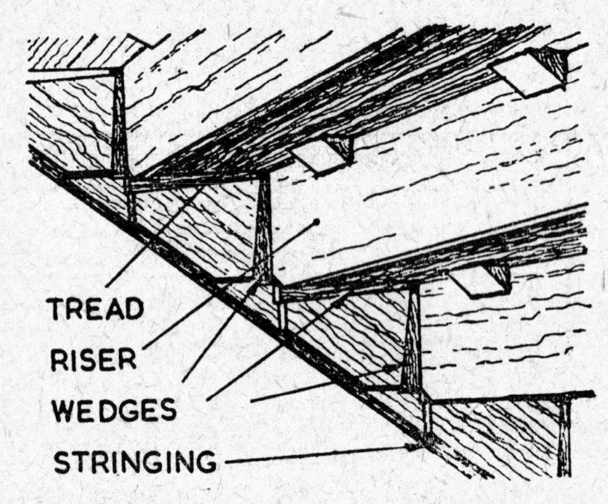

Fig. 26 Staircase Construction

into position to hold the tread to the riser. If you do this, it would help to have a second person to stand on the stair concerned so that the angle iron takes up the slack between the tread and the riser.

If it is not possible to gain access to the underside of the stairs, the loose tread can be refastened by screwing through the tread into the edge of the riser. If this method is used, make sure that you countersink the head of the screw, otherwise it will damage your stair carpet or covering.

For the construction of a typical staircase *see Fig. 26*.

Treatment of Woodworm:

Under the stairs is one of the places to be inspected at regular intervals for woodworm, and any sign should be treated as described in HOUSEHOLD

PESTS, *see page 116*. In any case, it is a wise precaution to treat the woodwork with one of the liquid preventives which can be either brushed or sprayed on.

VENTILATION

GOOD VENTILATION is not only hygienic — it makes working in the kitchen much more pleasant if steam can be kept to a minimum and cooking smells prevented from spreading through the home. In addition, excessive steam leads to condensation and in turn to possible dry rot.

Ventilation is also important in the bathroom, especially if you have a gas water heater or indulge in baths for each member of the family every day!

Activated Charcoal Hoods:

If your cooker has to be placed on an inside wall and ducting is impossible a charcoal hood will absorb steam and fumes and keep the air of the kitchen reasonably clean. The charcoal bed used in this hood has to be replaced once a year, but the cost is reasonable. The air is cleaned at a rate of about 65 cubic feet per minute. These hoods also have strip lighting built into them which is directed straight on to the cooker, thus avoiding shadows which could be cast by the hood. They are very quick to install — 2 screws are all that is needed.

Air Bricks:

This is one of the oldest forms of ventilation. It is still used to give underfloor ventilation *(see* FLOORS, *page 110)*. Air bricks are also fitted in walls to allow steam and fumes to pass through and out into the air. They have been outmoded by the extractor fan and in many new houses builders install fans instead.

Extractor Fans:

There are many makes of electrically-operated extractor fans — some small, some large, some powerful, some not so powerful. But their principle is the same — to rid the room of steam and smells and keep fresh air circulating. An extractor fan can be fitted in an existing window; in the place of an existing air brick; by making a new opening in the wall; over the cooker; or in its own canopy.

The actual site for the fan must be chosen so that the flow of air through the fan is not short circuited. If this is allowed to happen, you will not get a properly ventilated room and therefore the fan is not doing its job. If the fan is sited on the wall near a door or window which is allowed to remain open, then the flow of air will by-pass most of the room and pass only between fan and door or window. The ideal site is opposite the main air inlet.

If the fan is to be fitted in a kitchen with a boiler, be sure that there is an alternative air inlet other than the door or the fumes from the boiler might be drawn into the room.

The size of the fan depends on the cubic volume of the room and at what rate the air should be changed to get good ventilation. For example, a kitchen 12ft. long × 10ft. wide × 8ft. high has a volume of 960 cubic feet. Therefore, if ten changes of air per hour are wanted, the fan chosen must be capable of extracting at a rate of 10,000 cubic feet an hour. If fifteen changes are wanted, then the fan must be able to cope with 15,000 cubic feet an hour.

Louvre Windows:

Louvre windows provide controlled ventilation and help to prevent condensation. They come in a variety of sizes and you can fit them into existing metal or wooden window frames. The louvre blades are of 32 oz. glass. They slot into the louvre units and are held there by spring clips. Windows with 2 to 5 blades have a single central lever, 6 to 10 blades have two independent control levers, and a 11 to 15 blade window has three independent control levers. From this you can see that you will have a considerable amount of control over the intake of fresh air.

The metal units in these windows are rustproof and all blades can be cleaned from the inside. Also each control lever has a special locking device so that the window cannot be opened from the outside.

Non-Mechanical Ventilators:

These are fitted in the window glass and have central cords which open and close the louvres to the desired amount. Some cost less than £2, and can be fitted into glass panes up to $\frac{3}{8}$ in. thick.

WALLS

Inside Walls:

For the treatment of cracks and hair lines, *see* CEILINGS, *page 93.* If the walls are badly marked through damp or because of other work you have done to the walls (i.e. laying new damp course) and you find you have some large patches to make good, it is worth considering stripping the old plaster completely and putting on new.

Beginning at one end of the wall, pin 3 battens (or laths), $\frac{3}{4}$ in. thick, to the brickwork at about 18 in. intervals. Using a steel float, lay on an undercoat of plaster about $\frac{1}{2}$ in. thick, covering the area bounded by the battens.

The undercoat mix should be 1 part cement, 1 part lime, 6 parts sand, 1 part gypsum plaster, 2 parts sand. While the undercoat is still wet, make a key of criss-cross lines with the point of a trowel. As the areas dry out and harden, so the battens are moved on and the undercoat laying is repeated. The battens should be left in position on the last section of the wall so that, when the undercoat has dried out and hardened, they can be used to keep the top-coat level.

The top (or finishing) coat can either be neat Class B gypsum plaster or a mix of 1 part plaster and $\frac{1}{3}$ part lime. If Class B plaster is used, you should tell your supplier what it is going to be used for. Do not forget to wet the undercoat before laying the top coat. The channels left by the battens should be filled with the same mixes used in two stages, i.e. a keyed undercoat, then the top coat, which is made level with the new plaster on either side of the channel.

The smooth hard surface of a plaster wall is obtained by rubbing the wall in a circular motion with a metal float, using clean water brushed on to the float to keep the plaster in a workable state. Warning: If you overdo the watering, you will get an uneven and poor surface.

It is worth noting that this method could be employed on large patches as it would help the new plaster to meet the old at the correct level.

Beam and Plasterwork walls:

Plaster being of a porous nature and wood being subject to thermal expansion, there is a tendency to gaps or cracking where they meet. The plasterwork must be given a good wash down, as described in RENDERED WALLS, *page 138*, and the whitewash or paint may have to be removed to effect a good repair. The cracks between wood and plaster can be filled with the mastic filler described in CRACKS ROUND DOOR *and* WINDOW FRAMES, *see below*.

Small cracks in the actual plaster can be filled with one of the many plastic fillers now available. Larger patches should be filled with a plaster made up in the proportions: 3 parts silver sand, 1 part slaked lime, and 1 part white cement. The method for filling is as for RENDERED WALLS, i.e. fill half, make key, let dry and then add topcoat. For making good large areas, use batten method described in INSIDE WALLS, *see above*.

Cracks Round Door and Window Frames:

It is possible to fill these cracks, if they are large enough, with the 3 to 1 mix mentioned in RENDERED WALLS, *page 138*, but it is better to use a mastic filler. This type of filler will take up the differences in the expansion between wood and brick or cement.

You can make up your own mastic filler as follows: 5 parts dry clean sand, 5 parts whitening, 1 part red lead. These materials should be mixed with boiled linseed oil until you have a fairly stiff but workable paste. The paste (filler) is then pushed into the cracks after cleaning out dust and loose mortar. If it is done neatly, and the filler not allowed to spread over on to the woodwork or brickwork, it will be almost impossible to see. If the crack is a deep one, you will make a much better job of filling it if you do it in two stages.

This paste can be decorated but it may discolour existing paint on woodwork, which is why care should be taken when filling cracks. The same method can also be applied to window frames set in ordinary brick walls.

Lath and Plaster:

The repair of this type of wall is rather more difficult but again, with a little care, it can be done. Some lath and plaster walls are naturally uneven, but this sign alone should not be taken to mean that the wall is defective or that it is caused by dampness.

It could be that the laths have broken or are breaking away from the studs (stud is the term applied to the wooden supports to which the laths are nailed). If this has happened, it can usually be discovered by sounding the wall by tapping with the handle of a trowel. If the tapping gives off a hollow sound, then there is a defect. Tap round the suspect part of the wall until you get a rough idea of the extent of the bad patch. To keep the rather charming uneven look of the wall, chisel the plaster away and, if necessary, replace any faulty laths. In replacing laths, it may be necessary to cut away good plaster because these laths must be fixed to the studs. Nail the new laths into position at the same distance apart as those already fixed.

Now press the plaster over the laths so that it spreads out behind them and so forms a support for the rest of the plaster. This plaster is a mix of 1 part cement, 2 parts lime, and 8 parts sand. If a stronger mix is used, it will cause damage to the laths when it dries out. A wooden or metal float can be used to finish off the wall.

Another way to repair this sort of wall — if you think you are not able to fix new laths — is by fixing a piece of plasterboard to the studs and then plastering over. You need to be especially careful with this type of plastering repair, otherwise it will show.

Plugging a Wall:

The most common method of plugging walls is by using a 'jumper' and a hammer. Mark the position of each hole, place the point of the jumper against it, and then tap with a hammer. Tap gently to begin with — otherwise you could crack the plaster. As you continue to hit, rotate the jumper to clean the hole of dust *(see Fig. 27)*.

There are several types of plug which can be used — plastic, compressed fibre, and some which are mixed with a little water, rolled and pressed into the hole. There is also a variety of spring toggles, gravity toggles, anchors, bolts, H toggles, and bolts for fixing into cement and masonry. In fact, there is a fixing for every type of wall.

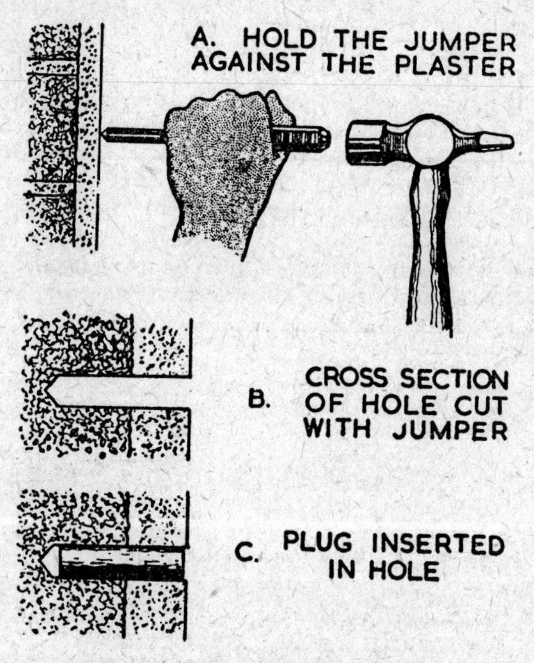

Fig. 27 Inserting Wall Plug

Uneven Walls:

Uneven walls can be plastered as explained in INSIDE WALLS, *page 133*. If they have been painted, the walls must be thoroughly chipped with hammer and chisel to form a key for the plaster.

Another method is to pin a series of battens to the wall. Pin sheets of $\frac{1}{8}$-in. hardboard to the battens and fill the joins with one of the many fillers available. You can use enamelled wallboard instead of hardboard if you prefer.

Uneven walls in a kitchen can be corrected by tiling the walls concerned. If you use standard glazed tiles, make sure that you soak them before fixing. A glass cutter will cut the glazed front cleanly and neatly if you need a piece of tile to complete the wall.

Polystyrene wall tiles are stuck to the wall with contact adhesives. Make sure the wall is free from grease and dirt before applying the adhesive. *Warning:* If the wall is very uneven, this method will not be very successful as you cannot build up to a specific level with an adhesive in the same way as you can with a mortar mix.

Outside Walls:

To repair brick or rendered walls, you will need the following tools: Trowel, club hammer, line and pins, floats, bricklayer's hammer, bolster with chisel edge, spirit level (with cross or plumb tubes), raker, and a bucket or watering can for mixing cement.

Damp Course and Prevention of Damp:

In many old houses, rising damp occurs in floors and walls. This is because either there is no damp course at all or because the original damp course has deteriorated so much that it fails to do its job.

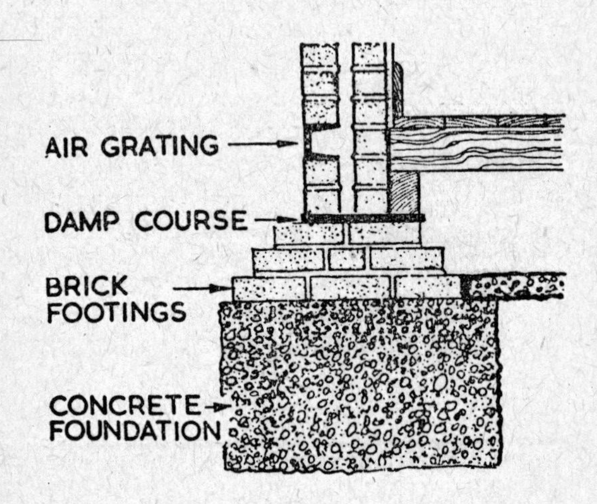

Fig. 28 Cross Section of Wall Base

1. If the wall is brick and safe, the job of renewing the damp course or putting one in should not prove too difficult *(see Fig. 28)*. Beginning at one corner of the house, remove three layers of brick (known as courses) down to where the damp course is to be laid. To avoid the possible collapse of the wall (!), the area to be worked at any one time should not be more than 3 bricks deep by 1 yard wide. Your damp-proofing felt should be cut into

handy rolls so that you can work with it in this opening. Old mortar should be cleaned from all the bricks, and you would be well advised to get in a few spare bricks in case you break any while getting them out. Work round the house in this way until you have made a complete circuit. There should be an overlap of 6 in. where you have to join the felt. The cement mix for this work should be 3 parts clean dry sand and 1 part cement. The re-pointing

Fig. 29 Damp-Proofing Exterior Walls

of the outside wall can then be done with the same mix *(see* RE-POINTING WALLS, *page 140*, INSIDE WALLS, *page 132*, for how to make good interior walls after laying a new damp course*)*.

2. If the wall is very old, it may be made of plaster and bricks or stone or a combination of the three, and any interference could result in the whole wall falling to pieces. This is because these walls are often filled with rubble

and not bonded together like normal walls. With this type of wall, you should really get in a builder to lay a damp course. If you cannot afford to do this, the following method should stop the damp coming through the walls: First, dig a trench down to the foundations of the wall and then brush and clean the wall free of earth. Apply two coats of cement, to which a water-proofing substance has been added, to the wall. Key the undercoat with the point of a trowel *(see* RENDERED WALLS, below*)*. Let this harden, dampen, then apply the top coat. If it helps, this job can be done between battens that have been nailed to the wall. Fill holes left by battens after the cement has hardened *(see Fig. 29, page 137)*. This rendering should come up the wall to at least 6 in. above ground level. When it has hardened and dried out, the trench should be filled with rubble. The trench will take the worst of the rain from the wall. If land drains are laid at each end, it will also help to keep the water from the wall. The rubble can now have a top soil put on it and grass sown if desired.

A new idea in the fight against damp is to inject a natural rubber latex siliconate composition into the brickwork to create a liquid dampproof course. The technique is quick and thorough, and walls do not have to be pulled down and rebuilt. The composition is injected into holes drilled in the mortar between bricks near the source of the damp. The pointing of the wall after these injections should be carried out with water-proofed cement.

Use of Liquid Silicones:

Another cause of damp penetration is when the brickwork becomes soft and porous. Until fairly recently there was only one way in which to treat this condition successfully — have a new wall built — but modern silicone waterproofing liquids now have an answer to the problem.

When brushed on to the wall, these colourless liquids do not alter the colour of the brickwork so the mellowed look is retained. To enable the liquids to do their job properly, any faulty pointing must be repaired *(see* RE-POINTING WALLS, *page 140)*.

This method can also be used on the plaster walls of beamed cottages. Before the liquid is applied, this type of wall must be washed down and the paint or whitewash stripped to the plaster if possible.

Rendered Walls:

To repair walls that are cement-faced — this includes smooth, rough cast and pebble-dashed walls — proceed as follows: Wash down with strong soda water, using a stiff-bristled brush, and then rinse with clean water, with a hose if possible. This should remove all the dirt and grime and help you to spot cracks and blisters that may need attention.

It is important that you should deal with hairline cracks in this type of wall because it is through these that damp can penetrate. All cracks should be sounded to see if they are just cracks or if the surrounding cement has become loose on its foundation. Sounding is done by tapping the cement surface with the handle of a brush or trowel. If it gives off a hollow sound, it is almost certain that the surface needs renewing.

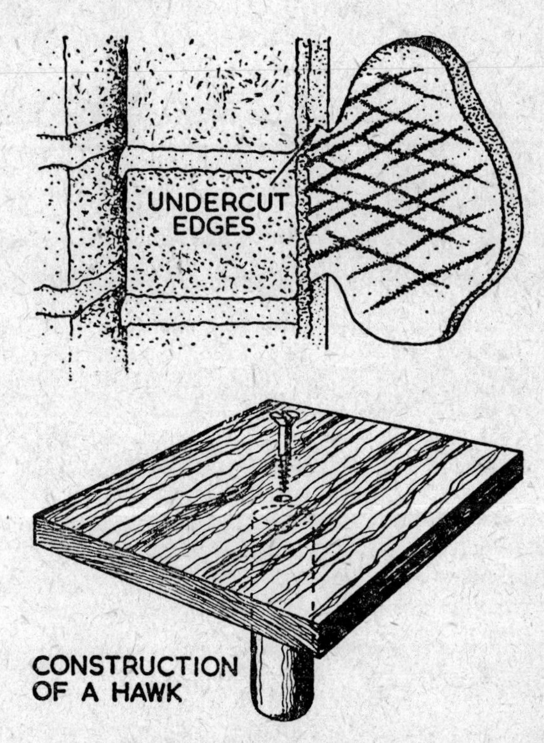

Fig. 30 Re-pairing Walls

You should also inspect the surface that runs down to the ground and which covers the damp course. Damp can creep up between the rendering and brick wall. In so doing, it by-passes the damp course and will sooner or later spoil your interior decorations.

Another check you should make while inspecting the walls is for cracks between window and door frames and the wall. These cracks are usually caused by the woodwork shrinking.

Cracks should be cut back wider at the base than at the top. This will give the necessary key for the cement filling to adhere to. Wet the cracks with an old distemper brush and fill with a cement mix of the proportions 3 parts sand to 1 part cement. Any 'blistered' or loose areas of a rendered wall should be chiselled away down to the foundation brickwork and sideways until you meet solid rendering which should be undercut to form a key *(see Fig. 30)*. The brickwork pointing should be scraped out to a depth of ½ in., and then the whole area moistened with water. The mix of 3 to 1 should then be laid over the area, filling it by half its depth. This undercoat should be scored by running the point of a trowel across the patch both vertically and horizontally to form a key for the top rendering. When the undercoat has hardened, the topcoat should be applied. Remember to wet the undercoat first, and then level off in line with the old rendering.

The wall has now been repaired but not finished. Whichever of the following finishes you choose must be done before the topcoat has dried and hardened:

Smooth finish: smooth with a trowel or float.

Trowelled finish: Rub the cement surface with a trowel or float in a circular motion as it dries — add a little water to the trowel or float as needed.

Rough cast: To match up the repair to the existing wall, mix washed gravel with the cement. This mixture should be cast at the area concerned before it has had a chance to harden — the 'casting' can be done with a small household coal shovel. The 'cast' should then be patted lightly into the cement surface with a float.

Pebble dash: The method is the same as for rough cast except that you do not mix cement with the gravel. Here again, try to match the new to the old.

Re-Pointing Walls:

Re-pointing of walls should be done when the existing mortar between the bricks begins to flake and crumble. The old mortar should be cleaned out to a depth of ½ to ¾ of an inch with a raker (a tool specially designed for this job) and all loose dust brushed away.

The mortar mix for re-pointing should be 3 parts clean sand to 1 part cement. This should be well mixed to a fairly stiff consistency by adding water a little at a time — do not mix more than you can use at any one time because it will not keep. You must keep to thc same amounts of sand and cement for your mix for the whole job in hand, otherwise your pointing will not be uniform in colour.

Wet the gaps between the courses of bricks that are to be re-pointed with an old distemper brush and a bucket of water. The mix should be on either a float or a hawk and close at hand. *(For construction of hawk, see Fig. 30, page 139.)* Have a can or bucket of water handy so that the mix can be kept in a workable state. Lay the cement mix into the gaps with a trowel and finish so that the pointing slopes out from under the upper layer (course) of bricks to the outer edge of the lower course — this allows water to run off the brickwork and not to settle in crevices.

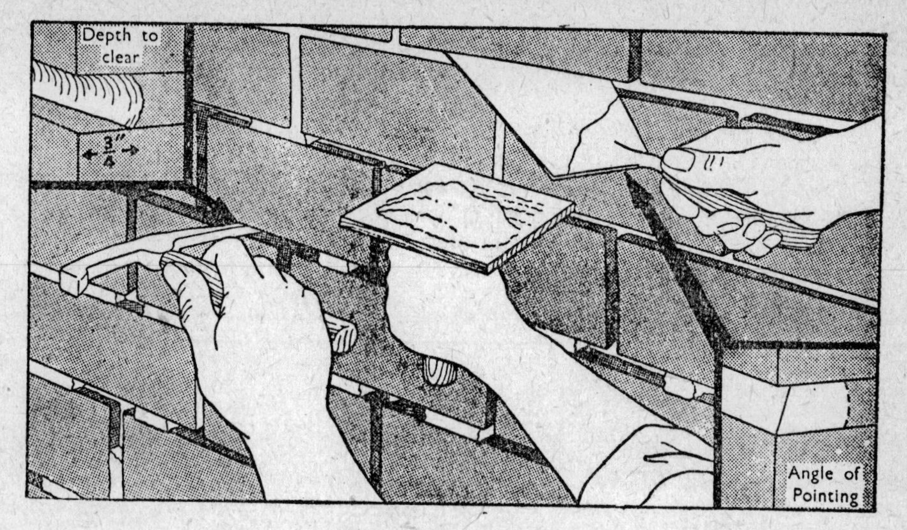

Fig. 31 Repointing Walls

If you come across soft and crumbling brick while you are scraping out, it should be removed *(see Fig. 31)* and replaced with a second-hand brick of the right colour and type. A new brick will look out of place, especially if your house is of the older type with brickwork which has mellowed with age. If it is not possible to find a 'new' brick, then the old one should be taken out carefully. Make a hole with a chisel, then insert an old hacksaw blade and cut through the mortar holding the brick. Butter it well with cement and gently tap it back into position, protecting the brick with a piece of wood.

If the brickwork is discoloured with grime, it should be restored by brushing with a wire brush or with a stiff bristle brush and plain water. To remove some stains, it may be necessary to wash the wall with household ammonia added to the water. Afterwards the wall should be rinsed down several times with clean water and then left to dry out. It is important that this cleaning should be done before any attempt is made to re-point the wall.

WINDOWS

Reglazing:

This is quite simple to do, but be careful if the job requires the use of a long ladder. Do ask yourself if you can work at heights AND use both hands on the job — not for hanging on to the ladder. If you feel at all uneasy about it, get your local builder in.

Tools required are: chisel, putty knife, light hammer, pair of pliers, and a hacking knife. Materials needed: glazing putty, glazing sprigs, and the new sheet of glass.

First, all the old glass, sprigs or nails, and putty must be removed from the frame. Hardened putty can be removed with a hammer and a hacking knife or by heating and then scraping away with a knife.

The rabbet must be cleaned of all old putty, etc. because any uneven surface could result in the breaking of the new piece of glass as you put it into the frame. The rabbet should also be painted with a primer to preserve the woodwork.

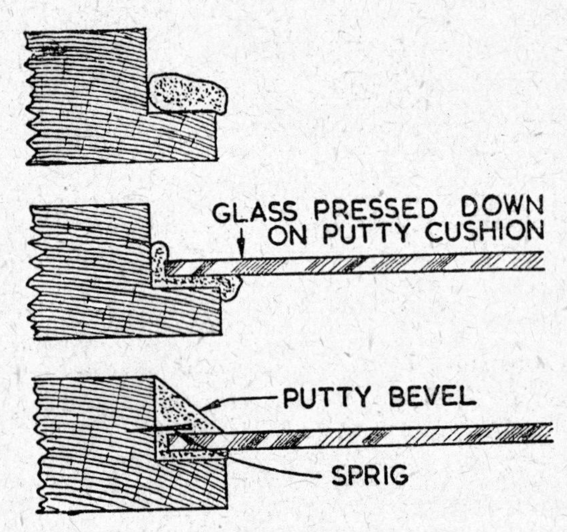

Fig. 32 Reglazing

Window glass is usually 21 oz. but, if you are not sure what weight you require, take a piece of the old glass to show your supplier. When measuring for the new glass, the inside measurement should be taken and $\frac{1}{8}$ in. subtracted all round. The corners of the new pane should be nibbled away with a pair of pliers to allow for easier fitting. Next press the putty into the rabbet *(see A, Fig. 32)* to form a cushion for the glass. Insert the glass and press gently but firmly on to the putty until you can see that it has flattened and formed a seal *(see B, Fig. 32)*. At intervals round the frame, knock in sprigs and lay putty level with a putty knife *(see C, Fig. 32)*. Clean away surplus putty on the inside of the window but do not paint until the putty has hardened.

This method is also applied to metal windows except that the priming paint should be for use on metal and there is a special putty for use with metal frames.

Reglazing Leaded windows:

These are a little more difficult to repair, and particular attention must be given to making them waterproof.

Press the broken pane from the inside, thus forcing the lead lip around the pane outwards. Protect your hands while doing this with gloves or several layers of cloth. The new pane must be of the correct weight so do take a piece of the old glass along to your supplier. The new pane should be a fraction of an inch smaller than the opening, and it may be necessary to open up the lead strip a little more to get it into position. Before inserting the new pane, run a thin layer of one of the many plastic sealers into the lead channel. Insert the new pane and press the lead strips back into position against the glass. Smooth out any wrinkles in the lead by rubbing gently — but with even pressure — with a piece of hardwood. If the lead should split at the corners, repair with a soldering iron, but do not get the iron too hot or it will melt the lead strips.

If a leaded window has been broken beyond repair or needs renewing because of its age and you cannot afford to have one made to match your other windows, the following method could be used: Take out all the old leads and glass from the frame and reglaze as for an ordinary window *(see* REGLAZING, *page 141)* but do not add the finishing putty on the outside. There is a do-it-yourself kit available which contains strips of lead and special adhesive. The kit can be used to make windows match. Using the special adhesive, stick the strips of lead into the same pattern as the other windows, allowing the ends of the lead strips to run right to the edge of the frame. Apply the finishing putty so that the ends of the lead strips are covered with a layer of putty. An alternative method of finishing is to cut out and fix quarter round beading to the sides of the frame. Before fixing, butter with putty or a sealing compound to take up the small gap between the beading and glass made by the lead strip.

You can take a 'bow' out of a leaded window by unscrewing the window from the frame and laying it 'bow' upwards on a flat surface. Now lay a piece of $\frac{1}{4}$-in. ply or hardboard on the bow (making sure that it does not overlap into the framework) and then across this and over the centre of the bow lay a length of $1\frac{1}{2} \times 1\frac{1}{2}$ in. batten which should cover the full witht of the frame. You will now need two clamps, one at each side of the frame, to bind the frame and batten together. Tighten each clamp alternately, a little at a time, until the bow has been straightened out. During this straightening process, keep an eye on the glass panes — they may need a little help to keep them in position. If necessary, open up the lead channels a little so as to give the glass freedom of movement. Plastic sealer should then be applied before pressing the lead back into position. Once again, wrinkles can be smoothed out with the aid of a piece of hardwood as described previously.

Renewing a Stone Window Sill:

Broken and cracked sills are a source of damp penetration which in time will spoil your inside decorations.

Hack away the old sill, under the window frame as well. Make a mould of 1-inch timber and fix to the brickwork at the side of the window so that the front edge of the mould is an inch lower than the bottom of the window frame. Fix a length of sash cord in the bottom of the mould to make the 'drip'.

When this mould is in position, it should be filled to a depth of about $1\frac{1}{2}$ in. and then reinforced. Folded chicken wire is a good material for this purpose, and it should not only be laid on the cement but run up under the wooden window frame. Now fill the mould with the concrete mix. Finish by smoothing with a trowel, making a gentle slope down from the window frame to the front edge of the mould.

It should be left to harden for about a week before the mould is removed. Let the new sill weather for a few months before attempting to paint it.

Repair of Sash Cords:

The cords of sash windows should be checked at regular intervals. At the first signs of fraying, the cord should be renewed, otherwise it could be the cause of a nasty accident, particularly if it belongs to the upper frame. To allow for easier window working, you would be well advised to renew both cords so that you get an even stretch instead of the old cord straining against a new one.

Generally, the sash window works as follows: To each side of each window frame is attached a cord (sash cord), and attached to the other end of each cord is a cast-iron weight. These weights form the counterbalance to the window — the actual poundage is marked on the weights themselves. The window frame is fitted with special pockets which house the weights *(see Fig. 33)*.

The job of renewing the cords is always done from the inside of the room. For the lower window, remove the staff beads from either side of the window frame by inserting a wood chisel between the bead and the frame and bowing the bead outwards so that it can be sprung clear of the mitred corners. The window should now be in the closed position. Cut the sash cord just above the window frame and lower the weight into the pocket as far as possible by hand. Let the weight fall to the bottom of the pocket; repeat this operation on the other side of the window. The window can now be lifted out of the frame altogether.

With the window out of its frame, you will be able to locate the traps (at the bottom of the frame on each side) which allow access to the weights inside the pockets. These traps are not fixed in position and can be removed easily by inserting a chisel in the cut at the bottom of each trap and levering them upwards and outwards. With the traps removed, you will be able to see the weights resting in the bottom of the pockets. Take them out and remove the broken pieces of the old cord.

Using the old cord as a pattern, measure a new length of cord for each side, making sure that it is of the right thickness to carry the window and weights. Remove the other pieces of old cord from the window and attach the new one in the same way as the old was fixed. One of two methods will have been used: (*a*) the cord passes through a slot in the frame and its end is knotted, or (*b*) the cord is placed in a groove and fixed to the side of the

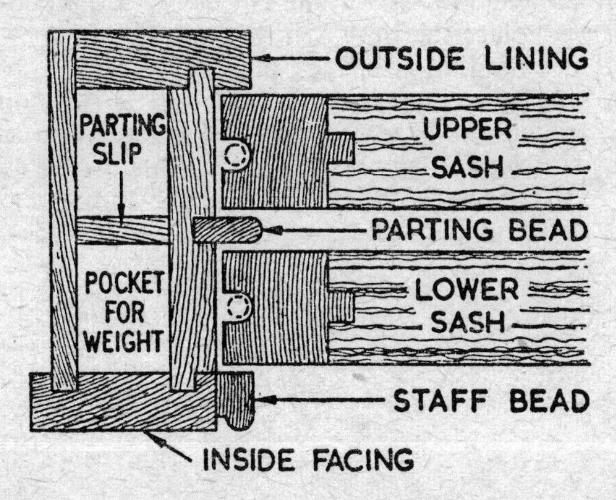

Fig. 33 Plan of Sash Windows

window with strong tacks. If you use (*b*), do not have the top tack too near the top of the window or there will not be enough 'slack' cord to go round the pulley when the window is in the up position.

Before going on to the next step you will need a 'mouse'. This is to facilitate the threading of the cords over the pulleys, down into the pockets, and so to the weights. (A mouse is a length of strong twine with a piece of lead attached to one end small enough to go over the pulley and through the hole above the wheel.) Now place the window in the frame in such a position that you can get at both pulleys and pocket openings. To hold the window in this position, knock a nail into the insides of the frame for the window to rest on. One nail will do for a small lightweight window, but use two for a heavy window (you will need help to get the window in position, especially if it is a heavy one). Attach the unweighted end of the mouse to the free end of the sash cord and then pass the weighted end (mouse) over the pulley, through the hole and down into the pocket. Feed it through until you can reach it through the pocket opening, and keep pulling the mouse until the sash cord has gone right through the pocket and the end hangs at the pocket opening. Untie the mouse and repeat the procedure for the other side.

Now push the window right up to the top of the frame and hold it in this position with nails fixed into each side of the frame. Pull the sash cords tight so as to take up any slack and thread the ends through the holes in the top of the weights. Knot securely and put the weights back into the pockets. The weights must hang free and NOT touch the bottom of the pockets. Remove the nails from underneath the window and, before replacing the trap, check that the window is working correctly — the cords might need slight adjustment. Replace the traps, oil the pulleys, and then pin back the staff beading. If the beading is broken or split, replace with a new piece.

The cord renewing procedure is the same for a top window, except that the parting bead will have to be removed as well as the staff bead. The parting bead should not be fixed but should fit tightly in its own groove — replace with a new piece if broken or split. If both upper and lower window need new sash cords, do the upper first.

How to Eat Wisely

COOKING AND RECIPES

BUYING FOOD AND STOCKING YOUR LARDER

WHAT to buy, WHEN to buy and HOW MUCH to buy—this is the day-to-day problem facing every housewife, no matter what the size of her family. Involved also is the whole question of meal planning, of one's individual habits in entertaining and eating, as well as the vital matter of balancing the housekeeping budget.

WHAT to buy is the first question. One could say shopping falls into two main categories — everyday supplies and emergency supplies. Everyday food includes all the staples such as sugar, tea, flour and so on, as well as such vital extras as herbs and seasonings, plus all the perishable foods — meat, fish, vegetables and fruit. Emergency food on the other hand is needed to cope with all those minor crises which occur in every household — the day mother is ill, the last-minute guest for dinner, the friends dropping in unexpectedly for tea or in the evening. With regard to everyday shopping, it is wise to familiarise oneself with the look of fresh meat, fish and poultry, as well as keeping an eye on the best seasonal buys, particularly in fruit and vegetables. As far as emergency foods are concerned — canned goods are a lifesaver. They will keep almost indefinitely, and the selection now available on the market is so large that you can find something to meet every occasion, from the prosaic to the exotic. It is a good idea to get into the habit of picking up the odd can of this or that, to store away for a future emergency. In this way you are never caught completely off guard, and there is no noticeable strain on your budget.

WHEN and HOW MUCH to buy is also a question which requires careful consideration. There is a great drive these days to popularise what could be described as 'bulk' buying — already an established North American habit. Giant bargain-size edibles, two-for-the-price-of-one and all sorts of other lures constantly tempt the housewife to put twice as much into her shopping basket as she intended. Now of course it is sensible to pick up a genuine bargain when you see one, but there is also no point in over-stocking your larder or buying 'bargains' you don't use. The other extreme is that kind of haphazard day-to-day buying, which can be hard on both nerves and shoe leather. The cake batter is in its last stages — and behold! — the bottle of vanilla is mysteriously empty. Somebody wants a late-night snack, but someone else forgot to pick up the bread, so there is barely enough for breakfast — let alone a sandwich. Such unhappy moments are bound to arise at some time in the life of every family, but they can be largely avoided by a little common sense, and working out a happy medium between buying too much and too little. My own preference is for planning on a weekly basis, working out in a general kind of way the main meals I will be serving in the following eight days. Saturday's shopping then covers basic supplies, plus whatever extras are necessary, macaroni for example, or a can of tomatoes for a casserole, and so on. Meat, fish, fruit and vegetables I like to buy on a day-to-day basis in order to ensure they are as fresh as possible.

But the real answer to the problem of shopping is for each family to evolve their own plan, one which is genuinely adjusted to the particular rhythm of the household. A little imagination and forethought will result in happier shopping expeditions, more satisfactory meals and the kind of larder which will never let you down.

STORING FOOD

FOOD	AT ROOM TEMPERATURE	IN REFRIGERATOR
Milk (covered and placed near evaporator)	4–5 hours	3–6 days
Butter (wrapped, placed near evaporator)	7 days	1–2 months
Margarine (wrapped, placed near evaporator)	7 days	1–3 months
Lard and Dripping (covered)	1–2 weeks	up to 3 months
Fruit Juice or Tomato Juice (In cans, they do not require refrigerator storage for long periods, will keep on shelf 6–8 months. Chill before serving. If cans are opened, pour contents into jug, cover and put in refrigerator)	1–7 days	2–3 weeks
Fresh Meat (wrapped or placed in special container provided)	24 hours	6–8 days
Fish (wrapped or placed in special container provided)	10–12 hours	2–3 days
Ice cubes	Refill trays when defrosting	
Frozen Vegetables and Fruits	Use immediately	1–3 days in evaporator only
Ice cream	Use immediately	1–4 days in evaporator only
Bacon (wrapped)	5–7 days	3–4 weeks
Cheese (wrapped)	1–3 days	2–4 weeks
Soft Cheese, Dutch or Cream (wrapped)	1–3 days	1–2 months
Refrigerator Biscuit Dough (wrapped)	2–3 days	2–3 weeks
Prepared Short Pastry Crumbs (in clean screwtop jars)	2–3 days	2–3 weeks
Dessert Custard Containing Milk (can be chilled uncovered for 30 minutes before serving, but cover for storage)	4–6 hours	2–3 days
Cooked Meat (wrap or place in special container)	2 days	5–6 days

Eggs in Shell (covered)	7 days	2–3 weeks
Stock (stored in covered jug)	1–2 days	7–10 days
Melba Sauce (in clean screwtop jar)	4–30 days	1–6 months
Chocolate Sauce (stored in clean screwtop jar)	1–2 days	7–10 days
Dried Fruits (in clean screwtop jar)	1–3 months	up to 6 months
Paprika (in clean screwtop jar)	2–3 weeks	2–3 months
Dry Cereals (in original packet or screwtop jar)	1–2 months	4–6 months
Salad Plants and Fresh Herbs (wrapped or in special container)	2–6 hours	7–10 days
Cauliflower (in special container)	1–3 days	3–8 days
Root Vegetables and Hard Apples (in special container)	1–2 weeks	1–4 months
Citrus Fruits (in special container)	1–7 days	2–4 weeks
Left-over Vegetables (in special container or covered)	1 day	5–7 days

N.B. All vegetables should be trimmed, washed and dried before storing in refrigerator. This keeps the refrigerator clean, takes less space and saves time.

Baking

If you want to be sure that your cakes are always a success, there are a few basic rules to follow:

1. Prepare your cake tins and baking sheets before making your cake.
2. Try to use the size of tin recommended in the recipe, and if this is impossible, always use a size *LARGER*, never smaller.
3. Measure all ingredients very precisely.
4. Remember that the more thoroughly your ingredients are beaten and mixed, the lighter your cake will be. However, the main mixing in a classic cake recipe should take place *BEFORE* you combine dry ingredients with wet. Once you reach that stage you should work as rapidly as possible.
5. *DON'T* be tempted to open the oven door before the full cooking time has elapsed, or your cake may fall.
6. Test your cake by pressing it lightly in the centre with your finger *WITHOUT* removing it from the oven. If the surface is firm, the cake is baked, if it is still soft, more cooking is needed. Or insert a clean metal skewer into the middle, and if it comes out clean, the cake is done.

COOKING FISH

Learning to cook fish properly is a skill which every housewife should acquire. It not only makes a tempting and nutritious dish but it is also one of the most economical foods available, and lends itself to a tremendous variety of dishes. The cardinal sin is overcooking, which ruins both texture and flavour. A little careful attention paid to correct timing and temperature will pay rich rewards.

To Bake Fish:

The oven temperature should be moderate to moderately hot and the fish should be covered with buttered paper in order to keep it as moist as possible. Butter the baking dish generously and add a little stock, milk or white wine. Baking time for fillets is approximately 12 to 20 minutes, cutlets will require about 20 minutes and whole fish 12 minutes per lb.

To Boil Fish:

Excepting in very rare instances, fish is never boiled. It should be very gently poached in water, milk or fish stock which is kept at simmering point. It can then be served hot or cold. Thin fillets require 7 minutes per lb. cooking time, thicker pieces 10 minutes per lb. For one large piece, or a whole fish, allow 12 minutes for the first lb. and 10 minutes for each succeeding lb.

To Fry Fish:

Fish may be fried in either deep or shallow fat. For deep frying, the most satisfactory method is to dry the fish, coat it lightly with seasoned flour and then dip in fritter batter. Make sure the oil or fat you are using is sufficiently hot. A thin blue haze rising from it indicates that the correct temperature has been reached. Immerse the fish. Allow 3 to 4 minutes cooking time for fillets, 7 to 8 minutes for cutlets or whole fish. Drain on absorbent paper. For shallow frying, dry fish, coat with seasoned flour as before, dip in egg, then roll in breadcrumbs. Melt oil, butter or fat in the pan, again making sure it is really hot before putting in fish. Allow 6 minutes cooking time for fillets, 4 to 5 minutes for thicker pieces or whole fish. Turn fish halfway through cooking time. Oily fish requires very little fat.

To Grill Fish:

Heat grill thoroughly before cooking and keep fish well brushed with melted butter during cooking time. With oily fish such as herring, fat is not needed. Thin fillets do not require turning and need only about 4 minutes. If wished, the heat can be reduced after the first 2 or 3 minutes. Thicker pieces should be grilled quickly, allowing 2 to 3 minutes for each side. Then reduce heat and cook for another 3 to 4 minutes.

COOKING FRUIT

THE SAME RULES apply with fruit as with vegetables — in other words, use the minimum of water and the minimum of cooking time. Fruit which contains a lot of water, such as rhubarb or apples, requires no water at all if cooked in a heavy covered saucepan. Add sugar and a squeeze of lemon juice, keep heat medium high under saucepan until the lid is hot to the touch, then reduce heat to low. The fruit literally cooks in its own juices.

COOKING MEAT

AS WITH ALL foods, the correct cooking of meat can spell the difference between a succulent and juicy dish and one that is dry and tasteless. There is considerable variation between the times necessary for the different types of meat. Pork, for example, needs long and careful cooking, as it can actually be dangerous to eat if not cooked thoroughly, whereas beef benefits by more rapid cooking. A chart for cooking times follows:

ROASTING	TIME	OVEN TEMPERATURE
Beef	15 minutes per lb. plus 15 minutes over	moderately hot
Lamb and Mutton	20 minutes per lb. plus 20 minutes over	as above
Pork	25 minutes per lb. plus 25 minutes over	as above
Veal	25 minutes per lb. plus 25 minutes over	as above

NOTE: The method of slow roasting has become increasingly popular in recent years, and is an added safeguard if you are not sure of the tenderness of your meat. For this use a very slow oven and double any of the cooking times mentioned above.

GRILLING OR FRYING	TIME
Beef	5 to 15 minutes, depending on thickness and personal taste
Lamb and Mutton	10 to 15 minutes
Veal	15 to 20 minutes

STEWING, BRAISING AND STOCKS	TIME
Beef	1½–3 hours
Lamb and Mutton	1½–2½ hours
Pork	2½ hours
Veal	1½–2½ hours

COOKING POULTRY

THE DELICATE FLAVOUR of poultry can easily be ruined by either over-cooking or cooking at incorrect temperatures. This applies to both young birds and to older fowl. Since chicken lends itself to such a delicious variety of dishes, learning to treat it with the proper respect is a necessary part of one's culinary art. Below you will find a few general rules as to proper temperatures and timing. I have also included the increasingly popular method of roasting in foil, as this gives particularly tender and flavourful results.

ROASTING	TIME	OVEN TEMPERATURE
Young Chicken	25 minutes per lb.	moderate
Duck and Goose	25 minutes per lb.	begin in hot oven, reduce to moderate
Turkey (under 12 lb.)	25 minutes per lb.	
Turkey (over 12 lb.)	20 minutes per lb.	

FOIL ROASTING: Wrap bird completely in double thickness of foil, turning edges over at least twice to completely seal. Set oven at hot. Place bird in pan breast upwards. Roast as follows:

		COOKING TIME
Turkey	8–10 lb.	2¼–2½ hours
	10–12 lb.	3 hours
	14–16 lb.	3–3¼ hours
	18–20 lb.	3¼–3½ hours
Chicken	3 lb.	1 hour

BOILING

Older fowl should be gently boiled or steamed, allowing 30 minutes to the lb.

GRILLING AND FRYING

Spring chickens can be halved or quartered and then fried or grilled until tender under a medium hot grill.

COOKING VEGETABLES

WHETHER COOKING fresh or frozen vegetables, there are two cardinal rules to follow: DO NOT OVER-COOK and use as LITTLE water as possible. Too much water results in loss of both flavour and nutritional value. When cooking fresh vegetables, bring water to the boil BEFORE putting in the vegetable, and cook cabbage, Brussels sprouts and broccoli in an open pot, unless you want to spoil both colour and flavour. With frozen vegetables, follow the directions on the package implicitly, and add a pat of butter just before the end of cooking time. Also be willing to experiment with method. Try baking or sautéeing your vegetables for a change — you will be delighted with the results.

• • •

WEIGHTS AND MEASURES

IMPORTANT NOTE: All weights and measures used in this book are British. When a tablespoon is referred to, it means a proper measuring tablespoon. 3 teaspoonfuls equal 1 tablespoon. The average British teacup is ¼ pint, or 1 gill. The average British breakfast cup is ½ pint or 2 gills. The British standard tablespoon measures *1 fluid ounce*.

SERVINGS: All recipes are for 4 servings, unless otherwise stated, or in those cases where an exact estimate is obviously impossible, as with cakes, canapés, etc.

• • •

Oven Temperatures

For the sake of consistency, all the recipes in this book will be found to conform with the chart below. No actual oven settings are given but by reference to the chart you will be able to establish what setting is correct for your own type of cooker.

However, since there is always a slight variation between different makes of cookers, and even between two cookers of the same make, this cannot be more than an approximate guide. Get to know your own cooker thoroughly if you do not already do so, and if you are ever in any doubt as to the temperatures given in some of these recipes, refer to your own manufacturer's temperature chart.

	ELECTRICITY °F.	GAS REGULO	CENTIGRADE EQUIVALENT
COOL oven	225–250	0–½	107–121
VERY SLOW oven	250–275	½–1	121–135
SLOW oven	275–300	1–2	135–149
VERY MODERATE oven	300–350	2–3	149–177
MODERATE oven	375	4	190
MODERATELY HOT oven	400	5	204
HOT oven	425–450	6–7	218–233
VERY HOT oven	475–500	8–9	246–260

Savoury Apple Flapjacks

4 oz. plain flour
2 tablespoons fine semolina
2 level teaspoons baking powder
shake black pepper
$^1/_4$ teaspoon salt
$^1/_2$ teaspoon dry mustard
good pinch dried sage
1 egg
milk
1 teaspoon chopped onion
1 large apple, peeled, cored and chopped
lard for frying

Sift flour, semolina, baking powder, seasonings and add onion. Make well in centre and add beaten egg. Stir, adding enough milk to make batter of a soft dropping consistency. Beat well until smooth. Stir in chopped apple. Melt a very small nut of lard on a heavy hot frying pan, griddle or electric hot plate. Drop batter from tablespoon, making as many circles as pan will take. Cook over moderate heat until bubbles form and burst and the flapjacks are golden underneath. Flip over and cook other side. As they are cooked slip them into teacloth. Serve freshly cooked and hot with butter and green salad; or with a sauce of freshly cooked tomatoes, and hot bacon or sausages. Mixed mustard or prepared French mustard is a 'must' for savoury flapjacks.

VARIATION: Add 2 oz. finely chopped cooked ham or bacon, or 1 oz. finely grated cheese instead of the apple.

• • •

Cheese and Herb Soufflé

1 pint milk
$^1/_4$ level teaspoon salt
2 rounded tablespoons fine semolina
$^1/_2$ level teaspoon or less dried herbs (such as basil, tarragon, sage)
3 oz. grated cheese
3 eggs, separated

Warm milk and sprinkle in salt and semolina. Bring to boil, stirring. Remove from heat and stir in cheese and herbs. Beat in egg yolks. Fold in egg whites, beaten to stiff froth. Turn into greased soufflé dish or casserole, filling not more than two-thirds. Bake in moderately hot oven until well risen and golden, about 35 minutes. Serve at once with prepared French mustard and green salad.

VARIATION: Add 4 oz. finely chopped boiled bacon or ham in place of the cheese and chives; or reduce cheese to half and add 2 oz. chopped ham.

Country-Style Bread and Cheese Bake

(4—6 Servings)

8 thin slices day-old bread, buttered
1 level teaspoon oregano (or other favourite herb)
4 thin slices ham (size as for bread slices)
4 slices Cheddar cheese (about same size as bread slices)
3 eggs
1 teaspoon made mustard
1 level teaspoon salt
good grinding pepper
1 tablespoon chopped onion
1½ pints milk
paprika

Butter a large shallow oven dish (about 12×7×2 inches). Dust oregano lightly over bottom. Arrange 4 slices of bread on bottom (cutting to fit). Cover with slices of cheese and ham. Top with remaining bread. Beat eggs well; add seasonings and onion and then milk, mixing well. Pour this over the bread. Sprinkle with paprika. Stand in a pan with 1 inch of hot water. Bake in a moderate oven for about 50 minutes, until lightly set and golden. Serve at once, hot, with green vegetables or salad.

• • •

Green Pepper Fondue

1 clove garlic
1 lb. grated Cheddar cheese
½ pint dry white wine
pinch cayenne pepper
pinch salt
1 level tablespoon cornflour
1 large green pepper

TO SERVE:

very small vol-au-vent cases

Butter the bottom and sides of a double saucepan and rub with cut clove of garlic. Pour in wine, reserving a little for blending the cornflour. Add grated cheese and stir over pan of hot water until the cheese has melted. Season, add cornflour and stir well. Remove stem and seeds from green pepper and dice very finely, stir into cheese mixture. Pour into chafing dish and keep warm at the buffet table. Pile warm vol-au-vent cases in hot dish and stand beside fondue so that guests can fill cases themselves with the cheese fondue.

Cheese-Stuffed Peppers

4 small peppers
8 oz. grated Cheddar cheese
salt and pepper
$^1/_2$ level teaspoon dry mustard
3 oz. fresh breadcrumbs
1 can anchovies
2 eggs (lightly beaten)

TO GARNISH:

tomato slices
parsley sprigs

Slice tops of peppers, remove core and seeds and wash well. Mix breadcrumbs with grated cheese, seasoning and mustard. Drain oil from anchovies, reserve four, and chop others. Add chopped anchovies to breadcrumbs and grind to soft paste with egg. Spoon filling into peppers and stand in well-buttered ovenproof dish. Bake in a moderate oven for $1\frac{1}{4}$–$1\frac{1}{2}$ hours until peppers are tender. Garnish with sliced tomato, parsley and curled anchovies. If serving cold, chill in refrigerator and slice.

• • •

Cheese and Sweetcorn Fritters
(16 Fritters)

4 oz. plain flour
salt and pepper
1 egg
$^1/_4$ pint milk
6 oz. grated Cheddar cheese
6 oz. sweetcorn

Sieve flour and seasoning into mixing bowl. Gradually beat in milk and lightly beaten egg, stir in cheese and sweetcorn. Place dessertspoonful in hot fat and fry until crisp and golden brown. Drain well and serve at once. May be served as a main dish, a cocktail savoury or as an accompaniment to chicken.

• • •

Cheese Straws

4 oz. flour
2 oz. margarine
2 oz. processed cheese
little water
few drops Worcester sauce
cayenne pepper

Rub fat into flour, add sieved processed cheese, pepper and Worcester sauce. Mix with water until dough holds together. Roll out $\frac{1}{8}$ inch thick. Prick with a fork and cut into fingers and put on greased trays. Bake in a very hot oven until golden brown.
This cheese pastry can be used to make cheese biscuits or to line individual patty tins for savoury fillings.

Anchovy Rolls and Twists

pastry as in cheese straws (see above)
1 can flat fillets of anchovy

Roll pastry into an oblong $\frac{1}{8}$ inch thick. Cut into two pieces 3 inches wide. Lay strips of anchovy fillet at intervals across one of the 3-inch pieces of pastry, cut between and roll pastry over each fillet as for sausage rolls sealing the edges. Cut the other piece of pastry in $\frac{1}{4}$-inch wide strips and twist two strips together with a strip of anchovy between. Place on greased baking sheet and bake until golden in a hot oven.

• • •

Cheese and Grape Tartlets
(18 Tartlets)

PASTRY:

7 oz. plain flour
pinch salt
4 oz. butter
1 egg (lightly beaten)
filling (see below)

Sieve flour and salt into basin, rub in butter and bind to stiff dough with the egg. Roll out thinly and line 18 2-inch patty tins. Prick base, line with greaseproof paper and fill with baking beans. Bake in a hot oven for 15 minutes, remove beans and greaseproof paper and bake for a further 5 minutes until golden brown. Allow to cool.

FOR THE FILLING:

6 oz. grated Cheddar cheese
1/4 pint double cream
8 oz. black grapes

Mix grated cheese with cream. Fill cases with cheese mixture.
Cut grapes in half, remove seeds and top each tart with 3 grape halves.

4 Savoury Spreads

Anchovy

2 oz. luxury margarine, 1 level teaspoon anchovy essence, salt and pepper to taste

Walnut

2 oz. luxury margarine, 1 oz. finely chopped walnuts, salt and pepper, 1 teaspoon lemon juice

Parsley

2 oz. luxury margarine, 1 rounded teaspoon chopped parsley, salt, pepper and cayenne pepper to taste

Cheese and Chutney

2 oz. luxury margarine, 1 oz. finely grated cheese, 1 level tablespoon chutney, salt and pepper

TO MAKE THE SPREADS: Simply place all ingredients in a small mixing bowl and beat together. Cover with foil or greaseproof paper and keep for up to a week in the refrigerator. Make up two spreads at a time with 4 oz. margarine. Wonderful for sandwiches of all kinds, as well as adding real zest to grilled steak or fish.

• • •

FISH DISHES

Salmon Patties With Mushroom Sauce

(8 Patties)

1 8-oz. can salmon
8 oz. cooked mashed potato

1 10½-oz. can condensed cream of mushroom soup

2 teaspoons lemon juice
1 dessertspoon parsley (finely chopped)
salt and pepper

TO COAT:

1 egg (beaten)
browned crumbs

Flake fish and mix with mashed potato. Stir in ½ can of soup, lemon juice, parsley and seasoning. Leave to stand for 30 minutes to one hour. Divide mixture into eight, shape into round patties, brush with egg and coat in browned crumbs. Fry in hot fat until golden brown on both sides.

FOR THE SAUCE: Put remaining soup in small pan, add 2 tablespoons milk and seasoning, and beat well. Heat gently and serve with patties.

Lobster Thermidor

2 medium size lobsters, boiled
2 tablespoons butter
½ teaspoon finely minced onion

dash cayenne pepper
2—3 tablespoons dry white wine (optional)
1 tablespoon tomato purée

8 oz. fresh mushrooms
¼ pint white sauce
Worcester sauce
2 oz. sieved processed cheese

Have the lobster halved lengthwise. Pick all the meat out of the shells and claws of the lobster, keeping the claws whole for decoration. Dice the tail portions, claws and coral — if any. Heat the butter and add the onion, lobster, cayenne to taste and white wine. Simmer gently for five minutes, stirring constantly. Add the tomato purée and seasoning. Cook another 5 minutes; place in the lobster shells. Cover with white sauce, sprinkle with cheese and bake in hot oven, until well heated and browned, or under a grill. Serve very hot.

• • •

MEAT DISHES

Curried Sweetbreads

(3–4 Servings)

4 calves' or lambs' sweetbreads (or 1 lb.)
flour and curry powder for coating
lemon juice
1 oz. butter

FOR THE SAUCE:

1 oz. fat
1 onion
1 oz. flour
1 level tablespoon curry powder
1 beef extract cube
1/2 pint hot water
1 apple
1 small tomato
1 level teaspoon brown sugar
1/2 level teaspoon salt
grated rind and juice 1/4 lemon
1/2 bay leaf
1 tablespoon mango chutney

Soak the sweetbreads for at least an hour in cold water, drain and put in a pan with cold water to cover and a squeeze of lemon juice; bring to the boil and simmer gently 5 minutes for lambs' sweetbreads, 10 minutes for calves'; plunge into cold water and then remove any gristle or skin. When quite cold cut in slices and sprinkle with flour mixed with a little curry powder. To make the sauce, peel and chop onion and apple, and chop tomato. Crumble beef extract cube and dissolve in hot water. Grate lemon rind and squeeze juice. Frying onion in fat add flour and curry powder, mixing and stirring for 1 to 2 minutes. Add beef extract liquid and stir until it boils. Add the remaining ingredients and boil gently for 30 minutes. Strain and reheat. Melt the butter and fry the prepared sweetbreads in it until very lightly browned; serve with the sauce and boiled rice.

Lamb With Rice

1 breast of lamb	*8 oz. rice*	*2 pints water*
2 oz. butter	*1 oz. raisins*	*8 oz. tomatoes*
1 onion	*2 beef extract cubes*	*salt and pepper*

Cut the meat into pieces and trim off excess fat. Melt 1 oz. butter in a saucepan. Chop the onion and cook with the meat in the butter for a few minutes. Cover with water, bring to the boil and crumble in the beef extract cubes. Reduce the heat and allow the meat to cook until tender — about 1 hour. In another pan, melt 1 oz. butter and cook the rice for a few minutes. Add raisins, chopped tomatoes, salt and pepper. Strain over the stock from the meat. Cook gently for 15 minutes. Strain off any liquid and make a ring of rice on a serving dish. Serve meat in the centre and garnish with chopped parsley.

• • •

Veal Stewed With Sherry

4 veal cutlets or chops (best end neck or loin)	*1 carrot (chopped)*	*1/4 pint dry sherry*
6 tablespoons olive oil	*1 onion (chopped)*	*salt and pepper*
1 stalk celery	*1 tablespoon tomato paste*	*chopped parsley*

Heat the oil and fry the meat until brown. Add the vegetables and mix well. Cover and simmer for about 10 minutes or until the vegetables are tender. Mix the tomato paste and sherry together and add to the meat, together with the seasoning. Cover and cook until the meat is tender — about 20 minutes. Add water during cooking if necessary to prevent burning. Sprinkle with chopped parsley. Serve with creamy potatoes or a pasta or boiled rice or any vegetable, though peas, carrots or spinach are nicest with veal.

• • •

Casserole of Beef With Cider

2 lb. beef (thin flank, blade, chuck or skirt)	*1 sweet pepper*	*1 level teaspoon salt*
2 oz. fat or oil	*1 onion*	*1/4 level teaspoon pepper*
2 level tablespoons flour	*1/2 pint tomato juice*	*8 oz. haricot or butter beans*
	1/2 pint cider	

Soak the beans overnight in plenty of cold water. Cut the meat in 1-inch cubes, removing all fat and sinew. Roll in flour to coat well. Slice the onion and the sweet pepper, removing all seeds. Heat the fat or oil and fry the beef in it to brown well. Remove. If the frying has not been done in the casserole, put the meat in this, otherwise lift out the meat while you fry the sweet pepper and onion until brown. Combine with beef and tomato juice. If frying has been in a separate pan use the tomato juice to swill out the pan and then pour it over other ingredients. Add the cider, seasoning and the drained beans. Cover and cook in slow oven for 3 hours. Serve from the casserole with a root vegetable and a green vegetable.

• • •

Barbecued Spare Ribs

4 thick chops
1/2 oz. butter or oil
1 small onion
1 stalk celery
1 level tablespoon brown sugar
2 level teaspoons dry mustard
1 level teaspoon salt
1/2 level teaspoon paprika pepper
2 teaspoons tomato paste
1 tablespoon Worcester sauce
1/4 pint water
1 tablespoon vinegar
2 tablespoons lemon juice

Peel and chop the onion. Wash and chop the celery. Squeeze lemon juice. Mix sugar, mustard, salt and pepper with the tomato paste and the liquids. Place the chops in a wide shallow casserole and bake uncovered for about 30 minutes or until well browned. Pour off any fat. Meanwhile fry the onion in the butter or oil until brown. Add remaining ingredients and pour over the chops. Cover and continue baking for about 45 minutes. Serve with potatoes and a green vegetable.

• • •

Devilled Neck of Lamb

2 lb. neck of lamb
1 oz. fat or oil
2 stalks celery
1 onion
2 tomatoes
2 level teaspoons dry mustard
2 level teaspoons salt
1 teaspoon Worcester sauce
1/4 level teaspoon pepper
1 beef extract cube
1/4 pint hot water
1/4 pint vinegar

Cut the lamb in pieces 1 inch thick. Chop the celery and the onion. Skin and chop the tomatoes. Crumble the beef extract cube and dissolve in hot water. Blend the seasonings with the beef extract liquid and vinegar. Heat the fat or oil in a saucepan or casserole and fry the meat brown in it. Add the vegetables and fry for a few minutes longer. Add the liquid mixture. Cover and simmer on top or in a very moderate oven for 1–1¼ hours. Serve with boiled potatoes or rice.

Veal Marengo

1 lb. veal (leg, breast or shoulder)
1 onion
1 oz. butter
$^1/_2$ oz. flour
salt and pepper
1 beef extract cube
$^1/_2$ pint hot water
2 tablespoons tomato purée
1 bay leaf
4 oz. mushrooms

Cut the meat into 1-inch pieces. Melt the butter in a frying pan and cook the meat until browned. Add the chopped onion and cook for a few minutes. Blend in flour and transfer ingredients to a saucepan. Add seasoning, tomato purée, bay leaf and the beef extract cube crumbled and dissolved in hot water. Simmer for 1 hour. Add chopped mushrooms and cook for 10 more minutes. Serve garnished with croûtons of fried bread and parsley.

Pork With Capers

1 lb. pork
1 onion
1 carrot
2 dessertspoons capers
$^1/_4$ pint red wine
thyme, bay leaf, parsley, pepper
2 oz. butter
1 oz. flour
1 beef extract cube crumbled and dissolved in $^1/_4$ pint hot water

Chop vegetables. Tie herbs in bouquet. Put these ingredients round the meat. Marinade 8 hours with red wine. Drain. Put liquid in a casserole. Melt the butter and brown the meat. Stir in flour. Blend in marinade and gravy. Season. Bring to the boil, cover and cook slowly for 2 hours. Serve meat in slices and reduce the sauce in casserole. Stir in the capers at the last moment and pour the sauce over the meat.

Braised Beef With Prunes and Wine
(4–6 Servings)

2 lb. piece of lean beef (flank, rib or chuck)
1 large piece of bacon rind or lean scraps of bacon
1 oz. fat
8 oz. onions
8 oz. carrots
8 oz. prunes, cooked
$^1/_2$ level teaspoon salt
$^1/_4$ level teaspoon pepper
$^1/_2$ pint red wine
8 oz. noodles
grated Parmesan cheese

Chop the onions and carrots. Wash the bacon rind. Melt the fat in a deep saucepan or enamelled cast iron casserole. Fry the meat in it until brown all over. Remove the meat. Put the bacon rind in the bottom and the vegetables on top. Add the seasoning and wine and return the meat. Cover and cook gently in a slow oven for $2\frac{1}{2}$–3 hours or until the meat is tender. Just before dishing-up time, boil the noodles in salted water; drain and arrange round the edge of the platter. Carve the meat and arrange slices in the middle of the noodles and put the vegetables, prunes and sauce round it. Sprinkle the noodles with cheese and serve with peas, green beans or spinach.

Aberdeen Sausage

(8–10 Servings)

1 lb. lean steak, except shin
8 oz. bacon
1 small onion
4 oz. rolled oats
1 tablespoon Worcester sauce
1 egg
1 level teaspoon salt
$^1/_4$ level teaspoon pepper
dried breadcrumbs

Mince steak, bacon and onion together until very fine. Add the oats, Worcester sauce, beaten egg and seasoning and mix well. Shape into a long, thick sausage, and wrap carefully in aluminium foil, sealing the ends well. Either bake on a tray or in a baking tin in a slow oven for 2 hours, or boil or steam. Have the dried crumbs ready on a piece of greaseproof paper. Remove the foil carefully and roll the sausage in the crumbs to coat thickly. Leave until cold and store in a cool place. Slice thinly. Serve with any salad, pickles or chutney, or for breakfast with slices of tomato.

• • •

CHICKEN DISHES

Curry of Chicken

1 oz. dripping for frying
12 oz. chopped onions
1 clove garlic
1 small apple chopped
1 dessertspoon curry powder
1 dessertspoon flour
$^1/_2$ pint stock (from chicken bouillon cube)
few drops Worcester sauce
1 tablespoon coconut
1 tablespoon sultanas
cold roast or boiled chicken pieces
1 dessertspoon lemon juice
1 teaspoon tomato purée or 1 tomato
1 tablespoon condensed milk
1 oz. rice per person, cooked and drained well
parsley and paprika for garnish

Melt fat, fry onion and garlic. Add apple. Stir in curry powder and flour. Add bouillon, gradually bringing to boil whilst stirring. Add Worcester sauce. Cover. Simmer gently with rest of ingredients for 30 minutes. Add lemon juice, tomato purée and milk. Blend, then add chicken and heat gently until thoroughly hot. Dish with a rice border, garnish with parsley, paprika. Hand small dishes of crisp bacon squares, slices of cucumber and lemon, banana and lemon, fresh grated coconut, mango chutney, chopped salted peanuts, fan-shaped gherkins, decorated with chillies.

Chicken Mischief

1 roasting chicken
2 tomatoes
2 tablespoons oil
2 level tablespoons honey
$^1/_4$ pint stock
1 level tablespoon cornflour
4 oz. dripping
2 onions
2 tablespoons pickle
3 tablespoons soya sauce
2 tablespoons vinegar
4 tablespoons water

Melt the dripping, joint the chicken and fry gently until well cooked and golden brown. Skin and chop the tomatoes, chop onions. Heat oil and fry tomatoes, onion and pickle for 5 minutes. Add stock, soya sauce, honey and vinegar and bring to the boil. Simmer for 10 minutes. Blend cornflour with the water and add to the sauce. Bring to the boil, stirring. Serve the chicken and pour the sauce around. Or the sauce may be served separately, the chicken joints being eaten with the fingers and dipped in the sauce.

Chicken Forcemeat Pie

4 chicken joints
1 oz. seasoned flour
1 oz. lard
1 $10^1/_2$ oz. can condensed chicken with rice soup
seasoning
$^1/_4$ pint stock or cold water
12—16 forcemeat balls

Roll chicken joints in seasoned flour and fry until golden brown in melted lard. Place in bottom of shallow ovenproof dish. Pour soup and water over chicken, season and bake in a moderately hot oven for 45 minutes. Arrange forcemeat balls round chicken joints and cook for further 20 minutes. Serve hot.

• • •

SALADS AND SALAD DRESSINGS

Iced Cheese and Pear Salad

3 level tablespoons mayonnaise
1 red pepper (canned)
4 oz. crumbled Cheshire cheese
$^1/_8$ pint double cream
2 large pears
4 lettuce leaves
sprigs watercress

Turn refrigerator up to maximum. Mix mayonnaise with Cheshire cheese, chopped red pepper and the cream, and spread in ice tray. Place in freezing compartment of refrigerator, and stir every 30 minutes until mixture is frozen, i. e. about 1–1½ hours. Wipe pears (peel if skins are tough) cut in half and remove core. Place each half pear on a lettuce leaf, pile iced cheese mixture on pear and garnish with watercress sprigs. Serve immediately.

Chilled Salad Medley

CHEESE BASE:

$1/_4$ pint water
$3/_4$ oz. butter
$1^1/_2$ oz. potato powder
salt and pepper
$1/_2$ level teaspoon dry mustard
6 oz. grated Cheddar cheese

SALAD:

2 oz. mushrooms
lemon juice
olive oil
salt and pepper
2 medium sized tomatoes (sliced)
1 hard-boiled egg (sliced)
watercress sprigs

To make the cheese base, heat water and butter in a saucepan and add potato powder. Beat well and add seasoning and grated cheese. Press this potato cheese mixture into an 8-inch circle, stand on a plate and chill in the refrigerator for one hour. To prepare the salad, wipe mushrooms and slice thinly, put into a shallow dish with a squeeze of lemon juice, olive oil and seasoning, (the olive oil will be absorbed very quickly, so allow sufficient). Arrange sliced mushrooms, sliced tomatoes and egg attractively on top of the cheese potato base and garnish with watercress sprigs.

• • •

Cheese and Orange Salad

8 oz. cubed Cheddar cheese
2 oranges
2 medium-sized onions
4 $1/_2$-inch slices bread
fat for frying
watercress

FRENCH DRESSING:

6 tablespoons olive oil
2 tablespoons lemon juice
1 tablespoon orange juice
grated rind 1 orange
salt
pinch cayenne pepper

Place cheese in mixing bowl. Remove rind and pith from oranges, and separate orange segments. Peel onions and slice thinly, separate into rings. Cut bread into $\frac{1}{2}$-inch cubes, heat fat to smoking point and fry until golden brown, drain. Wash watercress. Make dressing by mixing all ingredients for dressing together. Toss all ingredients in dressing separately and arrange in circles overlapping towards centre.

Mayonnaise

2 egg yolks
1 level teaspoon dry mustard
1 level teaspoon salt
$^{1}/_{4}$ level teaspoon pepper
$^{1}/_{4}$ level teaspoon paprika
4 tablespoons vinegar
8 tablespoons salad oil
1 tablespoon chopped capers

Put the egg yolks into a basin. Add the mustard, salt, pepper and paprika and mix thoroughly together. (The mustard helps to emulsify the dressing and prevent curdling.) Add 2 tablespoons vinegar slowly and stir well. Then add the oil drop by drop, stirring hard with a wooden spoon until the mayonnaise is thick and smooth. Add the remaining vinegar gradually and beat vigorously. Finally, add a tablespoon of chopped capers, and serve with a salad platter of salmon, lettuce, olives and finely sliced orange. Or omit capers and use for any recipe in which mayonnaise is required.

• • •

Parisian Salad

8—12 oz. cold boiled veal (knuckle or hock)
2 hard-boiled eggs
2 small onions
4 tomatoes
French dressing (see below)
1 lettuce
2 teaspoons chopped parsley

Boil the eggs and cool. Boil the potatoes and cool. Put the onions in water, bring to the boil, drain and cool. Wash and drain the tomatoes and lettuce. Chop the parsley. Make the dressing. Cut the meat in thin strips. Dice the potatoes and chop the onion. Slice the tomatoes and slice or chop the eggs. Mix the meat, potatoes, onion, eggs and tomatoes. Combine with dressing. Add the lettuce torn roughly or left whole if the leaves are small. Sprinkle with the parsley and serve.

FOR THE DRESSING:

1 tablespoon oil
pinch pepper
pinch dry mustard
$^{1}/_{4}$ teaspoon salt
$^{1}/_{2}$ tablespoon vinegar

Mix the oil and seasoning, add the vinegar. Stir before using as the ingredients separate out.

'One-Stage' Peach Cream Shortcakes

(12–14 Shortcakes)

4 oz. luxury margarine
2 oz. castor sugar
8 oz. sieved self-raising flour
1 egg
1 tablespoon milk

FOR THE FILLING:

1 small can peaches, drained and sliced
$^1/_4$ pint whipped cream

Put ALL the shortcake ingredients into a bowl, and mix very thoroughly with a wooden spoon into a smooth firm paste. Turn out on to a lightly floured board, and roll out until $\frac{3}{4}$ inch thick. Cut into rounds with a 2-inch cutter. Place on baking sheet, brush tops with water and sprinkle with castor sugar. Bake near the top of a fairly hot oven for 10–15 minutes. Cool on a cake rack. Cut each in half and sandwich the halves together with sliced peaches and whipped cream.

• • •

Apple and Orange Charlotte

7—8 slices two-day old bread, buttered
1 lb. apples
grated rind of an orange
2 tablespoons orange juice
2 tablespoons lemon juice
1 oz. butter
4 oz. sugar
2 egg yolks
4 tablespoons soft breadcrumbs or small bread cubes
extra sugar
cinnamon

Remove crusts from bread and cut into fingers. Line bottom and sides of a small cake tin, about 6 inches across, with bread, buttered side to tin. Peel, core and slice apples, and cook gently with the orange rind, fruit juices, butter and sugar until just tender. Remove from heat and beat in egg yolks. Spoon mixture into lined tin in layers with the crumbs. Cover with rest of bread, butter side up. Bake in upper half of moderate oven for 35–40 minutes. Cool a little and turn out. Serve warm, sprinkling top with sugar and cinnamon.

Cheese and Apple Meringue Pie

(4–6 Servings)

FOR THE PASTRY:

6 oz. plain flour
pinch salt
pinch cayenne pepper
$^{1}/_{2}$ teaspoon mustard
3 oz. butter
3 oz. grated Cheddar cheese
2 egg yolks

FOR THE FILLING:

$1^{1}/_{2}$ lb. cooking apples
1 oz. butter
2 oz. castor sugar
2 tablespoons cold water

FOR THE CHEESE MERINGUE:

2 egg whites
2 oz. grated Cheddar cheese

Sieve flour and seasonings into mixing bowl, rub in butter until mixture resembles fine breadcrumbs, mix in grated cheese and bind to a stiff dough with egg yolks. Knead lightly. Roll out to $\frac{1}{4}$ inch thickness and use to line 7-inch fluted flan ring. Line flan ring with greaseproof paper and fill with baking beans. Bake in a hot oven for 25 minutes, or until golden brown. Remove baking beans and paper. Peel and slice apples, place with butter, sugar and water in pan and cook gently until pulped, beat well. Allow to cool. To make meringue, whisk egg whites and salt until stiff and fold in cheese. Fill cheese flan with apple purée and top with meringue. Bake in a moderate oven for 20 minutes. Serve hot or cold.

• • •

Creole Temptation

(6–8 Servings)

2 eggs
1 heaped teacup breadcrumbs
$^{1}/_{4}$ pint evaporated milk mixed with $^{1}/_{4}$ pint water
4 bananas, mashed
juice and rind of 1 small orange and lemon

Beat eggs and mix all ingredients together. Pour into mould or basin, stand in tin of water, cook in very moderate oven until set. Serve on hot dish with jam heated with a little water and rum or rum essence.

Orange Meringue Bake
(4–6 Servings)

$^3/_4$ pint water
pinch salt
3 oz. fine semolina
1 oz. butter
2 tablespoons each orange and lemon juice, strained
2 oz. sugar or to taste
finely grated rind 1 orange
3 eggs
small can mandarin segments
4 oz. extra sugar
few glacé cherries or angelica pieces

Warm water and salt; sprinkle in semolina and bring to the boil, stirring. Beat in the butter, orange and lemon juice, sugar, orange rind, egg yolks and 1 beaten egg white. Pour into a buttered oven dish and bake in a moderate oven for about 20 minutes. Top with drained mandarin segments, reserving a few for garnishing. Whisk the 2 egg whites to a stiff froth with extra sugar and pile on top. Return to the oven to crisp the meringue, about 10 minutes. Garnish with mandarin segments and cherries. Serve hot or cold.

Raspberry Cheese
(4–6 Servings)

8 oz. grated Cheddar cheese
1 lb. raspberries (keep a few for garnishing)
3 oz. castor sugar
1 teaspoon lemon juice

FOR GARNISH:

mint sprigs
wafers

Whisk grated cheese, sugar, raspberries and lemon juice together and divide between individual dishes. Chill. Garnish with remaining raspberries, a mint sprig and wafer. If you have an electric blender use it to mix all ingredients.

Cream Mousse
(6 Servings)

1 fruit jelly (1 pint packet)
$^3/_4$ pint hot water, or $^1/_2$ pint water and $^1/_4$ pint fruit juice
1 large can evaporated milk
1 dessertspoonful lemon juice
orange quarters
angelica
cherries or nut strips to decorate

Make up 1 pint packet of jelly to a little over $\frac{3}{4}$ pint and allow to cool but not set. Whisk evaporated milk until thick, add lemon juice and re-whisk. Whisk thick jelly to a foam and fold into milk. Pile mixture into sundae glasses. Decorate with orange quarters, angelica, and nut strips.

Crunchy Crust Raspberry Pie
(6 servings)

FOR THE CRUST:

4 oz. luxury margarine
2 oz. castor sugar
2 level tablespoons golden syrup
8 oz. crushed digestive biscuits

Dissolve margarine and golden syrup in a small saucepan and bring almost to the boil. Add this to the crushed crumbs and castor sugar in a mixing bowl and mix thoroughly together. When slightly cooled, knead well and press into an 8-inch pie plate or flan ring. Place in refrigerator until firm and set. Pile filling into crust just before serving and decorate with whole raspberries.

FOR THE FILLING:

1/2 pint double cream
1 packet frozen raspberries or 1 small punnet, fresh raspberries, sweetened to taste

Whisk the double cream until stiff and fold in the raspberries, keeping back a few for decoration.

• • •

Coffee Chiffon Pie
(6–7 Servings)

2 oz. margarine
2 oz. castor sugar
12 oz. cake or sweet biscuit crumbs
coffee chiffon filling (see below)

Cream margarine and sugar, add the crumbs and press this mixture into a flan ring or sandwich tin, completely coating the base and sides. Leave to set in a refrigerator or cold place, or bake in a moderate oven for 10 to 15 minutes.

FOR THE FILLING

3 teaspoons gelatine
3 tablespoons cold water
3 egg yolks
1 tablespoon castor sugar
4 level teaspoons instant coffee
3 egg whites
1 1/2 oz. castor sugar
1/4 pint evaporated milk
1/4 teaspoon cinnamon
1 teaspoon castor sugar

Dissolve gelatine in water. Place egg yolks, the tablespoon sugar and instant coffee in the top of a double boiler or a basin over hot water and beat until foaming and thickened. Add gelatine, stirring continuously until it coats the spoon. Remove from heat and cool slightly. Add egg whites, previously beaten until stiff with the sugar, carefully folding them in. Whip the evaporated milk until similar to a very thick cream. Fold lightly into the mixture. Pour into a pie shell. Mix cinnamon with the teaspoon sugar and some crumbs and sprinkle over the pie. Chill thoroughly.

• • •

CAKES AND SMALL CAKES

Chocolate Iced Cherry

4 oz. whipped up fat
4 oz. castor sugar
2 eggs
1 egg yolk
6 oz. self-raising flour
4 tablespoons milk
1/4 teaspoon salt
6 oz. mixed dried fruit
2 oz. glacé cherries (cut in half)
1 oz. finely cut angelica
1 oz. chopped walnuts

Put all the ingredients into a mixing bowl. Mix for 1 minute and turn into a greased 7-inch cake tin. Bake in a moderate oven for approximately 1 hour. Cool.

TO DECORATE:

8 oz. icing sugar
1 egg white
glacé cherries
walnuts

Beat together the icing sugar and egg white until it stands up in peaks. Spread over the cake. Decorate with cherries and walnuts.

Date Shorties

6 oz. butter or margarine
3 oz. castor sugar
6 oz. self-raising flour
6 oz. fine semolina
8 oz. stoned dates, chopped
1 tablespoon honey
1/2 level teaspoon ground cinnamon
8 tablespoons cold water
1 tablespoon lemon juice

Melt butter; add sugar and when dissolved stir in sifted flour and semolina. Grease a Swiss roll tin or shallow baking dish (or two 8-inch sponge tins) and spread half the crumbly mixture in it, flattening down well. Heat the dates, honey, spice, water and lemon juice, stirring until soft and smooth. Spread this over crumble in the tin. Put the remaining crumble on top, pressing down lightly. Bake for 20–25 minutes in a moderate oven. Cut at once into small sections but leave in tin until cold.

'One-Stage' Chocolate Cake

4 oz. luxury margarine
4 oz. sieved self-raising flour
5 oz. castor sugar
1 heaped tablespoon sieved cocoa
2 eggs
1 tablespoon milk

FOR THE FILLING:

2 oz. plain chocolate
2 oz. luxury margarine
2 dessertspoons hot water
1 oz. castor sugar
1 dessertspoon milk

Mix ALL cake ingredients quickly in a mixing bowl, then beat well with a wooden spoon for 1–2 minutes. Put mixture into two 7-inch sandwich tins greased with margarine and with the bottom lined with greaseproof paper. Smooth tops. Bake in the middle of a moderate oven 20–25 minutes. Cool on a cake rack.

FOR THE FILLING: Melt chocolate carefully over hot water (don't let it get hot) then cool it slightly. Now whisk margarine, chocolate and castor sugar in a small bowl for 1–2 minutes. Add water, then milk, then whisk again. Sandwich cakes together with chocolate filling. Dust top with sugar.

• • •

Biscuit Log

12 digestive or wholemeal biscuits
fruit squash or sherry
3 tablespoons strawberry or raspberry purée or jam
4 oz. plain chocolate
sugar flowers and maidenhair fern (to decorate)

Soak each biscuit for a few seconds in the squash or sherry, being careful not to allow them to become soggy. Place the first biscuit on a flat board and spread fruit purée evenly over the top. Continue to stack the biscuits and spread with purée, so forming an upright cylindrical shape. Melt the chocolate very slowly in a basin over a pan of hot water. Beat thoroughly. Spread evenly around the sides and across the top of the log. Turn on to its side and coat the other flat end. Decorate with sugar flowers and maidenhair fern. To serve cut the first slice at an angle across two or three of the biscuits. Cut the other thin slices parallel to this.

Crispy Delights

(Approximately 15–18 Biscuits)

3 oz. table margarine
1 oz. salted peanuts, chopped
2 oz. castor sugar
2 oz. soft brown sugar
½ beaten egg
½ level teaspoon ground ginger
4 oz. plain flour
½ level teaspoon baking powder
castor sugar to dredge

Cream the margarine, chopped peanuts and all the sugar together in mixing bowl, until light and fluffy. Beat in the egg. Sieve the ginger, flour and baking powder together and mix into the other ingredients to form a soft dough. Divide and shape the dough as directed in any of the following ways *(see below.)* Place on a baking sheet, previously brushed with melted margarine. Bake in a pre-heated moderately hot oven on second shelf from top for 12–15 minutes. Dredge with castor sugar. Cool on a wire tray.

6 WAYS WITH CRISPY DELIGHTS:

1. Mould into small rounds, about ¾ inch in diameter and press flat with a fork. When baked, dredge with castor sugar.

2. Mould into small, even-sized rounds about ½ inch in diameter. Place them together in threes. Press flat with a knife (in the shape of a clover leaf) and put a piece of glacé cherry in the centre of each. When baked, brush over immediately with boiling apricot jam.

3. Mould into small even-sized rounds about ½ inch in diameter. Place them in a line of three or four. Press flat with a knife. When baked brush immediately with boiling apricot jam and sprinkle with chopped peanuts.

4. Mould into small rounds about ¾ inch in diameter and press flat with a fork. When baked and cooled, mix 8 well-heaped tablespoons sieved icing sugar with 3 dessertspoons warm water and beat thoroughly. Spread evenly over each cookie and decorate with a small piece of crystallised ginger.

5. Mould into small sausage shapes about ½ inch wide and 2 inches long, then press each flat with a fork. When cool, sandwich together in pairs with peanut butter. Dredge with sieved icing sugar.

6. Coarsely chop 2 oz. plain chocolate, and knead into the cookie mixture. Shape into rounds about ¾ inch in diameter and press flat with a fork or knife.

• • •

Chocolate Tangerine Cake

2 heaped tablespoons cocoa
4 tablespoons hot water
8 oz. self-raising flour
8 oz. luxury margarine
10 oz. castor sugar
4 eggs
2 tablespoons milk
tangerine icing (see below)

Sieve the cocoa, and mix smoothly with the water. Cool. Sieve the flour. Cream the margarine and sugar thoroughly together. Beat the eggs in separately, one at a time, adding a little sieved flour with each egg after the first. Fold in the remaining flour and the milk. Divide equally between two sandwich tins $8 \times 1\frac{1}{2}$ inches, lined with greaseproof paper, and brushed inside with melted margarine, and bake for 35—40 minutes in a moderate oven on the middle shelf. Cool on a wire tray. When cold cut open, and sandwich all the layers together with the tangerine icing, attaching the first layer to an 8-inch cake board with a little icing before beginning to fill. Ice all over and mark in a pattern with a fork, or slap and pull up in points with a palette knife. If liked, pipe borders and rosettes of icing at top and bottom edges, using a rose tube. Decorate with orange and lemon slices, or sliced jelly sweets.

• • •

FOR THE TANGERINE ICING:

3 dessertspoons tangerine juice
grated rind 2—3 tangerines
8 oz. icing sugar
3 oz. luxury margarine

Sieve the icing sugar. Beat margarine until creamy, then beat in half the icing sugar until light and fluffy. Add remaining icing sugar and the juice and the grated rind and again beat thoroughly until smooth and ready to spread on cake.

• • •

Royal Icing

1 lb. icing sugar
2 egg whites
few drops lemon juice

Sieve icing sugar until all lumps are removed. Lightly beat egg whites and lemon juice and gradually stir in the icing sugar, beating well, until a smooth, shiny mixture, which only just finds its own level in the basin, is obtained. It should coat the spoon smoothly.

Jap Cakes

3 egg whites
6 oz. castor sugar
6 oz. ground almonds
chocolate vermicelli (for garnish)
chocolate and vanilla butter cream (see below)

Grease and line a Swiss roll tin with rice paper. Whisk the egg whites until 'white' but not stiff. Add 1 dessertspoon sugar then fold in the remainder and the ground almonds. Mix well. Spread the mixture evenly into the tin and flatten, using a palette knife. Should the knife drag dip it into cold water. Bake in a moderately hot oven for 10 minutes. When the top is firm press with a 1½-inch plain cutter. Return to the oven until golden and firm — about 10–15 minutes. Remove the tin from the oven, lift out the rounds. Sandwich the rounds together with chocolate butter cream. Spread a little round the sides and roll in chocolate vermicelli. Pipe the tops of the cakes with alternate stripes of chocolate and vanilla butter cream.

FOR THE BUTTER CREAM:

3 oz. butter
8 oz. icing sugar
2—3 oz. unsweetened chocolate
few drops vanilla essence

Combine butter and icing sugar. Cream butter, gradually add sugar, beat until light and fluffy. Flavour one third of mixture with vanilla, the remainder with the melted chocolate.

Dundee or Rich Fruit Cake

2 oz. glacé cherries
4 oz. blanched almonds
½ pint water
10 oz. margarine
8 oz. currants
8 oz. sultanas
4 oz. mixed chopped peel
finely grated rind 1 orange and 2 lemons
1 large can condensed milk
10 oz. plain flour
pinch of salt
¾ level teaspoonful bicarbonate of soda

Chop cherries and half of blanched almonds, place with water, margarine, fruit, chopped peel, grated rinds and condensed milk in a saucepan. Bring to the boil stirring all the time, lower the heat and simmer for 3 minutes. Remove and cool. Sieve flour and salt into a mixing bowl. Add bicarbonate of soda to cooled fruit mixture and stir briskly. Add to the flour, etc., and mix quickly together. Put into an 8-inch tin lined with greaseproof, and brush with margarine. Spread evenly. Put remaining halved almonds on the top. Bake 2¾ hours on middle shelf in slow oven. Cool for about 5 minutes in tin. Turn out on to wire tray. Half the ingredients as above may be used, baking in a 6-inch tin for 2 hours as directed above.

'One-Stage' Lemon Fingers

(12 Fingers)

4 oz. luxury margarine *2 oz. castor sugar* *5 oz. plain flour, sieved*

FOR THE FILLING:

lemon curd

Put the margarine, sugar and plain flour into a mixing bowl. Mix well together, then beat the mixture thoroughly for 1–2 minutes with a wooden spoon until it is soft and creamy. Spread mixture in a Swiss roll tin, making lines along the top with the back of a fork. Bake near the top of a moderate oven for 20–25 minutes. Cut into fingers, and cool on a cake rack. When cool, sandwich fingers together with lemon curd filling.

Valentine Cake

(Uncooked)

UNCOOKED FUDGE CAKE:

4 oz. luxury margarine
3 level tablespoons cocoa
1 oz. castor sugar
1 tablespoon golden syrup
8 oz. crushed sweet biscuits
glacé icing (see below)

Put the margarine, sugar and syrup in a pan, melt but do not boil. Put the cocoa and biscuit crumbs in a mixing bowl, add the melted ingredients and mix all together. Brush the inside of a medium sized heart-shape tin with melted luxury margarine, and press the mixture well down into the tin, smoothing the top with a palette knife. Leave to set preferably in a refrigerator overnight. Turn out of the tin before icing.

FOR THE ICING:

6 oz. sieved icing sugar
2—3 dessertspoons hot water
few drops red colouring
1 yard ribbon

Put the sieved icing sugar in a mixing bowl, stir in the hot water and mix to a coating consistency. Place one tablespoon of the icing in a small bowl and add a few drops of red colouring and mix thoroughly. Pour the white icing over the top of the heart cake and while still wet pipe lines of pink icing about ¾ inch apart across the heart cake. Then with a pointed skewer or knife, draw lines at right-angles across the pink icing to give a feathered effect. When set tie a ribbon around the sides.

How to Kill the Fatted Calf

ENTERTAINING

BARBECUE ENTERTAINING

THE BARBECUE — one of America's favourite outdoor pastimes — now shows signs of becoming almost equally popular in Britain. In spite of the uncertainties of the climate, an increasing number of intrepid Britishers are happily singeing their eyebrows and charring their steaks over an outdoor fire. And the truth of the matter is that the barbecue DOES provide a very gay and informal method of either feeding your family or entertaining your friends.

One begins with the equipment — which can cost as little as £3 for a simple charcoal grill — or as much as £33 for an elaborate American import with an electrically turned spit. In between these two extremes are a number of other models, such as a smaller version of a grill with an electrically operated spit, which is available at somewhere between £7 and £8. It is also wise to spend a little extra on properly designed tools. Charcoal fires generate a lot of heat and if you want to avoid both burnt food and burnt fingers you should at least invest in a long-handled fork and fish slice, and a pair of asbestos gloves. With regard to operating your grill, manufacturers' instructions should naturally be followed, but there are also five basic rules which will contribute greatly to the success of both your fire and your cooking:

1. DON'T use kindling to start the fire. Choose methylated spirits or firelighters.

2. Start the fire well in advance of the time you want to use it. All flames should have died down before you begin to cook, and the coals should have acquired a thin film of ash, so that they look grey by daylight, but will glow red when darkness comes.

3. When the fire is ready for cooking, add reserve charcoal around the edge, keeping the centre bed open and roughly the same size as the food you will be cooking.

4. A shallow fire is best for broiling, but *rôtisserie* cooking requires a deep coal bed.

5. To reduce heat, lower the firebox if it is adjustable, or raise the grill. For quick heat, tap the ashes off the coals with tongs. The food you serve can be as simple or as elaborate as you desire, but don't forget that the whole purpose of a barbecue is to create an easy and informal atmosphere. Also the rich tangy flavour of most barbecue cooking makes it desirable for all accompaniments to be as simple as possible. Your appetiser should be something like chilled tomato juice, or jellied consommé served in paper cups. Or a bowl of olives handed round with carrot sticks and celery curls or a tangy cheese dip *(see recipes on page 188)*. Your main course could be hamburgers with barbecue sauce, marinated steaks or kebabs *(see recipes below)*, or meat or fowl roasted whole on the spit. A big salad is an excellent accompani-

ment, as are hot rolls or bread, particularly if spread with herb or garlic butter and heated on the grill *(see below)*. For dessert you could serve a fruit or cream pie or cake, but fruit and cheese, fruit salad or ice cream are really the most refreshing after a spicy main course. And when the garden is dark and the embers of the fire are burning low, why not let everyone toast marshmallows in the true barbecue tradition, eating them right off the end of the stick; delicately crisp on the outside, melting soft within. Such a meal as this, served with wine or beer, or a cold, tangy fruit punch will result in a feeling of blissful well-being for everyone, including the hostess.

Barbecued Hamburgers

1 lb. ground beef
1 tablespoon Worcester sauce
1 onion, finely chopped
1 teaspoon salt
pepper
barbecue sauce (see below) or butter for basting

Combine all ingredients, shape into ovals (for some reason this helps the patties to grill more evenly). To keep them tender, handle as little as possible. Baste with barbecue sauce while grilling and serve with a good spoonful of sauce on top. Foil-baked potatoes *(see below)* are a delicious accompaniment. To serve hamburgers on buns, spread with softened butter before grilling. Provide plenty of garnishes. French mustard is a 'must' as are onions, either fried or raw, and sliced very thin. Cucumber or sweet pickles are also important. The genuine American hamburger always has at least two or three garnishes, so don't be afraid to experiment.

BARBECUE SAUCE

2 onions, chopped fine
2 tablespoons vinegar
1 tablespoon Worcester sauce
1 tablespoon brown sugar
1 tablespoon chilli powder
½ pint tomato ketchup
about 2 tablespoons water
4 tablespoons oil

Cook onions in oil until tender and golden. Add all other ingredients, stir well and cook gently for 10 to 15 minutes. This sauce is equally good for basting and serving with either meat or chicken. For variation try adding a chopped green pepper and a few stalks chopped celery.

Barbecued Kebabs

cubes of lamb
mushrooms, tomatoes, green peppers, onions, sliced
marinade (see below)

FOR THE MARINADE

1/4 pint salad oil	*3 tablespoons vinegar*	*1/4 teaspoon pepper*
3 tablespoons soy sauce	*1 1/2 teaspoons sugar*	*2 large onions, sliced*

Pour marinade over cubed meat, placing sliced onions on top. Cover, leave to stand in the refrigerator or in a cool place for several hours or overnight. When ready to cook meat, place cubes on skewer. On separate skewers, place alternate pieces of the vegetables. Some recipes suggest alternating vegetables with the meat, but experts agree they are better cooked separately, as the vegetables tend to toughen the meat. Grill the kebabs about 4 or 5 inches from the heat. After the first 15 minutes turn and cook for another 15 minutes. Baste with the marinade while cooking. Grill the vegetables the same way, but they should only require about half the cooking time. *(This marinade is equally good for steaks.)*

French Bread in Foil

Slice the loaf, without cutting all the way through to bottom. Spread with slices of herb or garlic butter, made by blending butter with about half a clove of crushed garlic, a couple of teaspoons chopped herbs or some grated Parmesan cheese. Spread butter on slices, wrap loaf in double thickness of foil, doubling edges over securely. Heat on grill for 10 to 15 minutes, turning once.

Baked Potatoes in Foil

Scrub potatoes. Brush with salad oil, wrap each securely in square of foil, overlapping ends carefully. Bake 45 to 60 minutes on grill or right on top of coals. Turn occasionally. Pinch to see if they are done.

BUFFET DINNERS

THE BUFFET DINNER has become one of the most deservedly popular forms of modern entertaining. It is easy for the hostess, relaxing for her guests and adaptable to all sorts and conditions of household, budgets and tastes. To make your buffet a success, remember to keep the atmosphere as gay and informal as possible; pottery dishes and richly coloured tablecloths are a happy choice, and do remember to let your guests serve themselves. You have a wide choice in the food you serve. The main dish can be as simple as a great steaming tureen of soup (such as the recipe for Clam Chowder given below), served with plenty of crusty French bread and a big salad to follow. Or you might like to try Chicken Mischief *(see page 166)* plus as many glamorous extras as you may feel inclined to provide. What could be described as the classic buffet dinner usually consists of a really succulent casserole, such as Braised Beef with Prunes and Wine, or Veal Marengo *(see page 164)*, served with a salad and either rice, noodles or potatoes, with perhaps Cheese and Apple Meringue Pie or Raspberry Cheese to follow *(see pages 170, 171)*. And don't forget that plenty of really good coffee will provide the perfect ending to your meal.

Clam Chowder

1 pint clams from can, or mussels
1 chopped onion
2 oz. fat
2 cubed large potatoes, cooked
salt and pepper
4 oz. flour
$^1/_2$ pint boiling water
$^1/_2$ pint evaporated milk
clam juice made up to $^1/_2$ pint with water
1 oz. butter
4 cracker biscuits

Strain the clams and cut up in small pieces, fry in the fat with the onion. Put a layer of potatoes in a casserole, cover with a layer of clams, sprinkle with flour and salt and pepper. Repeat until all are used. Add $\frac{1}{2}$ pint boiling water and simmer for 20 minutes. Add the milk and clam liquid and pats of butter, bring to the boil. Add the biscuits, soaked in milk. If required, the liquid may be thickened with a little cornflour blended with the milk.

CHILDREN'S PARTIES

WHEN PLANNING a children's party, do keep in mind the ages and interests of the group you are going to invite. Small children of nursery school age, for example, have lots of energy, so running and marching games are always a good way of helping them let off steam. However, they tend to lose interest in things rather rapidly, so there should be plenty of variety in the games you suggest. Older children enjoy competitive, imaginative games, and don't forget to have lots of prizes, even if they are only tiny ones. It is also fun to plan a theme for your children's party and carry it right through from the invitations to the decorations and the games you organise. For instance, a Pussy Cat Party for small children could include such games as Puss-in-the-Corner, Pinning the Tail on Pussy and Hunt the Mouse in which a small rubber mouse is used instead of the proverbial slipper. And the birthday cake would, of course, be Kitty-the-Kitten *(see below)*. For older children a Pirates'-Party is a colourful idea. It can include such games as Walking the Gangplank. (Draw a straight line on the floor, each child's eyes are bandaged, and they must walk along the line. If they fall off they are in the sea.), a Pirates' Tug-of-War and, of course, a Treasure Hunt. There is also the game in which a number of small objects are brought in on a tray, everyone has a minute or two to look at them, then they are taken away and the person able to remember the most objects wins the game. In this case, the tray can be full of pirates' treasure — pieces of costume jewellery, old coins, thimbles, anything else which could be considered as 'booty'. And as the crowning touch to your Pirates' Party, why not have a 'Treasure Chest' birthday cake? Bake your cake in a deep oblong pan, then cover it with chocolate icing, to suggest an oaken chest. Pipe on 'silver' locks and bindings in white icing, and use the tiny silver balls (of the type usually found on Christmas and wedding cakes) to suggest silver nail heads. With regard to the food you serve at children's parties, it is much wiser to make it simple and nourishing rather than rich and starchy. For this reason, I am inclined to favour serving something else besides sandwiches. Small children, for example, could be given a simple salad, such as tomatoes stuffed with chopped egg and served with tiny rolls. (Little children love small things, so do remember to make everything in miniature.) All they will require besides this is some ice cream, served in paper cups, a few small cakes and, of course, the birthday cake. Older children would greatly enjoy frankfurters on toasted rolls (served with French mustard and sweet chopped pickle), or baked beans and hot rolls with ice cream to follow, plus the birthday cake and a couple of plates of small cakes and sweet biscuits.

Kitty the Kitten

CAKE:

6 oz. table margarine
6 oz. castor sugar
3 eggs
1 tablespoon milk
8 oz. self-raising flour, sieved

ICING AND DECORATION:

3 oz. table margarine
8 oz. icing sugar, sieved
3 dessertspoons milk
6 oz. desiccated coconut
1 skewer
one 7-inch silver cake board
large sweets
8 oz. almond paste
2 long sticks spaghetti
small piece of stiff white paper
red colouring

TO MAKE THE CAKE: Cream the table margarine and sugar together until light and fluffy. Beat in the eggs, one at a time, adding a little of the sieved flour with every egg after the first. Fold in the remaining flour and the milk. Turn the mixture into a ½-pint and a 1½-pint pudding basin, previously brushed inside with melted margarine. Bake in a pre-heated very moderate oven on middle shelf for 45—50 minutes for the small cake and 1¼ hours for the large cake. Turn out and cool on a wire tray.

TO MAKE THE ICING: Cream the margarine and half the icing sugar together until light and fluffy. Beat in the remaining icing sugar and the milk until again very light.

TO MAKE KITTY THE KITTEN: Trim the cakes into two rounds with a sharp knife. Cover them all over with icing and roll in desiccated coconut. Place the smaller cake on top of the large one and secure together with a skewer. Stick cake on cake board with a little icing. The 'feet' and 'tail' are made from large sweets or moulded almond paste, covered with icing and coconut. Sweets or coloured almond paste are used to make the 'eyes', 'nose' and 'mouth', and pieces of spaghetti make the 'whiskers'. Cut the 'ears' out of stiff white paper; paint one side with red colouring; ice the other side and cover with coconut.

CHRISTENING PARTIES

A CHRISTENING PARTY is most commonly a tea party, although some people turn it into a more formal occasion, and serve a cold buffet luncheon. If you decide you are going to serve a luncheon, your wisest course is to plan the kind of meal which can be almost entirely prepared the day before. A simplified version of the Wedding Luncheon Buffet *(see page 192)* is probably the best choice, using perhaps three of the courses suggested. A tea party on the other hand should provide a tasty assortment of sandwiches and bridge rolls, as well as such extras as a cream pie or a trifle well laced with sherry. And whether your christening party is to be large or small, a Bell cake will do much to add a festive air to the occasion.

Bell Cake

Dundee cake (see page 177
almond paste — double quantity (see below)
3 tablespoons apricot jam
1 lb. royal icing (see page 176)
round cake board

Make the Dundee cake and bake in a very well greased 2-pint fireproof pudding basin. Prepare almond paste, reserving a small piece for the ring Brush the cake all over with the heated and slightly diluted jam, then cover firmly with almond paste, building up the top and forming a ridge round the base to give the characteristic bell shape. Place cake on board. Make up the royal icing and with it ice and decorate the cake. Shape the remaining piece of almond paste into a ring and place on top of the cake. Finish with a bow of silver ribbon. Decorate base with seasonal flowers and any other appropriate trimmings.

FOR THE ALMOND PASTE

$1^1/_2$ lb. ground almonds
2 teaspoons lemon juice or rum
8 oz. icing sugar
8 oz. castor sugar
10 level tablespoons condensed milk
$^1/_2$ teaspoon vanilla essence
6 drops almond essence

Sieve ground almonds and sugar. Mix in rest of ingredients and knead until smooth.

COCKTAIL PARTIES, OPEN HOUSE AND WINE PARTIES

THE COCKTAIL PARTY as such appears to be waning in popularity, which is probably just as well. I have always felt that the procedure of jamming as many people as possible into your sitting room in order to fill them up with large amounts of strong drink and very little food is a somewhat barbaric method of entertaining. However, a party of this type does offer a solution to the knotty question of how to provide entertainment to the maximum number of people with the minimum of effort. Particularly for the city dwellers, the accumulation of social obligations is a recurrent problem. Suddenly the day comes when you realise you owe invitations not only to far too many people — but also to far too many different *kinds* of people. How then to combine Aunt Margaret, Mr. Blakeley from the office and that gay young couple who live upstairs, in such a manner that all will remain happy? One solution is to hold not a cocktail party but an open house. Also, you might be interested in the method evolved by a friend of mine to avoid the crush in her sitting room ever reaching unbearable proportions. What she did was invite her guests in shifts. Business associates, and anyone else she wanted to have in for a short drink, were invited early — say between 5 and 7 p.m. This group also included elderly relatives, and anyone with buses or trains to catch. A few chosen friends were let in on the plot and invited early, in order to help spread the proper spirit of gaiety. The remaining batch of guests were invited to come between 7 and 9. The surprising thing about this method is that it really does work. The overlapping between groups is relatively slight, and even if Mr. Blakeley from the office *does* stay beyond his appointed time, he often turns out to be the life of the party.

Food and drink at a party of this sort can be much more flexible and imaginative than at the conventional cocktail party. There is no need to lay on lashings of expensive drinks, particularly in cocktail form. It may be necessary to provide whisky and gin, if you can afford it, and if some of your guests drink nothing else. But a great many people prefer wine, sherry or beer. Around Christmas time a punch bowl or mulled wine can be very successful as the main drink, with some extra bottles of wine or beer laid on for those people who prefer their drinks untampered with. Canapés can be at once simple and reasonably substantial. Hundreds of tiny biscuits and squares of toast dabbed with this and that are incredibly tedious to prepare and definitely unsatisfying to eat. In my opinion it is much better to have an assortment of five or six really delicious things, of which at least one should be served hot. One or two cheese dips, or a Tahiti dip *(see recipes below)* are always successful and very easy to prepare. Miniature vôl-au-vent cases filled with creamed mushrooms, chicken or tiny shrimps can be prepared well ahead of time and popped into the oven ten minutes before serving. Baby frankfurters *(if you want to save money, buy the large ones and cut them in 2-inch pieces)*, speared with toothpicks and served with a bowl of Barbecue sauce *(see page 182)* are always popular. Or you might like to try the Cheese and Grape Tartlets, Anchovy Rolls and Twists, Cheese Straws or Cheese and Sweetcorn Fritters *(see pages 159, 158)*.

It is also sensible to stretch expensive ingredients by combining them with other things. For example, try mixing chopped shrimps with chopped green peppers, cream cheese, a dash of Tabasco and Worcester sauce and enough sour cream to make the mixture of spreading or dipping consistency. The cream cheese and sour cream combination are also delicious if mixed with tiny shreds of smoked salmon. It is also nice to provide a few extras such as bowls of olives, crisps, pretzels and salted nuts.

An even simpler method of giving a party, and one that is steadily increasing in popularity, is the cheese and wine party. For this all you require is as many bottles of wine as you can afford and your guests are likely to drink, plus a good tray of assorted cheeses. In order to please every taste, you should provide at least one of the creamy cheeses, such as Brie or Camembert, as well as a nice, bland Dutch Gouda and one of the sharper flavoured cheeses such as Roquefort, Danish blue or Stilton, plus a good chunk of honest cheddar. Don't forget to provide a good variety of biscuits (hot French bread is also delicious with the creamy cheeses) and a few such extras as crisp celery curls and olives.

Cheddar Dip

8 oz. grated Cheddar cheese
salt to taste
about 8 tablespoons single cream or top of the milk
good pinch cayenne pepper
add flavouring as liked

Mix the cheese and cream together to a soft consistency. Add the seasonings and any flavouring as liked. Serve in an attractive bowl and hand potato crisps or small biscuits with the dip.

during this treatment look for moth. Methods of preventing moth attack are to use regularly, keep in a cupboard with moth repellent, or best of all in cold storage. Professional cleaning will de-infest furs. Insecticides should not be used as they encourage dust and spoil the lustre.

Professional cleaning is recommended once a year, but home cleaning can e attempted as follows. Beat and brush as above. Cover with warm bran fig dust, leave for several hours, then comb out with a wide-toothed comb. greasy collar can be treated with a grease solvent, but this must not be too often and the solvent must be kept from the pelt which it would

GOLD – TO CLEAN

GOLD OBJECTS should be polished with jeweller's rouge. Specially impregnated cloths can also be used and the polishing should then be done with a chamois leather. Wash gold chains in warm soap and water, brushing out the dirt with a soft brush.

GREASY PANS – TO CLEAN

BOIL UP GREASY PANS with water and a little soda (unless they are aluminium), scrub round and pour this away before washing. Alternatively wipe round with newspaper which can be burned. Both these are good methods of keeping excessive grease out of the washing-up water.

GUM ARABIC – TO USE

TO STIFFEN HAT VEILS, etc., make a solution of 2 oz. gum arabic in ½ pint of water by heating together in a double saucepan. After straining keep this in a bottle. When required take 1–4 tablespoons and add to 1 quart water. Rinse the article in this and iron when damp.

HATS – TO STORE AND CLEAN

THESE SHOULD BE stored carefully where they will not be crushed. Brush hats whenever they have been worn. To prepare a hat for storing for a long period stuff it with crumpled paper so that it will keep its shape, put moth repellent among this and wrap the whole hat in paper to exclude moth and dust.

A felt or velour hat is cleaned as follows: take out the band and clean with a grease solvent. Hold the hat in the steam of a boiling kettle, stuff with paper to give it shape and leave to dry. Press the brim with a warm iron over a damp cloth. Straw hats which have lost their freshness should be brushed then painted with milliner's varnish, or with straw dye to change their colour.

HOT-WATER BOTTLES – TO USE AND PRESERVE

STONE OR METAL hot-water bottles should not be used without a c[illegible] except for airing beds. Rubber hot-water bottles should not be filled [illegible] boiling water. Pour in the hot water, then squeeze till it rises to the st[illegible] hole thus expelling all air. Screw in the stopper. After use hang rubbe[illegible] water bottles upside down to drain. Tie the stopper to the neck for convenience. Store rubber hot-water bottles in the dark during summer to prevent the rubber perishing.

IRONING

VOILE, ORGANDIE, linen and rayon should be ironed damp; cotton and silk less damp; nylon and terylene almost dry; shantung and rayon with a dull and suede finish, quite dry. If cotton articles are too dry sprinkle them with water, roll up and leave for 1 hour then iron, when they will be nicely damp. It is not advisable to dampen rayon in this way as it may become spotty.

A hot iron should be used for cotton, organdie and linen (except crease resistant linen); a fairly hot iron for voile and shantung; a warm iron for silk; a coolish iron for crease resistant linen and rayon; and a cool iron for nylon and terylene.

Iron all articles till they are completely dry or they will look crumpled, then place in an airing cupboard. Air dresses, shirts, blouses and skirts on hangers to avoid creasing. Iron double parts, such as hems, on the inside first. Then iron all small parts like collars and pockets. Iron all articles along their length, except for certain rayons which must be ironed across to keep their shape and lace curtains which should be ironed diagonally.

IRONING BOARD – TO RE-COVER

THIS WILL NEED periodically re-covering. Use several layers of old blanket or some other thick material. Cut this out and tack to the under side of the board with large-headed tacks. To prevent wear and keep clean use a cover over this padding made from linen or cotton material which can be changed and washed.

IVORY – TO CLEAN

TO CLEAN IVORY, make a paste of whiting and lemon juice and coat the ivory with this, leave to dry, rub off and polish with furniture cream. If more seriously discoloured wash with soap and water and bleach in the sun; then rinse and polish. For methods which do not use water *see* PIANO KEYS.

JEWELLERY – TO CLEAN

IT IS BEST to have this cleaned professionally but it can safely be washed in soap and water, not with detergents. Pieces which are of no great value and which do not contain pearls, opals or turquoises can be cleaned at home in this way: cover them with methylated spirits and leave them for a little while. Take out and allow the methylated spirits to evaporate, then use a soft brush to polish them. *See also* GOLD AND SILVER.

KID – TO CLEAN

DO NOT ATTEMPT to clean kid gloves at home but send them to a clear
Shoes of white kid can be cleaned with a special cream sold for the purr

KNIVES – TO MEND

TO RE-FIX A KNIFE BLADE, clean out the hole in the handle usin a skev r, then fill this with powdered resin topped by a pea-sized piece of candle ax. Heat the tang of the blade till it will melt a piece of resin, then force it home into the hole and at once hold under warm but not hot running water. Trim off surplus wax.

LAUNDERING

PLAN YOUR WASH by dividing lightly and heavily soiled articles into two lots and washing the lightly soiled first. Use water of about 110°F. — a cooler temperature for woollens and coloured clothes — and not too much soap. If the water is hard add soda, but this is not necessary if you are using soapless detergents. Do not put in too many articles at once.

Heavily soiled articles may be put to soak for 12 hours in cold water to which borax is added — 1 tablespoon per gallon. Then wash as above but using more soap if necessary.

Coloured articles should be tested before washing. If no small sample is available take a corner of the article and tie it tightly with a piece of tape.

Dip and squeeze it in the water you are proposing to use, rinse, half dry, untie the tape and iron on the wrong side with a warm iron on top of a piece of white cotton. It will then be easily seen if the colours run.

Wring all articles before rinsing them as this will eliminate soapsud marks. Rinse in ample water, twice if necessary.

Handkerchiefs and other small badly stained articles can be boiled in a boiler over the kitchen stove. Add soap flakes and a little borax and boil briskly for 15 minutes or stew slowly for 1 hour. Blueing will then give the best results. Make a blue bath, testing the strength by scooping up a handful of the water and seeing that it is a strong but not dark blue. Dip the articles twice but do not leave in the bath. To remove excess blue, soak in vinegar and water then wash.

LAVATORY – TO CLEAN

A DAILY CLEAN is advisable and the floor should be washed twice weekly. Once each week pour a solution of soda in hot water, 1 oz. to 1 pint, into the pan, work round with the brush and flush. Pour in some carbolic disinfectant and leave to stand in the pan as long as possible. Keep disinfectant well out of the reach of small children.

Scouring agents which contain grit or sand are not recommended for they are liable to damage the glaze. If there are stains which cannot be removed by normal methods use a solution of *citric acid* (1 teaspoon in 1 glass warm water) for rust marks — wet the marks with this and leave for a time before washing off; use vinegar for blue-green scum marks or hard white calcium marks, rubbing on with a cork.

If any of these fail use a chloride bleach, many of which are sold under brand names.

LEATHER – TO CLEAN

LEATHER STRAPS, harness, bellows, etc., should be treated with neatsfoot oil. Leather handbags may be polished with shoe cream.

LINEN – TO WASH

WASH LINEN in very hot water. It will stand up to hard treatment in the wash and can be boiled, rubbed and even scrubbed with a soft brush if necessary.

To keep linen white when storing, wrap it in blue paper and put blue paper between the folds.

MANGLE – TO CLEAN

CLEAN DIRT OFF the working parts of a mangle with a paraffin rag. Clean the rollers by scrubbing with soap and water.

MARBLE – TO CLEAN

WASH MARBLE MANTELPIECES, ornaments, etc., with soap and water. Use abrasive to remove marks, or if this does not work use vinegar or lemon juice on a rag. Rinse after a few moments for these acids will easily spoil the surface.

MIRRORS – TO CLEAN

CLEAN MIRRORS by washing with a damp leather and then rubbing up with a leather cloth, or by using a proprietary window cleaner which is allowed to dry on the surface and then rubbed up. Whiting may be used in a similar way and rubbed up when dry. Another method is to use a cloth damped with *carbon tetrachloride* or with methylated spirits, but be careful not to let these touch the frame. After either of these rub up with a damp cloth.

MOPS – TO CLEAN

MOPS SHOULD be washed weekly in soapy water to which soda has been added. Keep mops, like brooms, hanging up when not in use.

NYLON – TO WASH

NYLON SHOULD NOT be boiled and should not be dried by heat as it will melt at quite moderate temperatures. It can be rubbed fairly hard during washing but should not be twisted.

OIL PAINTINGS – TO CLEAN

IF THESE ARE of value it is extremely unwise to attempt to clean them at home for damage may be done. For paintings of no great value wipe the surface very gently with a rag damped with methylated spirits.

ORLON – TO WASH

WASH FREQUENTLY in warm water. Do not boil and let it drip dry away from direct heat. If desired iron with a cool iron.

PATENT LEATHER – TO CLEAN

BELTS, HANDBAGS, etc., made of this should not be treated with polish but rubbed up with a dry cloth. Occasionally a little petroleum jelly may be applied to prevent them from drying out and cracking.

PEARLS – TO CLEAN

TO KEEP PEARLS in good condition they should be worn, for this gives them the light, air and oil they need. But they may become too oily and lose their sheen. They should then be covered with powdered *magnesia,* left a night and brushed clean with a soft brush. Never have pearls strung on metal, for this discolours them. A silk thread should be used.

PEWTER – TO CLEAN

THIS IS USUALLY an alloy of tin and lead. It does not tarnish readily but may gradually acquire a darkness which can be removed as follows: mix whiting powder and linseed oil; rub this on strongly with a rag. Take another rag, rub off and polish with a chamois leather.

PIANOS – TO CLEAN AND PRESERVE

DAMP IS THE GREAT ENEMY of a piano and for this reason it should either be placed away from a wall, or against an inside wall. It should not, however, be placed near a fire. If damp is suspected put a shallow tin of unslaked lime inside at the bottom.

Keep a piano's lid closed. Dust it regularly and polish the wood as other wooden furniture. Watch for moth on the felts and if there is any sign of this take professional advice.

PIANO KEYS – TO CLEAN

TO CLEAN PIANO KEYS take a piece of muslin, dip it in methylated spirits and rub.

For badly yellowed keys use flannel damped with *eau-de-Cologne*. Another method is to make a saturated solution of *potash* and into this mix enough whiting to form a paste as thick as putty. Put this on to the keys and leave overnight. In the morning remove, taking care to prevent any falling between the keys, and polish with chalk.

PICTURES – TO CLEAN

CLEAN POLISHED WOOD picture frames with furniture polish. Clean gilt frames with a rag dipped in warm turpentine. Clean the glass of pictures with a proprietary window cleaner or with a cloth damped in methylated spirits and a leather damped with water and wrung out. *See also* OIL PAINTINGS.

PILLOWS – TO CLEAN AND RE-COVER

PILLOWS can have feathers or down stuffing or a mixture. Down is softer but feathers are cooler.

Pillows can be washed but the work is heavy and drying prolonged. Use a good lather and deep bath. Knead thoroughly, rinse and hang out of doors to dry, shaking occasionally to loosen the stuffing.

To re-cover pillows tack together the open ends of the old and new covers, then shake the stuffing from one to the other. Rub beeswax over the inside of the new cover before filling to prevent feathers from penetrating.

PLAYING CARDS – TO CLEAN

A DOUGH of breadcrumbs is the best means of cleaning these. Rub gently, being careful not to buckle the edges. India-rubber is not suitable for it roughens them and they become unsatisfactory to use.

PRESSING

WHEREAS in ironing the iron travels over the material, in *pressing* the iron is pressed firmly on to a damp cloth placed above the material. Use a damp but not wet cloth and press till it is nearly dry.

When pressing heavy materials, to avoid giving them a flattened appearance place flannel below and above between the material and the damp cloth.

To prevent seams giving a glazed appearance on the right side of the material, press them over a pressing roller. This can be improvised from a rolling pin or tightly rolled magazine sewn into flannel then cotton. Place this along the seam on the outside and press from the inside. The seam edges will then fall away from the iron.

To press a pleated garment pin tops and bottoms only of the pleats to the ironing board.

For pressing collars, etc., make a pressing bag 9 inches square of any strong material, and stuff it with rags or kapok.

RAYON – TO WASH

WHEN WASHING RAYON, or artificial silk as it is still sometimes called, be careful not to stretch or twist. It is advisable not to boil or bleach rayon, but wash in warm water, rinse several times and dry away from direct heat. Use a cool iron.

ROLLER BLINDS – TO CLEAN

THESE CAN BE WASHED without taking them from their rollers as follows. Take down the blind and spread it on a table. Brush off dust and dirt. Scrub gently with warm soap and water (to which 1 tablespoon borax may be added if the blind is white). Repeat on the reverse side. When nearly dry iron with a hot iron. If the blind is to be starched it must be taken from its roller but on the whole this is not advised as it is then more likely to lose its shape.

RUST – TO REMOVE

ANY IRON or steel articles in the house (except stainless steel), or any articles which are tinned (i.e. made of iron or steel with a thin surface of tin) are liable to rust. Lanolin may be rubbed on metal objects such as fire-irons, carpentry tools, etc., which are being stored; lard may be rubbed on kitchen scales, baking-tins, etc. Lacquers are also used, and as long as these remain unbroken rust will be prevented. Paint of adequate quality will prevent rust. So does galvanising, i.e. coating the iron or steel with a surface of zinc.

To remove rust, rub with a paraffin rag, but the paraffin must not remain on the metal or more rust will occur. Deep patches of rust will require more violent treatment and emery paper must be used. Before repainting a rusted article, every patch of rust must be completely removed or rust will continue to develop under the paint.

Fabrics which lie next to steel or iron articles are liable to become rust marked. Treat with a solution of *citric acid* — 1 teaspoon to 1 pint warm water — but make sure first that this will not damage the fabric or discolour it.

SHOES – TO CLEAN AND PRESERVE

PUT SHOES on shoe trees as soon as they are taken off and while they are still warm. Trees will keep them in shape and prevent creases developing which eventually become cracks. Stuff wet shoes with newspaper. Dry in a warm but not hot place.

Ideally shoes should be cleaned after each wearing. Brush off the mud with a stiff brush (or if very muddy wash off with warm water). Apply polish with one brush, use a second one for polishing. For a fine shine rub with a very soft pad or duster.

Patent leather shoes should not be cleaned with shoe polish but rubbed up with a duster. Occasionally apply a little petroleum jelly. Crocodile shoes should be rubbed over with a colourless shoe cream. Canvas shoes should be brushed clean then whitened (or coloured) with wet whiting and set to dry. If very dirty they may be scrubbed first. Suede shoes should be brushed with a rubber brush. Spots can be removed with a grease solvent. Rubber shoes need no treatment except washing clean.

Sometimes heavy leather shoes or boots are required to be waterproof rather than shiny, and to achieve this clean them then rub in dubbin very thoroughly.

SILK – TO WASH

WASH SILK in warm water and soap or detergent, squeezing gently with the hands. Do not rub or the fibres will be frayed. Rinse thoroughly and to the last water add some vinegar. Rinse in gum arabic to stiffen.

When washing silks of several colours add salt to the water, which should be cool, and use detergent not soap. This will help to prevent the colours from running.

SILVER – TO CLEAN

THE SIMPLEST METHOD of keeping silver clean is to dry it after washing with a specially impregnated drying cloth; or use a different type of special cloth for rubbing it when it has been dried before putting it away.

To clean silver a proprietary cleaner may be used provided this is not gritty. If it is in powder form, wet it with methylated spirits. Other makes come ready mixed and need only be shaken thoroughly in their tins before putting on to the silver with a cloth. Use a soft toothbrush to clean corners. When it has almost dried use a leather to rub up. A cleaner can also be made by dissolving fine whiting in methylated spirit. This should be used in the same way.

There are also specially impregnated cleaning wools which may be used to wipe over the silver before rubbing it up with a clean cloth.

A method of cleaning badly tarnished silver is to boil it in an aluminium saucepan of water to which is added $\frac{1}{4}$ oz. soda per pint. Leave in for a few minutes only then wash in soap and water and dry. Remember not to leave the soda solution standing in the saucepan or it may be damaged. Silver plate may be cleaned in the same way.

To store silver for a long time place it in an airtight container wrapped in a special non-tarnish paper, or if not in soft paper then layers of newspaper.

SOOT – TO REMOVE

IF ANY of this gets on to the carpet when a chimney is being swept, brush it off gently with a soft brush, vacuum clean the patch and then rub vigorously in a circular direction with a cloth damped with *carbon tetrachloride*. Do not use salt for this gets into the carpet and absorbs moisture in damp weather.

SPONGES – TO CLEAN

Natural sponges:

If hard and gritty when bought, soak them in cold water, squeeze out gently and put into boiling water for 5 minutes. Repeat this 3 times, washing out the saucepan between. Even if new sponges do not need this treatment they should be soaked for a full day to allow them to expand.

When sponges become greasy, wash free from soap and soak in 1 quart water to which 2 tablespoons vinegar or lemon juice have been added. Leave in this for 1–2 hours. Or scald them in boiling water.

Artificial sponges
(Rubber, plastic, cellulose, etc.*)*:

Rinse them in a solution of bicarbonate of soda, $1\frac{1}{2}$ oz. to 1 pint warm water. Leave for a time, then rinse thoroughly in cold water.

SPRING CLEANING

THIS SHOULD be done one room at a time, starting from the top of the house. Have chimneys swept first, do any alterations that are to be done and any re-decoration. Send curtains and pelmets to the cleaner, or if not take them down and lay on newspaper then vacuum them clean. Vacuum clean all furniture, using the special attachment provided. Vacuum clean carpets then take them and their felts out of doors and vacuum clean them from the back. Dust ceilings, walls, etc., then wash woodwork and other washable surfaces.

STAINLESS STEEL – TO CLEAN

THIS METAL, which has been made with chromium, will stand up to all wear without staining. Stainless steel sinks and draining boards can be occasionally cleaned with a little whiting powder.

STAINS – TO REMOVE

SPECIFIC REMEDIES are listed below, but there are a few general principles in dealing with stains which should be followed:

1. Treat all stains as soon as possible after they have occurred.
2. Shake the garment and brush thoroughly to remove loose dust.
3. Treat the spots individually according to their nature.
4. Do not only treat the exact spot but the surrounding area as well.
5. Wash out all chemicals thoroughly.
6. If you have no specific remedy use warm soap and water. In any case, it is often worth trying this first.
7. If possible test chemicals to be used on a piece of the same material to see that they do not damage it.
8. When using *benzine* or any other inflammable chemical work out of doors.

Acid:

Treat with a weak solution of washing soda or borax, 1 teaspoon to 1 pint water. Household ammonia may be used, 1 part in 3 or 4 of water, but test this on a separate piece of fabric as it may bleach the colours.

Blacklead:

Remove with turpentine and wash.

Blood:

Soak in cold salty water for 1 hour, then rinse in warm soap and water.

Candle grease:

See WAX.

Cocoa:

Sponge the stain with warm borax and water, 1 pint water to 1 oz. borax.

Coffee:

Treat as cocoa stains.

Creosote:

Sponge with *benzine (benzol)* then rinse in warm water.

Dye:

These stains are very difficult to remove and it may not be possible. Try a mixture of household ammonia and methylated spirits in equal parts.

Egg:

Wash off in cold, not hot, salt and water, 1 teaspoon to 1 pint. Remove egg yolk stains with a grease solvent such as *carbon tetrachloride.*

Fruit:

Soak in warm borax solution, 1 teaspoon to 1 pint water, rubbing gently. Rinse and dry. Fruit stains should be dealt with promptly.

Grass:

Sponge with methylated spirit.

Grease:

Use a grease solvent such as *benzine* or *carbon tetrachloride,* or a propietary brand which contains these. Either are suitable for the greasy edges of collars and cuffs. *Carbon tetrachloride* is non-inflammable and has this advantage over *benzine,* but should not be inhaled as it is a mild anaesthetic. It is safe on wool, cotton and silk but may damage some rayons, and should be tested first on a sample piece. Lay the fabric on a flat surface on a pad of material. Work round the grease mark, then gradually towards it.

Ice cream:

Sponge at once with warm water and then rinse. If a grease stain remains use a grease solvent such as *carbon tetrachloride.*

Indelible pencil:

Rub out with methylated spirit. Be careful when using this on rayon for it will damage certain kinds and should be tested first on a small piece where it will not show.

Ink:

Use a solution of *citric* or *oxalic acid,* 1 level teaspoon to 1½ pint water. If these are not available use lemon juice then rinse. For red ink stains spread freshly made mustard over, leave for 30 minutes then wash.

Stains made by ball point pens can be removed with methylated spirits. Indian ink and marking ink stains are very hard to remove but citric acid solution may be tried, or if this fails use *permanganate of potash,* ½ teaspoon to 1 pint water, rinse and then use hydrogen peroxide.

Iodine:

Soak the affected area in a dilute solution of *sodium thiosulphate,* ½ level teaspoon to ½ pint warm water, then wash with warm soap and water and rinse.

Iron Mould:

Either soak in a hot solution of *oxalic acid,* or cover the stain with salt damped with lemon juice, leave for 30 minutes then rinse in warm water and ammonia.

Lipstick:

These stains will usually wash out, but if not use a little *carbon tetrachloride;* or *hydrogen peroxide* may be used to bleach them out.

Mildew:

This is difficult to remove but try *permanganate of potash,* ½ teaspoon to 1 pint water, then rinse and sponge with *hydrogen peroxide.*

Milk:

Washing in soap and water will normally remove these stains but if a greasy mark remains use *carbon tetrachloride* or *benzine.* Methylated spirits may also be used.

Nail polish:

Sponge with *acetone,* testing the material first. Then wash in warm soapy water.

Paint:

Turpentine or turpentine substitute will remove wet paint, but if it has dried use turpentine mixed with household ammonia. Rub on gently with a piece of flannel.

Paraffin:

Rub with *benzine* on a rag.

Perspiration:

Soak for 1 hour in warm water with some ammonia added but no soap. If this fails, sprinkle the stain with lemon juice. Finally wash in the normal way.

Salt water:

Soak in warm soft water for 10 minutes, then wash in soap and water to which a little ammonia has been added.

Scorch:

If white material is scorched make a paste with bicarbonate of soda and water, spread on and leave for a time, then wash. If the fibres of the material have been seriously damaged it will not be possible to remove these marks but if the scorch is slight it should be sponged with borax and water. Another method is to damp it with lemon juice then expose to sunlight.

Sealing wax:

Brush on naphtha or methylated spirits to dissolve the spots.

Shoe polish:

Wipe with a rag dipped in turpentine, then with another dipped in methylated spirits. Repeat alternately.

Tar:

Remove by scraping and then apply *benzine (benzol)*, or if this fails use paraffin.

Tea:

Either soak in a warm solution of borax and water (1 oz. to 1 pint) or (for white linen and cotton material) use a *chlorine* bleach in a dilute solution.

Wax:

Lay blotting paper over the stain and iron above this with a hot iron. The blotting paper will absorb the wax. If a greasy mark is left treat with *carbon tetrachloride* or *benzine*.

Wine:

Either rub on salt and lemon juice, then wash in warm soap and water; or treat with a hot solution of borax and water, 1 oz. to 1 pint. Soak till the water is cool then wash; or if the stain is old and the cloth white use a *chlorine* bleach — not for silk, rayon or wool.

STARCH – TO USE

STARCH MADE FROM RICE is best for cotton and linen. A fine fabric or a new fabric will not need as strong a solution as an old or weak fabric.

Starch may be applied boiled or unboiled. Boiled starch is made with 3 times as much cold water by volume as starch. Mix this to a smooth paste then add boiling water till the starch clears, stirring all the time. Dilute with between 2 and 8 times as much water depending on the strength needed. Dip the washed garment thoroughly. Iron with a hot iron when still just damp.

Unboiled starch is made by mixing 1 tablespoon starch with twice as much cold water, then adding just under $\frac{1}{2}$ pint cold water. Strain and dilute further in similar proportions to boiled starch solution. Dip, dry and iron in the same way as above.

STEEL – TO CLEAN

CLEAN ORDINARY STEEL with a hard abrasive, for example, bath-brick, if it is rusty or badly stained. In extreme cases use emery paper, or steel wool and paraffin. Normally when washing up articles a little proprietary powder cleaner and steel wool will be sufficient.

When storing steel articles rub them all over with lanolin or petroleum jelly to prevent rust.

STOCKINGS – TO WASH

ALL TYPES of stockings last better if washed as soon as they have been once worn, especially nylon and silk. Dip in warm soap and water, knead gently but do not wring. Never put nylon stockings into hot water and do not expose to heat when drying.

SWEEPING

USE SHORT STROKES, gather the dust in a pan as soon as any quantity has been collected, and sweep towards the fireplace so that any upward draught will help to carry the dust away. Use well washed tea-leaves or torn-up damp paper to lay the dust when sweeping carpets, but not salt, which will get into the carpet and take in moisture in damp weather.

A sweeping compound can be used for tiled or wooden floors consisting of $\frac{1}{3}$ sand, $\frac{1}{3}$ sawdust, $\frac{1}{6}$ paraffin and $\frac{1}{6}$ water with some pine oil added for a pleasant smell and as a disinfectant.

TABLE LINEN – TO PRESERVE

THIS SHOULD be laundered and cared for in the same way as other household linen. Embroidery should be ironed on the reverse side on to a soft cloth surface so that the pattern will rise.

TARNISHING – TO PREVENT

TO PREVENT METALS from tarnishing when storing them rub them with grease or petroleum jelly. For iron and steel use lanolin. Silver can be wrapped in impregnated paper.

TEAPOTS – TO CLEAN

IF A TEAPOT has become stained inside by a tannin deposit stand it for a time filled with a solution of soda or borax in hot water. Afterwards wash it out very thoroughly.

TOWELS – TO WASH

TOWELS SHOULD be washed with ample soap in hot water and rinsed several times. They should be frequently boiled and dried in the sun if possible. Before hanging out Turkish towels to dry shake them well to raise the pile. Such towels need only have their ends ironed.

TRICEL – TO WASH

WASH IN WARM WATER, using a detergent rather than soap. Drip-dry and iron with a cool iron.

TROUSERS – TO MAINTAIN

THESE NEED particular care if they are to retain their creases and good appearance. They should be brushed often and each time they are worn they should be folded up in their creases and hung on a hanger or put in a press. To replace creases which have been lost press with a steam iron or with a hot iron through a damp cloth. *(See* PRESSING.*)*

UMBRELLAS – TO PRESERVE

NEVER LEAVE an umbrella folded if it is wet. Open it and stand it on its side in a warm room. Do not put it close to a fire, especially if it is covered in nylon.

Most repairs to umbrellas are best done professionally but it is quite easy to re-attach the edge of the cover to the tip of a rib if these come apart as sometimes happens. Use strong thread, for there is considerable strain at this point. The ferrule, if it comes off, may be refixed with strong waterproof glue. Small slits should be patched on the inside with identical material. When the patch has been sewn into place it should be darned down on to the cover.

VASES – TO CLEAN

WHEN VASES have become badly discoloured put some vinegar and some silver sand in them, then stand and shake alternately.

VEILS – TO WASH AND PRESERVE

WASH VEILS very gently in warm soap and water, then pin out on a flat surface to dry. To stiffen hat veils which have become limp, *see* GUM ARABIC.

VELVET, VELVETEEN – TO CLEAN AND PRESERVE

BRUSH VELVETEEN and velvet frequently to remove the dust which is liable to collect in them. To improve the look of the pile hang it in a steamy atmosphere, for example in a bathroom where a hot bath is being taken.

Velvet can be sponged with *carbon tetrachloride* to remove marks but should not be washed at home as the pile is crushed and cannot be easily restored. Velveteen on the other hand can be washed in warm soapy water if treated very carefully, squeezing and not wringing. Rinse in several fresh waters, hang out to dry and shake to raise the pile. When just damp iron it lightly with a warm iron on the wrong side.

VENETIAN BLINDS – TO CLEAN

DUST REGULARLY. Occasionally take down and sponge each lath on each side with warm soap and water. Rinse, then hang out to dry in the sun or in a warm room before rehanging at the window.

VILENE – TO WASH

TRY TO AVOID crumpling in the wash; like paper nylon taffetas, it is best washed in the bath where there is plenty of space to swish it round.

WALLPAPER – TO CLEAN AND REPAIR

DO NOT WASH wallpaper or the damp will penetrate and bring it away from the wall. Clean it with a soft broom round the head of which a duster is wrapped. Clean off grease spots with grease solvent on a rag, rubbing gently in a circle round the mark. If there is serious soiling use a dough of new breadcrumbs. Use paper which has been specially treated to resist damp in the bathroom and kitchen.

It is not difficult to cover up bad marks on wallpaper with a patch. There is no need to remove the old paper. Just tear a patch of the right shape (do not cut it out) and paste down, matching the pattern.

WASHING MACHINES – TO USE

LARGE MACHINES will take about 8 lb. of washing, smaller ones about 4 lb. Do not mix cottons and woollens, for woollens need a warm temperature only — about 95°F., and cottons and linens a hot temperature of about 150°F. There will be a temperature dial which you can adjust to the correct heat for the fabric to be washed. Rayons, silk, nylon and Terylene need warm temperatures only.

Before washing close all fastenings including zip fasteners. Small articles such as collars and handkerchiefs are best tied together. Badly soiled articles such as collars should have a little soap or detergent powder rubbed gently into them with a brush before they are put into the machine. See that the agitator is below the level of the water.

Approximate times for various fabrics are as follows: cottons and linens 10 minutes, woollens 3 minutes, rayon 2 minutes, silk 1–3 minutes, nylon and terylene 2 minutes.

WASHING-UP

FIRST FILL your bowl, or sink if it is small, with hot water and add soap powder or liquid detergent. Wash glasses and dry at once while they are hot to get a good shine. Wash silver next. Cups, saucers and plates come next and finally dishes, pans and other heavily soiled articles. New water may be needed for these and a stiff brush or mild abrasive. Only resort to metal cleaners if absolutely necessary for they cause wear and damage glazes. The same applies to the coarser abrasives.

WICKS – MAINTAIN

Do not cut wicks, but pat them level. Remove charred top with soft paper. The wick will be spoiled if a stove burns dry.

To change a wick, remove the flame spreader from its position at the centre of the wick then turn up the wick as far as it will go and pull out. Have paper handy, for it will come out dripping with paraffin. The wick is normally held in a perforated steel cylinder with claws to grip it. Force it free from these claws and pull it out. Fit the new wick into the cylinder; press it outwards to make the claws grip. A line on the wick will show at what point the top of the cylinder should come. Insert the new wick and cylinder, keeping loose threads away from the turning wheel which raises and lowers the wick. Do not light for 15 minutes, to allow time for the new wick to absorb paraffin.

WOODEN UTENSILS – TO CLEAN

WHEN WASHING wipe with a hot wet cloth and do not soak. If this is not sufficient scrub with the grain using a scrubbing brush and soap or a soapless detergent. Stains can be removed by scrubbing with salt water, and grease by scrubbing with hot water and soda. Dry by standing on edge and do not put away or lay flat while still wet.

WOOLLENS – TO WASH

WASH IN WARM SOAP and water and rinse in water of about the same temperature. Do not use alkalis. Knead gently and do not rub or the garment will be damaged. Never twist when wringing but squeeze and then pass carefully through a wringer. Fold delicate woollens in a towel for this purpose. To dry lay out in shape on a towel, and place out of doors or in a warm room but not near a fire or on a hot tank. When almost dry hang up to air.

ZINC – TO CLEAN

TO PREVENT WEAR do not use harsh abrasives on zinc articles but wash with warm soda and water.

How to be a Ministering Angel

FIRST AID AND NURSING

ACCIDENTS AND FIRE PREVENTION

ACCIDENTS IN THE HOME continue to cause more casualties than road accidents. A few sensible precautions will do much to avoid them:

1. Clothes:

DO NOT wear high heels or tight clothes when working in the house as this increases the possibility of accidents by constricting your movements.

2. Electrical:

Children will poke fingers or anything else convenient into plugs. To prevent this, have the plugs placed out of reach or fit sockets which close when the points of the plug are withdrawn. Fit switches which operate by a pulled string in bathrooms. Never touch a switch (except of the latter sort) with wet hands. Never place an electric fire on the edge of the bath. Never fit bulbs, or plug in electric kettles, fires, etc., when the socket is live. Examine electrical wires and equipment regularly for faults. Never use plugs or wires which are designed for a lower power than they will have to carry.

3. Fire Prevention:

CIGARETTES: Carefully put out and dispose of matches and cigarette ends. It is wise to always check ashtrays for burning cigarettes before you go to bed, particularly if you have been entertaining.

DRY-CLEANING: Do not use petrol or *benzine* for dry-cleaning inside a house. The vapour is dangerously inflammable.

ELECTRIC SWITCHES AND WIRES: See that all electric switches, including those connecting radio or television, are switched off at the wall when you leave the house. Be particularly careful never to leave an electric iron switched on. Replace old electric wiring.

FIRE-PROOFING MATERIALS: Curtains and other materials can be rendered non-inflammable. This is especially important for nursery curtains and upholstery and for small children's sleeping garments. Clothes for children which have already been fire-proofed are now available on the market. The method of fire-proofing materials at home is as follows:

Coarse fabric: 8 oz. *ammonium phosphate* and 1 lb. *ammonium chloride* to 3 quarts water.
Normal and fine fabric: 5 oz. borax, and 4 oz. boracic acid to 2 quarts water.

If the material is washed the fire-proofing must be done again, but ironing will not affect it. Before treating materials with these solutions test a small section to see that the colour will not be harmed. Nursery curtains and upholstery should be made fireproof.

FIRES: Guards should be used with all types of fires where there is an open fire or an exposed element. It is illegal to have unguarded fires with children under 7. (Fix electric fires in children's rooms high on the walls out of reach. Make small girls wear pyjamas rather than nightdresses.) Use a metal tray or sheet instead of a newspaper to draw up a fire. Do not transport burning coal from one fire to another. Never throw cupfuls of paraffin on to a fire to light it. Keep all rugs, curtains, furniture, clothes, cushions, etc., well out of the way of fires. Electric fires left burning near furniture are a common cause of fires.

GAS: Never look for a gas leak with a naked light.

OIL LAMPS, OIL STOVES AND CANDLES: Never leave these burning in an empty house, and take great care whenever they are being used. When filling stoves and lamps with paraffin, always extinguish them first and do not re-light till the paraffin can has been removed. Never use paraffin stoves in children's rooms unless enclosed by some protection.

SAUCEPANS: Do not leave pans of food cooking in an empty house or overnight. They will boil dry and the contents may eventually start to burn. If deep fat in a frying pan bursts into flames, don't run to the sink with it — cover the pan immediately and turn off the heat.

IF FIRE DOES BREAK OUT: Try at once to put it out. This is the first thing to do, not run or telephone for help. While attempting to put the fire out shout for someone else to telephone for help, if this is needed. Pour water on most fires, but if they are caused by electricity in any form put some sand or earth on them.
Shut all doors and windows to reduce draught.
If you have to enter a room full of smoke put a wet towel over your nose and mouth.
If it is necessary to leave by a window, do not stand on the sill and jump, but lower yourself to the full extent of your arms then drop. If walking on floors of rooms or passages which are dangerous, keep close to the walls.

IF CLOTHES CATCH FIRE: Prevent the person from running. Make him lie down and roll him instantly in a rug or blanket.

4. Pillows:

Until a baby is at least a year old he should sleep without a pillow. Otherwise he may smother himself.

5. Poisoning:

Always keep pills and other medicines out of the way of children, preferably in a locked medicine cupboard. Do not use laxatives made in the form of chocolate sweets or sweetened baby aspirins. It will greatly increase the danger of a child taking poison pills which he may find about if he has been taught to think of them as sweets.

6. Polythene Bags:

These very thin filmy bags are now widely used commercially, especially by dry cleaners. They can be extremely dangerous and MUST be kept out of the hands of young children. A number of fatalities have already been caused by children pulling them over their heads in play. The bags have a clinging quality and adhere instantly to the skin causing suffocation in a matter of minutes.

7. Scalding:

Always turn saucepan handles inwards on a stove, particularly when there are children about. Use a tablecloth the edges of which do not overhang the edge of the table, or tuck these under. Do not leave buckets of boiling water about. Put the cold water into a baby's bath before the hot.

8. Slipping:

Old people often slip on polished floors. Latex polishes give a less slippery surface than wax polishes. If the boards under rugs and mats are not polished there will be less danger of these sliding. Test rugs or mats beside baths for slipperiness on the floor, for this is a common place for old people to slip. Some sort of rail is useful here even if there is no mat, for water on linoleum can be slippery. Make sure that stair carpets are tacked down as well as held by rods. Tack down all carpet edges and cover or repair holes.

9. Step Ladders, etc:

Do not use ladders or stand on chairs and tables which are rickety, or too light to carry your weight, or in any way defective.

ANKLE, SPRAINED

BIND UP the injured ankle as soon as possible to reduce swelling. Pass the bandage under the instep, cross the ends over the foot and behind the ankle. Repeat this, pinning the ends at the side of the foot. Keep the bandage damp, and have the foot raised and cool. A doctor should ALWAYS be consulted, to rule out the possibility of a fracture, and advise on further treatment.

ARTIFICIAL RESPIRATION*

WHEN ARTIFICIAL RESPIRATION is required the vital need is to inflate the lungs even though the air has to be blown past any obstruction in the windpipe. Delay may prove fatal. If the patient is not breathing start mouth-to-mouth respiration immediately. To decide whether he is breathing see whether he is making breathing movements. As another test, if a mirror is handy, see whether a mist develops on it when it is held in front of the patient's nose and mouth: if there is a mist the patient is still breathing.

1. Take up a convenient position and work from the side. Hold the patient's head in both hands, one hand pressing the head backwards and the other pushing the lower jaw upwards and forwards.

2. Not infrequently it will be found that as soon as the air passage is open, the casualty will gasp and start to breathe. If the breathing does not start, open your mouth wide, take a deep breath and in the case of:

(a) A young child—seal your lips round his mouth and nose, blow gently until you see his chest rise, then stop and remove your mouth. Repeat this procedure at the rate of twenty times per minute.

(b) An adult—seal your lips round the patient's mouth while obstructing his nostrils with your cheek; it may be necessary to pinch the nostrils with the fingers. Blow into his lungs and watch for the chest to rise, then remove your mouth. Inflation should be at the rate of ten times per minute.

3. The first six inflations should be given as quickly as possible. Without leaving the patient arrange for an ambulance, or the nearest medical assistance to be called. Continue artificial respiration until spontaneous breathing occurs or until a qualified person arrives on the scene. A resuscitated patient should rapidly be sent to hospital by ambulance.

* *Method by courtesy of the St. John Ambulance Association.*

ATHLETE'S FOOT

A WHITE SODDEN appearance of the skin and cracks between the third and fourth or fourth and fifth toes. The infection can be spread by towels and bath mats. Keep clean and absolutely dry. The doctor will prescribe an ointment and dusting powder.

BED-MAKING FOR INVALIDS

A PATIENT who is confined to bed will require a mackintosh sheet which should be placed above the bottom sheet and should stretch from the pillow to his knees. Above the mackintosh sheet a draw-sheet should be placed. If a special draw-sheet is not available a normal sheet may be folded lengthwise to form a narrow sheet. This should be tucked in firmly at one side but not using more sheet than is necessary. The sheet at the other side which will be much longer should be rolled and tucked in.

The bed should be made twice a day. If the sheets are not to be changed proceed as follows. Gently turn back all coverings except one on to a chair at the foot of the bed. Untuck all remaining bedclothes and pull tight the bottom sheet before tucking in firmly. Unroll the long end of the draw-sheet and tuck in sufficient of this to secure it firmly. Carefully ease the draw-sheet under the patient till it is taut, roll up the opposite end which is now the long end and tuck in. It is much better to do this with the help of an assistant who can lift the patient while the draw-sheet is being moved across. Now turn and shake the pillows and replace the covering bedclothes.

If the bottom sheet has to be changed first remove the mackintosh and drawsheet. The bottom sheet should then be untucked all round and one half rolled up firmly close to the patient's back. The clean sheet is opened up and one half rolled up lengthwise. This is placed next to the roll of the soiled sheet and the patient gently rolled from the soiled to the clean sheet.

BITES see STINGS

BLACK EYE

PUT ON ICE-WET CLOTHS and bandage firmly. Go to a doctor as soon as possible so that he can make sure there is no damage to the eye itself or the skull.

BLOOD POISONING

IF GERMS GET into the bloodstream the condition can be very serious. Always take the utmost care in treating cuts and wounds and wash clean under running water. If the glands are swollen or you see a red streak running from the wound call the doctor at once. He will probably treat it with an antibiotic such as penicillin.

BURNS AND SCALDS

A BURN is caused by dry heat such as a red-hot poker, and a scald is caused by moist heat such as steam. Otherwise they present the same appearance and dangers and require similar treatment. The greatest dangers from burns and scalds are shock and sepsis. Shock is present in all cases and depends more upon the extent of the injury than its severity.

Burning clothing should be extinguished by laying the patient on the ground with the burning part uppermost, and smothering the flames by wrapping him tightly in a rug, blanket, curtain or something similar.

The treatment must be directed to: (*a*) the exclusion of air from the burn by the application of dressings that are sterile or at least made from fresh or freshly laundered material; (*b*) the relief of pain; (*c*) the prevention of treatment of shock.

If the burn is extensive and medical assistance is readily available: (*a*) at once cover the burnt area with a thick layer of cotton wool; (*b*) bandage lightly with clean dressings; (*c*) remove to hospital.

If medical assistance is not readily available: (*a*) promptly cover the area with cotton wool, linen, or anything that will exclude the air; (*b*) carefully remove the clothing from the injured part unless it is sticking to the skin, when it must be cut round with scissors and left in place; (*c*) if possible immerse the injured part in warm water (98.4°F.) until the dressings are ready (1 dessertspoon bicarbonate of soda added to 1 pint warm water will make a soothing lotion and should be used if easily available); (*d*) dress the wounds with strips of linen or gauze soaked in a fresh soda solution as above. In removing clothing and applying dressings, the injured area must be uncovered bit by bit, so as to expose it to the air as little as possible. As previously mentioned, all dressings must be sterile, or at least made of fresh or freshly laundered materials; (*e*) cover with a thick layer of cotton wool; (*f*) bandage lightly; (*g*) get the patient to hospital as soon as possible.

If dressings are not readily available, cover the injured area with cotton wool and bandage lightly.

If a child is severely burned it should be placed in a warm bath of the soothing lotion without removing the clothing, and kept there until medical assistance is obtained.

If the burn has been caused by lightning, shock is very severe; the 'treelike' burn markings are treated as an ordinary burn.

Burns from Corrosive Acid *(acetic, carbolic, hydrochloric, sulphuric acids):* Neutralise the acid by a weak alkaline solution such as bicarbonate of soda, or weaken the acid by pouring warm water over the burn. Then treat as an ordinary burn.

Burns from Corrosive Alkali *(ammonia, cement, lime, caustic soda):* Flood the part with warm water or neutralise the alkali with a weak acid solution such as vinegar or lemon juice and water. Then treat as an ordinary burn.

Burns From Sun-Bathing:

Treat as ordinary burns.

CHOKING

ANY OBSTRUCTION which prevents air from entering the lungs will cause choking.

If the cause is strangulation the first step is to remove the constriction from around the throat, then sprinkle the face with cold water and give stimulants.

If the cause is some object which has become lodged in the throat thump the back between the shoulder-blades. Hold a child completely upside down. If this fails try to put a finger down the throat and dislodge the object outwards. If a child has actually swallowed a piece of glass or any sharp object or if an object seems to be stuck in the gullet take the child to the casualty department of your nearest hospital without delay, as an X-ray will be necessary.

If the cause of choking is a sting or bite from a swallowed insect put hot cloths on the front of the neck and give sips of cold water or olive oil. If necessary give artificial respiration, and obtain medical assistance at once.

CRAMP

CRAMP is due to sudden involuntary and painful contraction of a muscle or group of muscles. It may be caused by chilling during exercise, bathing, or in several other ways. Cramp can also occur when there has been excessive loss of fluid from acute diarrhoea, vomiting or sweating. Some people are more prone than others.

Massage the affected part and apply warmth. If there has been excessive loss of fluid give plenty of water to which has been added half a teaspoon of salt to each two tumblers and inform your doctor.

DISINFECTANTS AND DISINFECTING

CARBOLIC ACID, *coal-tar* and *chlorine* in various chemical combinations are good disinfectants and there are also many proprietary disinfectants which are effective and simple to use. Boiling is a satisfactory way of disinfecting clothes and bedclothes which have been in contact with infectious illnesses. To disinfect china and crockery stand for 1 hour in a solution of disinfectant.

EARACHE

NEVER IGNORE earache, especially in a child, for it may lead to serious developments if not attended to. Consult a doctor at once.

There are a number of possible causes: a hard lump of wax in the ear, a boil in the external ear canal or inflammation of the middle ear. If there is a discharge the latter is the usual cause.

Syringing an ear to remove wax should not be attempted except by a doctor or under his instructions, but a little warm olive oil or a few drops of *hydrogen peroxide* dissolved in 3 parts water may be put into the ear and this may soften the wax and ease discomfort.

ELECTRICAL INJURIES

IN THE CASE of any electrical injury it is essential to act quickly and with great caution.

1. Switch off the current. If the switch cannot be found immediately and the supply is through a flexible cable the current may be cut off by removing the plug or even breaking the cable or wrenching it free. Do not attempt to cut the cable with a knife or scissors.

If it is *impossible* to switch off or break the current:

2. Remove the patient from contact with the current. The greatest care is necessary; insulating materials *must* be used and they must be dry. Rubber gloves are good and a dry cap, coat or other garment or a folded newspaper gives fair protection. If possible stand on some insulating material such as rubber-soled shoes or boots or piles of newspapers.

3. Unless the patient is breathing — give artificial respiration, for some hours if necessary.

4. Treat for shock (*see page 238*).

5. Treat any burns (*see page 228*).

6. Transfer to hospital or seek medical aid.

ENEMA

ENEMAS are given to evacuate the bowel, or to give nourishment. Fluid is introduced into the bowel by way of the rectum. No one should attempt to do this without a doctor's advice. The following is an outline of the method. Prepare the fluid and place it on a tray with the rubber tubing, a clip to close this, a glass funnel, Vaseline and a towel. Give the patient a hot-water bottle at his feet as he may feel faint if he is seriously ill. Turn him on his left side and make him draw up his knees and bring his buttocks to the edge of the bed. Have the bed-pan near and warm it with hot water. Fix the funnel into one end of the tube and the clip a few inches from the opposite end. With the clip open fill the funnel. Close the clip when the tube is full. Very gently insert the clip end of the tube up to 3 inches into the patient's rectum, using Vaseline to ease it in. Holding the funnel no higher than the top of the patient's buttocks, release the clip to allow the liquid to flow in.

It should take at least 5 minutes for 1 pint of liquid to enter and for this reason the funnel should never be held higher. Nor should it ever be allowed to empty until injection has been completed or air bubbles will be caught by the fresh liquid.

After the patient's bowels have acted he should be sat up in bed and given a warm drink.

Enemas should always be given at 98°F. (body temperature). Medicinal enemas are normally: 1 oz. Castile soap (never scented or coloured soap) to 2 pints water; or 6 to 8 oz. olive oil. The latter is given when constipation is severe to soften the hard faeces and is always followed 30 minutes later by a soap enema. Enemas given for nourishment are various, depending on the patient's complaint.

FAINTING

THIS MAY be due to a variety of causes such as excessive bleeding, nasty smells, lack of ventilation, over-feeding, under-feeding, or disturbed emotions, such as those caused by fright or pain.

Lower the head and encourage better circulation in the brain. Give *sal volatile* or smelling salts. On recovery give a non-alcoholic stimulant — a sweet hot drink is best. If a person feels faint in a stuffy crowded room, press the head down between the knees, and the patient will usually recover sufficiently to walk out with assistance. If fainting is due to lack of food give food sparingly at first: beef-tea or soup in sips will be found beneficial. In all cases, treat the fainting condition first and then the cause, calling in your doctor if necessary.

FEVER

NORMAL BODY TEMPERATURE, is approximately 98.4°F. Temperatures above this indicate fever, and temperatures above 103°F. indicate high fever. Whatever illness is causing the fever, certain similar signs often show its approach. A shivering fit, general feeling of chilliness, headache and lassitude are the most common.

To take a person's temperature place the bulb of a clinical thermometer under his arm or under his tongue and leave there for about 2 minutes. Before inserting the thermometer shake down the mercury past the narrow part of the tube so that the reading is not more than 95°F. To read the thermometer hold it in the light and twist it a little until the thread of mercury is seen. After taking a temperature rinse the thermometer in cold water to which a little mild disinfectant has been added, then wipe dry with a clean cloth. Alternatively it can be left standing in a jar containing a weak solution of disinfectant.

Do not take the temperature in the mouth immediately after the patient has eaten or drunk hot or cold foods or after any physical exertion as the reading may then be distorted.

Take the temperature of a very young child by inserting the bulb of the thermometer in the rectum, first wiping it with petroleum jelly. Always use one place for a particular patient and do not vary from mouth to under the arm, etc. There may be variations between different places on the body.

FRACTURES

THESE ARE DIVIDED into a number of different types.

Simple fractures: In these the bone is broken but not the skin.

Compound fractures: In these the skin as well as bone is broken.

Comminuted: When there are more than 2 pieces of broken bone.

Complicated: When the fracture involves a joint, or an internal organ or artery.

Impacted: When the broken ends of bone are driven into each other.

Incomplete: When the bone is only partly broken, for example the green-stick fractures which young children suffer in which the convex part of the bone is severed and the concave only bent.

To decide whether there is a fracture, ask the victim what happened. He will often be able to say that he felt or heard the bone break. Next compare the injured limb with the opposite limb. Signs which may be noticed are swelling or bruising, crookedness, inability to move the limb, shortening of the limb.

A good rule is never to move the patient unless you have a sound knowledge of first aid. Such movement carried out by unskilled people is very dangerous and may easily turn a simple fracture into a compound one or cause other internal injuries.

To prepare the patient to be moved to hospital splints must be fixed and any suitable material should be used, such as walking-sticks, broom handles, umbrellas, pieces of packing case, etc. The splints must be long enough to fix the joints above and below the fracture and must be padded with cloth, cotton wool, etc. When the splints are ready, help will be needed. The limb must be held above the fracture and a steady pull exerted below the fracture. The splints are then tied on with torn rags, handkerchiefs or bandages. Never lift or carry a patient before the splints have been fixed, and then use a stretcher if possible. If not, let one person carry the splinted limb with both hands while others carry the patient. If the injury is to the spine never move the patient until the doctor arrives.

HEAT-STROKE

THIS CAN ARISE from exposure to the sun (sun-stroke) or to other sources of heat. Symptoms usually begin gradually and may include preliminary headaches, and sometimes a sudden giddiness or loss of consciousness. The pulse may become rapid and irregular, there may be vomiting and if the case is serious the temperature may rise rapidly. Call a doctor. If there is a high fever, treat by putting the patient in a cool place and spraying him with cold water, but do not allow his rectal temperature to fall below 103°F. As soon as he can swallow give him ample quantities of salt and water to drink, 1 teaspoon to the pint.

INFECTIOUS DISEASES

INFECTIOUS DISEASES are those which can be transmitted from one person to another by the breath, sneezing or coughing, and in other ways. Several of them, such as smallpox and diphtheria must be notified to the local Medical Officer of Health immediately they occur. It is against the law for a person suffering from such a disease to enter a public conveyance or public place without taking proper precautions to prevent the spread of the disease. The Local Authority can close any school where an epidemic has occurred or may exclude from school any children liable to carry the infection. Infected bedding, clothing, etc., must be disinfected and the Local Authority will provide for this. The following table lists some of the most common of these. It is ESSENTIAL to call your doctor as soon as symptoms begin.

	SYMPTOMS	INCUBATION PERIOD	QUARANTINE FOR PATIENT	QUARANTINE FOR CONTACTS
Chicken-pox	Rash on face, head, trunk. Small red, raised spots become blisters and itch	12–20 days	When all scabs have fallen off	20 days
Diphtheria	Rash on mucous membrane in the throat. White-grey patches	1–6 days	When certified free from infection by the doctor — may be about 6 weeks	7 days
German Measles	Rash on face, then neck and whole body. Pink oval spots, like measles but paler	14–28 days	10 days from appearance of rash	28 days
Measles	Rash behind ears, forehead, mouth, then rest of body. Dark crimson, very small slightly raised spots which later join up in a blotchy rash	7–14 days	14 days from appearance of rash	14 days
Mumps	Earache, difficulty in swallowing. Swelling of large salivary glands in front of ears, sometimes glands in abdomen and testicles	12–28 days	Until all glands have subsided	28 days
Scarlet Fever	Rash on trunk, then face and limbs. Very small bright red spots with an underlying flush of the skin	1–7 days	When certified free from infection by the doctor	7 days
Smallpox	Rash on face and wrists but not trunk at first. Like chicken-pox but with more shot-like feel if pressed	7–16 days	When certified free from infection by the doctor	18 days

	SYMPTOMS	INCUBATION PERIOD	QUARANTINE FOR PATIENT	QUARANTINE FOR CONTACTS
Typhoid	Rash on abdomen then back, chest and rest of trunk. Pale, rose pink spots	10–14 days usually	Until certified free from infection by doctor	4 weeks
Whooping Cough	Cold and catarrh, cough, which is worse at night. Whoop is heard after 7–10 days, vomiting may follow	7–14 days	at least 6 weeks	14 days

INVALID COOKERY

IN ANY INVALID DIET the food should be easily digestible and nourishing; try to make the meals, however small, look as attractive as possible on the tray. You will have to build up the patient's appetite gradually, and several regular small meals and snacks may be more attractive to him than a few large meals.

The following are recommended to those on a liquid diet: beef tea, meat jellies and broth, barley-water, gruel, lemon squash, black currant tea. Those who are permitted milk may also have soda-water and milk, arrowroot blancmange, baked egg custard, junket, milk jelly, caramel pudding. On a light diet the following are suggested: steamed egg, chicken soup, mutton broth, steamed lamb cutlets, fish soufflé, boiled chicken, stewed sweetbreads, brains on toast, minced liver, steamed fillet of sole or plaice, white or brown bread, rice pudding, semolina pudding, tapioca pudding, bread and butter pudding, apple fool. In a light diet milk is one of the most important items, and unless strictly forbidden by the doctor, fresh fruit and green vegetables should also be included. Avoid strongly flavoured foods, spices and herbs.

Those who are suffering from disorders of the stomach or diarrhoea should avoid fruit or vegetable dishes.

MEDICINE CHEST

A FAMILY MEDICINE CHEST is essential. All bottles should be clearly labelled. Poisons should be kept in dark green glass bottles with ribbed sides. All poisons and medicines intended for external use should be kept on a separate shelf. The medicine chest MUST be kept locked if there are children in the house. The bathroom is not the most suitable location as steam may detach the labels. Its contents should include the following:

General equipment:

Medicine glass, clinical thermometer, pair of scissors, tweezers, eye bath, eye dropper, safety pins, small enamel basin.

Dressings:

Medical plaster, adhesive dressings, lint, roll of cotton wool, several bandages of different sizes and thicknesses, triangular bandage.

Medicines and Antiseptics:

Proprietary antiseptic (such as Dettol or T.C.P., bicarbonate of soda, brandy, some mild aperient (such as aga or liquid paraffin), aspirin, calamine lotion, Kaolin Mixture B.P., antiphlogistine, olive oil, hydrogen peroxide, Vaseline or petroleum jelly, zinc ointment.

NOSE BLEED*

(1) Sit patient down.
(2) Pinch nose between fingers for five minutes, telling patient to breath through his mouth.
(3) Apply cold compress to nose.
(4) If bleeding persists, send for doctor.

* *By courtesy of the St. John Ambulance Association.*

POISONING

ALL CASES OF POISONING MUST be seen by a doctor as soon as possible, preferably in the casualty ward of a hospital if this is not too far away.

POISON	TREATMENT
Alkalis (found in ammonia)	Do not make the patient vomit. Give plenty of water to dilute the alkali. Add if possible 2 tablespoons of vinegar, orange, lemon or lime juice, to a pint of water.
Arsenic (found in weedkillers, rat poisons)	Make the patient vomit. Give soothing drinks.
Aspirin	Make the patient vomit. Give water to which 2 teaspoons of bicarbonate of soda to the tumbler may be added. Give strong tea or coffee.
Carbolic Acid (Phenol) and Lysol	Do NOT induce vomiting. Wash face and mouth with lots of water. Give egg white or milk.
Carbon Monoxide (found in gas stoves or exhaust fumes)	First turn off the gas. Then remove the patient to fresh air if possible. If not, open windows. Apply artificial respiration *(see page 226*. Give oxygen if available — can be obtained at some garages and chemists.
Chloral, Luminal, Veronal and the other Barbiturates (found in sleeping tablets)	Make the patient vomit. Give a dessert-spoon of Epsom or Glauber's Salts in a tumbler of water. Give hot coffee. Keep the patient awake.
Mercury	Give white of egg in water followed by milk. Then make the patient vomit. Give more egg white.
Paraffin, petrol	Do NOT induce vomiting.
Phosphorus (found in rat poisons)	Make the patient vomit. Give water copiously with, if possible, a few crystals of permanganate of potash to each tumbler. Never give oils, fats or milk.
Prussic Acid (found in oil of bitter almonds)	Act at once. Make the patient vomit. Apply artificial respiration.
Strychnine (found in vermin killers)	Make the patient vomit, unless spasms have begun. Keep very quiet. Do not restrain movements. If breathing stops apply artificial respiration.

PULSE

THE NORMAL PLACE to take the pulse is the radial artery at the wrist. Lift the patient's wrist, which should be relaxed, and feel for the pulse beat on the thumb side with the fingers. Do not use the thumb or the pulse of the person taking the reading may be taken accidentally. When it can be felt begin to count and continue for a full minute.

Adults normally have a pulse rate of between 70 and 80 beats per minute. Children have a quicker rate and old people slower. A high rate of pulse beat is usual in fevers.

QUICKLIME

IF QUICKLIME is splashed into the eye do not rub but wash out with warm water into which a little olive oil or castor oil has been dropped, then bandage a pad of cotton wool over the eye, and visit a doctor at once.

SHOCK – GENERAL TREATMENT*

REMEMBER that excessive loss of blood whether to the exterior from an open wound or internally at the site of a fracture or other internal injury, leads to shock and this can be fatal. Therefore, in any injury (other than a minor one) or in any sudden illness:

(1) Lay the patient down on a bed if possible.
(2) Keep quiet; do not fuss.
(3) Keep warmly covered.
(4) Do *not* apply extra heat, e.g. hot-water bottles.
(5) Do *not* give anything to drink.
(6) Send for your doctor.

* *By courtesy of the St. John Ambulance Association.*

SPLINTERS

THESE CAN often be removed by the use of a needle, which must be sterilised in boiling water or the flame of a spirit lamp. First clean the skin with surgical spirit or antiseptic. Pierce the skin and ease out the splinter by squeezing very gently from the farthest point to which it has entered. If the splinter cannot be seen it should not be probed but a hot fomentation should be applied, and a doctor consulted, as a serious infection can result.

STINGS AND BITES

Bees and Wasps:

These stings need not be considered dangerous unless they are numerous, or they occur in the throat and may cause swelling and suffocation. In these cases see a doctor without awaiting developments. A wasp does not leave its sting behind, but a bee does, and it should be extracted if possible by scraping. For bee stings, apply an alkali such as weak ammonia, soda, *sal volatile* or a solution of bicarbonate of soda. For wasp stings apply vinegar or lemon juice. Methylated or surgical spirit, or a wet 'blue bag' may also be used. If the sting is inside the mouth, use a mouthwash of 1 dessertspoon bicarbonate of soda in 1 pint of tepid water. Place a hot compress on the front of the neck. If collapse occurs, give *sal volatile* or diluted whisky and call a doctor.

Dog Bites:

A dog bite should be well washed out, treated with an antiseptic such as Dettol or T.C.P. and bandaged with a sterile dressing. If there is the smallest suspicion of rabies, keep bitten part low, encourage bleeding and call a doctor at once. If for any reason there is a delay in the doctor's arrival, the wound should be cauterised PROVIDING NOT MORE THAN 30 MINUTES HAS ELAPSED SINCE THE BITE OCCURRED. Cauterise by applying carbolic or nitric acid on a match end. Each tooth mark must be cauterised separately. Apply a sterile dressing.

Jelly Fish:

Water will not dissolve the acid deposited on the skin by jelly fish. Olive oil should be applied as soon as possible, as the longer the treatment is delayed, the more the acid will burn the skin. If there are many jelly fish, in the sea, a bottle of olive oil should be taken to the beach.

Mosquitoes:

Apply insect repellent creams to keep mosquitoes away at night. Treat bites with soda or household ammonia. Gnat and fly bites may be similarly treated.

Nettles:

The spikes of nettles inject *formic acid* into the skin. The traditional remedy of rubbing with a dock leaf counteracts this and is justified by science. Bicarbonate of soda in solution may also be used.

STYES

MAKE A HOT SALINE SOLUTION: *1 teaspoon salt to 1 pint water,* and bathe the eye gently. If styes occur often there may be a lack of vitamins in the diet and plenty of fruit and green vegetables should be eaten.

TENNIS ELBOW

THIS IS CAUSED either by strain of the muscle on the side of the elbow or by inflammation of the bursa beneath this muscle. Treat by strapping the elbow with adhesive tape to give the muscle rest.

TOOTHACHE

A DENTIST must always be consulted but there is sometimes a delay before he can be visited. Soak a small piece of cotton wool in oil of cloves and pack this into the cavity. Or crush an aspirin tablet into the affected tooth.

UNCONSCIOUSNESS

CALL A DOCTOR at once in any case of unconsciousness. Keep the patient warm. Lie on the back with the head turned to one side and supported slightly. Give a few sips of cold water when consciousness begins to return.

How to be an Animal Lover

PETS

CANARIES AND BUDGERIGARS

BECAUSE they are decorative and easy to care for, birds are a favourite choice as pets. The R.S.P.C.A., although opposed to the caging of birds, does give advice as to the best way of keeping domestic breeds such as canaries and budgerigars. Canaries may be yellow, green, grey or buff or white with a short pointed beak. Budgerigars may have blue, green, yellow or white feathers. They have a curved beak like a parrot, and where the beak joins the head there is a small bulbous swelling, known as the ceres. In the adult male bird, this is bright blue, in the female, white or dark brown. When choosing your bird, remember they NEED company. It is always preferable to buy a pair.

Housing:

Do provide your bird with as large a cage as possible. A cage for two birds should be at least 3 ft. × 15 in. × 15 in., so that it is also large enough for breeding. The perches should be widely spaced to allow plenty of flying room. Avoid elaborate decorations and knick-knacks which can dangerously impede flight. Don't put the cage near a window where it will be exposed to draughts or the direct rays of the sun. Budgerigars and canaries can be kept in an outdoor aviary, providing their quarters are dry and free from draughts and some form of artificial heating is available in very cold weather. Electric heating is best as there is no risk of harmful fumes. Details for the proper construction of an outdoor aviary are available from the R.S.P.C.A.

Feeding:

The natural diet of both budgerigars and canaries is grass seeds and green stuff, and is essential for their health. Since most of the available bird seeds are deficient in proteins, vitamins and minerals, they should be augmented by special mixtures (of the type that contain the ingredients in the kernel). Green food such as lettuce leaves, cabbage, spinach and watercress should be washed before being given to your bird. A cuttle fish bone to nibble helps to provide him with minerals. Grit should be placed in a small pot, and not scattered over the cage bottom. Give salt in the form of either rock salt or sea sand. Fresh seed collected from smaller grasses and shepherd's purse should be washed and dried. It can also be stored in a tin for the winter. ALWAYS have water in the cage and change it daily.

Handling:

Let your bird get used to being handled. For the correct way of picking up a small bird, *see Fig. 34*. If he struggles don't tighten your grip. Be gentle and avoid sudden movement.

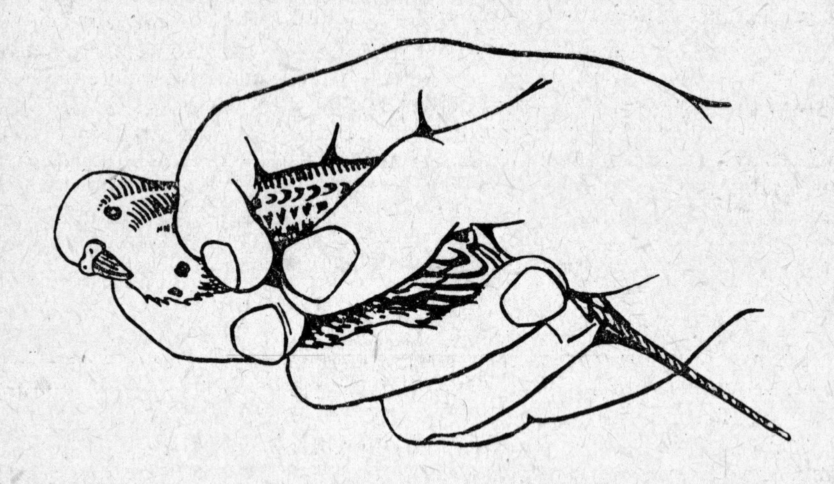

Fig. 34 Holding a Small Bird

Bathing:

Both species enjoy a bath. Put a saucer of tepid water in the cage before cleaning, as birds like making a great splash.

Amusement:

Ping pong balls or a cotton reel on a piece of thread are good playthings. Some birds like admiring their reflection in a mirror on the side of the cage. You can let a tame bird out of his cage occasionally, if you take precautions beforehand. Screen fires and open windows. Deep flower vases may be a trap. Budgies are very curious and tragedy can result if they are let loose in the kitchen when you are cooking. If you have a cat keep the cage well out of his reach and never let him in while the bird is loose.

Sickness:

If your bird is ill, take him immediately to either a veterinary surgeon or an R.S.P.C.A. clinic.

CATS

FOR MANY PEOPLE living in the city, a cat is an easier choice as a pet than a dog. It is perhaps not as companionable as a really friendly and domesticated dog, but it is a charming and affectionate animal, and needs relatively little fussing over, as cats are essentially independent, self-reliant creatures. And certainly there is no sight more comfortable and home-like than that of a cat curled up happily in front of a fire on a winter night.

Housing:

Cats are very susceptible to draughts, so the best choice for their bed is a large lidless wooden box turned on its side with a narrow board fastened across its front, or a stout basket raised from the ground. Cats also like their beds to be soft and yielding, as well as clean, so an old cushion covered with washable material and laid on several thicknesses of newspaper is probably the best choice. Country cats often prefer to stay out at night, but town cats are better kept at home.

Feeding:

Kittens require three to four meals a day once they are five to six weeks old and have ceased regular suckling. All cats like cream and milk, but if your milk is pasteurised, a few drops of haliverol should be added to your kitten's food to prevent rickets. A little yeast, Marmite or Bemax are also important additions to a kitten's daily diet. Allow him to slowly become accustomed to solid food and never give him food which is lumpy.

Adult cats should be fed twice a day, morning and evening. The quantity should be about 1 oz. to every lb. of their weight. They should NOT be given fish exclusively, as this can lead to a chronic skin disease. Give your cat fish every few days, in alternation with white and red meat. Cooked meat or fish should be cut up and mixed occasionally with green vegetables and also with a little finely minced liver or raw meat. Something to chew is also important for your cat — but NEVER GIVE HIM CHICKEN, RABBIT OR FISH BONES. They can cause great suffering and death by piercing his intestines. Water should always be on hand, especially in the summer.

Training:

Kittens can be trained by being provided with a box or tray filled with sand, dry earth or, better still, soft peat litter. Town cats will require a tray permanently placed in some convenient corner. It should be about 18 inches square and must be regularly cleaned, or the cat will not use it. Never use carbolic preparations as they are dangerous for cats.

Grooming:

Cats take very good care of their coats themselves, but they appreciate an occasional brushing and combing, especially during moulting time, as this prevents the formation of hair-balls, which can give them stomach illness. Don't bathe your cat to get rid of fleas or other parasites, but use some gammexane-containing insect powders. Dust both the cat, the cat's bed and its immediate surroundings with the powder, and then brush most of the powder out within two or three hours. Repeat the same process in a week's time. Do not use insect powders containing D.D.T.

Doctoring:

Males are best taken to a veterinary surgeon between the ages of three and four months. Females at about five months.

Breeding:

A cat about to have kittens should be provided with a comfortable bed in a sheltered place with no draughts where she can be quiet and undisturbed. Once the kittens are born, those which are not wanted should be painlessly destroyed. An R.S.P.C.A. Inspector will always assist, or they can be taken to the nearest R.S.P.C.A. clinic or to a veterinary surgeon. Drowning is not recommended. And please remember that it is not kind to deprive the mother of all her kittens. Leave at least one and if possible two for her to bring up. If all the kittens have to be taken away, or if they are born dead, move the mother immediately into another room. Give her a fresh bed and keep her away from the place of birth for some days, until she has had time to forget her loss. Kittens should remain with their mother until they are at least eight weeks old.

Sickness:

Loss of appetite, watery eyes, coughing, sneezing or vomiting are sufficient indication of illness for your cat to be taken immediately to an R.S.P.C.A. clinic or to a veterinary surgeon. Never dose your cat with patent medicines. Irritation of the ears, caused by a tiny mite in the interior, can be relieved by a few drops of warm olive or castor oil, but you will need expert advice for the safe destruction of the mites. Wax appearing at the ear's orifice can be removed with cotton wool, but it is unwise to poke about inside the ear. Skin diseases should also be treated by a veterinary surgeon. Many skin ointments that are harmless to other animals or to people can poison a cat because of his habit of licking off everything that is put on his fur or skin. NEVER apply paraffin or petrol to a cat's skin as it is poisonous.

Handling:

Cats are very sensitive and nervous and can easily be hurt, and children should not be allowed to pull them about or squeeze them. When you lift a cat, remember to support his hindquarters with your other hand, and don't lift kittens up by the scruff of their necks after their mother has ceased doing so. Never put a leather collar on a cat or tie a ribbon around its neck. Cat collars should be made of elastic about half an inch wide.

New Surroundings:

Cats aren't always happy about being moved and will sometimes wander back to the site of their old home. This can only be prevented by shutting your cat up in the new house for 48 hours, feeding him as usual and providing an earth try. Keep the windows closed and let him wander freely about the house to get his bearings. Let him go out for the first time about 20 minutes before feeding time, as this will ensure his return in practically every instance.

DOGS AND PUPPIES

Choosing Your Puppy:

Of all household pets a dog is probably the most rewarding, and providing you are willing to spend a little time and energy on training him, he will make a delightful addition to your family. However, do get your pup from either a reputable dealer or a private owner. A puppy bought from a pet shop or street vendor may well have been exposed to various virus infections and distemper, as well as fleas and lice, and may have been taken away from his mother before he was properly weaned.

There are a number of things to watch for when actually choosing him: Make sure his eyes are bright and his nose free from discharge. Pick him up to see if a heavy coat is hiding a skinny little body. His skin should be clean and free from bald patches and pimples, and examine his coat carefully, particularly behind the ears and elbows, and on the back near the root of his tail. Look for the black specks of flea dirt or ivory white specks the size of a pin head which may be lice. And lastly— make sure he has been properly weaned by seeing him eat some food BEFORE you take him away. Actually the best safeguard is to have him completely checked by a veterinary surgeon. Most reputable dealers will allow you to do this, and will refund your purchase price if disease is found, PROVIDING the examination is carried out within forty-eight hours.

Deciding on the sex of your puppy is sometimes difficult. A bitch is often more gentle and affectionate but she does present a problem when she is in heat. You need some means of shutting her up indoors or in a kennel for a period of three weeks every six months. Strong-smelling essential oils such as peppermint and eau-de-Cologne will mask the sex odours, but once a dog knows a bitch is in heat, nothing will keep him from your door until it is over. However, a simple method of neutralising the odour of bitches may prove the solution. Your veterinary surgeon should be able to tell you about it.

Housing:

A new puppy should be given a box or basket, taught when to go to it when told, and to sleep there at night. Put the box in a draught-free corner, make it large enough for him to move about freely. Line it with several newspapers and an old rug or blanket. Most dogs like to roll themselves up in their bedding. Shake the bedding out of doors every day or two and change the newspaper frequently.

When your dog is grown you may want to keep him in a kennel. Be sure it is weatherproof and put it in a dry and sunny spot with its mouth, when possible, placed south-west in the winter and north-east in the summer. It should be raised from the ground and if possible placed on concrete so that it can easily be cleaned.

Feeding:

After he is six weeks old the puppy wants more varied food than his mother's milk. He is able to gnaw, and has also begun teething, so a biscuit or rusk will be particularly appreciated. Puppies thrive on only three meals in twenty-four hours, but if you do feed your pup more often allow four hours to elapse between meals. Give him porridge, custard and milk pudding, adding a teaspoon or two of condensed milk, to prevent rickets. Start him with a little minced or scraped meat, particularly liver and tripe, and give him two or three drops of halibut liver oil or a teaspoon of cod live oil every day, plus one or two Vitamin B tablets or a piece of yeast the size of a hazel nut. A daily teaspoon of bone meal will avoid mineral deficiency. All change in diet should be made gradually, to give the puppy's stomach a chance to adjust.

When your dog is grown, he should be fed morning and evening at regular times. His meals should be more or less equal in bulk and the meat portion should be ONE QUARTER OF THE TOTAL DIET. Raw or lightly cooked fresh liver is invaluable. Otherwise, a yeast tablet should be added daily to his food, particularly during the winter. Most dogs are quite happy to swallow these tablets, regarding them as a kind of sweet. Give him household scraps, wholemeal biscuits or stale brown bread, but fruit and vegetables are not essential. He can occasionally have cabbage, onions or leeks, or a bit of apple or banana, but the quantity should be limited, as they may give him slight diarrhoea. Continue the halibut or cod liver oil during the winter. From six months on most dogs benefit from the occasional bone, but NEVER give your dog knuckle bones, fish, rabbit and bird bones. They tend to splinter and get stuck and may lacerate the stomach and intestine.

Training:

There are three vital words to remember when training your dog — KINDNESS, PATIENCE and CONSISTENCY. Always praise him when he obeys, never punish him unless he understands what the punishment is for. A dog who is harshly treated, shouted at or cuffed during training may easily become a coward and will be too nervous to understand what is expected of him. Whereas proper training will reward you with a wonderful companion who will understand everything you say to him and be willing to do whatever you wish. Your first task with a young puppy will be to house train him. Let him out of doors every two or three hours and do not be discouraged by a few messes, they are inevitable. Praise for good behaviour is much more important (and will lead to much more rapid results) than too much scolding over accidents. Then of course he must also get used to wearing a collar and lead. Introduce him to this gradually, inside the house at first. Make sure the collar is never too tight (you should be able to insert two fingers under the collar). As your dog gets used to obeying you there are other things you will want to teach him — such as coming to heel. Indeed, the importance of training your dog properly cannot be over-emphasised. Not only because it makes him easier to live with, but also because he will actually benefit from whatever education you give him. As with human beings, learning helps to develop a dog's intelligence and actually increases his enjoyment of life.

Grooming:

All dogs, puppies included, are better for a daily grooming with a brush, plus regular combing for the long-haired breeds. Any signs of fleas or lice should be dealt with promptly by a dusting of insect powder all over the dog, his bed and the surrounding floor. Two applications of gammexane-containing insect powders, allowing seven or ten days to elapse between treatments, should be enough to clear up both fleas and lice.

Licensing:

When your dog is six months old he MUST have a licence. Keeping him without one is against the law. He must also have the name and address of his owner on his collar. This is a simple but essential precaution, as you otherwise run the risk of having him irretrievably lost if he wanders away from home.

Exercising:

Don't over-exercise or overtire your puppy, and don't allow your children to pull him about too much. A daily romp outside plus the exercise he gives himself is quite enough until he is about six months old. All dogs need regular exercise to keep them happy and healthy but the amount naturally varies with the breed, and no dog should be allowed to jump or run long distances directly after a meal. Neither should you let him run out on to the road by himself — he should always be led on busy streets.

The R.S.P.C.A. has a leaflet which describes how to construct a simple and very useful running chain which is invaluable for tying your dog outside. If you are interested in this and in any other information on the care and training of your dog, all you need to do is to send them a stamped addressed envelope.

Sickness:

Among the most common diseases of puppyhood are distemper and certain of the virus diseases. However, there are now vaccines available for your dog's protection, and either an R.S.P.C.A. clinic or your veterinary surgeon will be able to advise you about these inoculations and their cost. With regard to your dog's general health don't immediately start worrying if he seems a bit 'off colour' and refuses one or two of his meals. Dogs are wiser than we are, and frequently correct any minor internal upset by fasting. If your dog has been kept on the type of diet suggested above, he should hardly ever suffer from constipation. If for any reason he does become constipated, liquid paraffin is quite harmless as a mild laxative. If a stronger dose is needed you can give him one or two teaspoons of castor oil. NEVER dose him with any of the so-called 'conditioning powders' or patent medicines, and don't allow an unqualified person to prescribe treatment. If he continues to feel unwell, for his protection and your own peace of mind take him immediately to an R.S.P.C.A. clinic or to your veterinary surgeon.

GOLDFISH AND TROPICAL FISH

GOLDFISH and coarse fish live in a cold aquarium. Avoid varieties which grow to a large size. Under suitable conditions, goldfish may live for twenty-five years or more.

TROPICAL FISH require a heated aquarium and come in a great many varieties. Not all live in harmony, so get your dealer to help you. Always buy young active fish, as they are old and worn out at three years.

Housing

GOLDFISH: Never keep your goldfish in a bowl. Fish have no eyelids, and require shelter from the light. You should use a rectangular aquarium, allowing 1 gallon of water for each inch of fish, and with the side facing the light painted green. Place about 1½ lb. of sifted loam at the bottom and cover with ½ inch well-washed coarse sand. Make sure any stones are placed at least 1½ inches away from the side, so there is no danger of fish becoming wedged. Don't use limestone as it makes the water too alkaline. Cover the sand with a sheet of brown paper, place a saucer on top and gently pour in tap water into the saucer until the tank is a one-third full. You are now ready for the plants which are necessary as well as decorative. They provide shelter, and such plants as *vallisneria, cabomba* and *anacheris* help keep the water fresh and the fish healthy. Buy healthy plants with their roots attached. Make a hole in the compost at the bottom of the tank with your finger or a stick, set plants in firmly but not too deeply, and press a little sand round the roots. Complete the filling of the tank and leave for several days to mature. When the water is quite clear, it is ready for your fish. The temperature can vary between 40–80° F.

TROPICAL FISH: First completely fill tank with warm water (about 75° F.). Fix your heater and thermostat in position and check the temperature with a small submerged thermometer fitted to the side of the tank away from the heater, When adjusted, switch off the current and empty the tank (never empty with the current on). Then set up tank as described above. Temperature should be maintained at 75° F. but raised to 80° F. if you want the fish to breed.

Cleaning:

From time to time scrape the sides of the tank to remove the green algae. Remove any sludge or black sand (due to decomposition of food) with a siphon. Replace any water, lost by evaporation, from the hot-water tap.

Garden Ponds:

If the surface of a pond freezes goldfish will suffocate, so keep the ice broken in severe weather. Chemicals such as glycol should never be added to the water as they will kill the fish. During a very cold winter, remove the fish from the pond to a tank.

Feeding:

GOLDFISH: Don't overfeed your fish, or you will foul the tank. Buy packets of dried goldfish food, spread a tiny pinch over the water once a day. The fish should finish it in a few minutes.

TROPICAL FISH require live food, which you can buy from dealers. Tuifex mud worms should be washed in running water for several hours before putting them in the tank as they may otherwise cause disease.

Sickness

Study your fish so you recognise unusual behaviour. Continued lack of interest in food, or sulking at the bottom of the tank, usually indicates something is wrong. A sick fish should be removed to a separate container (you can use an ordinary pail, providing the water is the same temperature as the tank). For treatment it is wise to seek the help of an expert.

HAMSTERS

HAMSTERS DID NOT EXIST in the modern world until 1930, when a female and her 12 babies were discovered in a burrow near Aleppo in Syria. It was the first hamster family to be found alive since before 1880. All hamsters now in existence are the direct descendants of this lady, and all are also Golden Hamsters, even though cross-breeding has produced many different variations in colour. The full grown Golden Hamster should be about 5 to 6 inches long with reddish brown fur on his back and a whitish belly and feet. As a baby, his fur will be mousy brown.

Choosing Your Hamster:

Size is nothing to go by. Examine the ears, which, if the hamster is young, should be covered with plenty of silky hair. An elderly hamster's ears are quite bald and shiny. A young hamster should be plump and well conditioned, his fur soft and thick. Scars or sores of any kind must be avoided as, even if they heal, your hamster may remain too highly-strung and nervous to make a good pet. With regard to sex — the female is old at two years and also tends to be peevish when in season, whereas the male lives up to four years and has an easier-going disposition. You can easily discover the sex of a hamster by remembering one simple rule — the male organs are a distance apart, the female close together.

Housing:

Hamsters are so clean and odourless they can be kept in any room. Aquarium jars and bird cages are not suitable homes for them, as they MUST gnaw to keep their teeth in trim or they will die of starvation. (They are rodents, although not related to rats.) A hardwood box at least five-eighths of an inch thick is the best choice. Its size should be about 24 in. × 12 in. × 9 in. Hinge the lid and replace one side by a glass panel. To keep your hamster warm, use a good ball of hay—straw is too coarse, and cotton wool can cause severe constipation. Some sawdust will help to keep the box clean. Hamsters can also be kept in a warm shed, but it MUST be mouseproof, as mice can cause disease if they get near a hamster's food. Hamsters do not like the English climate and should not be kept in the open as they are used to an even, equable temperature. When very cold they look quite stiff and dead. When this unfortunate event occurs they should be left to waken naturally, but some food should be put in the cage in case a spell of warm weather revives them.

Cleaning the Cage:

The cage should be cleaned once a week, the damp corner being changed as necessary.

Companionship:

Hamsters do NOT get on well together and are happiest living alone, providing they have a few things to amuse them, such as cotton reels, nuts, paper, etc. Plastic toys are dangerous. Two hamsters living together will fight fiercely, particularly if they are good breeders. Litters should be separated into male and female groups when they are four weeks old, or their offspring may grow up as weaklings. Groups of all-male or female hamster babies can live together happily until they are around eight weeks old, after which they should be separated.

Feeding:

The best basic food is damp mash, made from puppy meal combined with table scraps such as bits of meat, boneless fish, egg, cooked bacon rind, cheese, pudding, porridge, etc. Rabbit greens should also be provided, plus chicory, lettuce, broccoli, fruit, and, in winter, some raw root vegetables. Some hamsters dislike mash, and may be given Quaker oats, baked bread, dryish bread and milk, maize or mixed corn instead. Nuts and raisins as a special treat can be a great help in settling a hamster in, but DON'T give him chocolate. It is bad for him and can actually kill him. Give him his main meal once daily, preferably in the evening. He needs about a tablespoon of mash, plus greens. Always leave some dry food in the cage as he also likes the occasional snack. Indeed, hamsters tend to store more food than they eat, and this store should be cleared once a week. But don't take it away daily, or your hamster will grow to distrust you.

Handling:

The more he is handled, the tamer your hamster will become. Pick him up by placing your hand gently over his back and lift him so that his head faces your wrist. Do not place your hand beneath or poke your finger at him — he is short-sighted and may mistake you for food. Don't handle him when you are wearing dark gloves, as they can scare him badly. There should be little risk of his biting you, if you have bought him from a reputable dealer. Hamster bites are not poisonous, though they should, of course, be washed and dressed.

Sickness:

Hamsters which have been bought from a shop should always be given mainly green food and fruit, with water or milk to drink for the first few days. Quite often they will have been fed previously on nothing but corn, and unless given greens may suffer severe constipation, followed by diarrhoea. If this should happen, in spite of the precautionary diet, take your hamster immediately to the nearest R.S.P.C.A. clinic or veterinary surgeon. Give him nothing but water for 24 hours or you may lose him.

MICE

PARTICULARLY if your household contains a small boy, at one time or another you are likely to find it necessary to welcome one or several pet mice into your family.

Housing:

A cage which measures 18 in. × 18 in. × 8. in. is the smallest possible home for two or three mice. If you can manage to have it 18 in. high it can be fitted with little ladders and swings on which the mice can disport themselves. Never put revolving wheels into the cage.

Cleaning:

A zinc tray fitted to the bottom of the cage is helpful in keeping it clean. Strew the floor with sawdust and give the mice a fresh bed of hay every week. About once a month wash the cage with boiling water containing a little disinfectant, although you cannot entirely avoid a certain 'mousy' odour. Keep an extra cage to house your mice while you are cleaning their home.

Feeding:

Morning and evening give about a tablespoon of oats, coarse oatmeal or canary seed, or a mixture of these. In the evening reduce the corn and seed, and substitute bread and milk. A piece of brown or wholemeal bread about the size of a tangerine is enough for 4 mice. Soak in boiling water, squeeze until nearly dry and add a little fresh milk. Any left-over food should be removed immediately. They also enjoy a bit of green food at midday, such as dandelion leaves, chick-weed, groundsel, watercress, lettuce, and an occasional bit of carrot or apple. Put all food in a china jar or saucer and scald feeding vessels regularly. Put fresh water in the cage every day.

Handling:

The more time you spend with your mice, the friendlier they will become. Pick a mouse up near the root of the tail and immediately put him on your hand. You'll have to take great care to stop him jumping off at first, but he will soon be quite content if you stroke him with one finger or gently groom him with a silk handkerchief. All show mice must be very tame, so that they will stay on the judge's hand.

Breeding:

Provide a smaller box with a 2-inch hole in one wall, so the mother mouse can have her family in privacy. Give her a little cotton wool to make a warm nest, but NEVER disturb the nest to look at the babies until they show themselves outside, or the mother may kill them.

RABBITS

TAME RABBITS make ideal pets for children because they are gentle and easy to handle. Providing it is given regular periods of exercise outside its hutch, a rabbit will remain healthy and happy, and live from 4 to 12 years.

Housing:

Hutches should be not less than 4–5 ft. long and 2 × 2 ft. in height and width, and divided into two compartments. The sleeping compartment should be about 1–1½ ft. wide and have an outside door as well as an inside entrance to the day compartment. A door of wire netting (½–1 in. mesh) should extend over the whole front of the day compartment. The floor of the hutch should have no ledge so it can be scraped with a hoe from back to front when cleaning. The roof should be covered with tarred felt, sloping from front to back and extending 3–6 inches over the front. Place the hutch on a bench or on four legs, where the midday sun will not blaze down on it, and where it does not face the prevailing rainy quarter. When constructing a hutch the rabbits' natural passion for gnawing wood should be kept in mind. The best bed is a layer of peat moss litter, scattered with straw and wood chips. The females, called does, like to hollow out a cosy nest for themselves. When they are expecting babies they line this nest with soft wool plucked from the surface of their bodies.

Food:

Food is generally given twice daily. Give all garden greenstuffs, grass, meadow and clover hay, cow parsley, dandelion leaves and the green tops of root crops such as carrots, turnips and swedes. Rabbits also love clover hay in winter. Frozen greenstuff MUST be thawed before giving, and wet greenstuff should have the moisture shaken out of it. Bran can be damped to a crumbly mass that holds together when squeezed. DO NOT GIVE green raw potatoes, potato haulm, rhubarb, chrysanthemum, foxglove, geranium, hemlock, henbane or any evergreen such as laurel, privet and yew. Remove ALL stale and uneaten food every day. Keep food and water bowls scrupulously clean and give fresh water every day.

Exercising Your Rabbit:

Since rabbits can both burrow under and climb wire fences, the safest way of giving them exercise is to use the long, triangular-shaped pen, made entirely of wire netting and called the 'ark'. It can be moved about on grass or lawns and the rabbits can eat grass through the floor mesh. Diagrams for making this and also for designing a rabbit hutch are available from the R.S.P.C.A.

How to have Green Fingers

GARDENS AND PLANTS

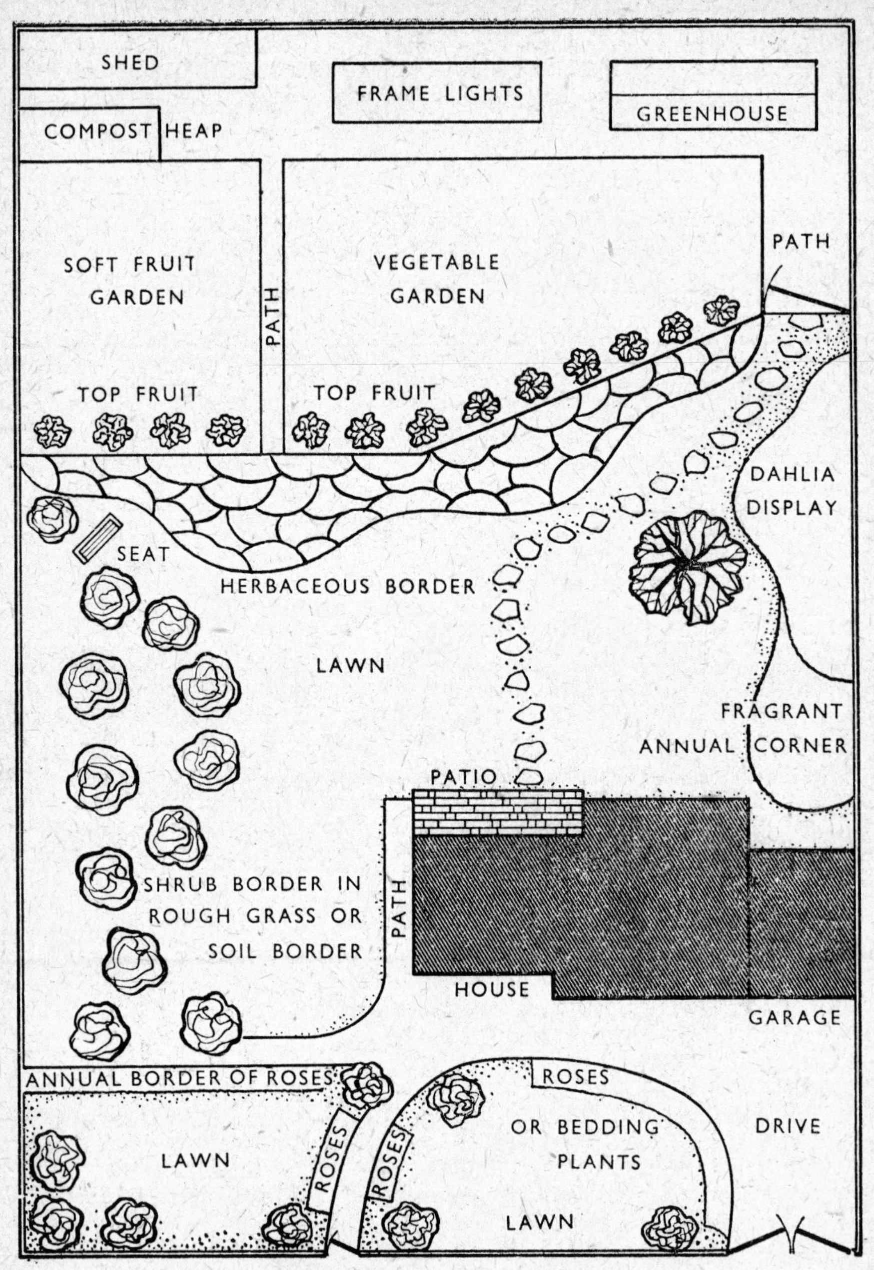

Fig. 35 Plan for a 'Busy' Garden

PLANNING YOUR GARDEN

THIS IS THE REALLY EXCITING PART! Here's the opportunity to plant that wonderful garden and fill it with your favourite plants. Many of our gardens, especially those on the new housing estates, are quite small — somewhere in the region of 80 ft. wide and 200 ft. long. They come in all shapes too. Not all are of nice proportions — some may be long and narrow and others a triangle. Each site will present its own difficulties, but what a worthwhile challenge it is.

The awkward-shaped site can be a great help, for by its very shape it may well lend itself to unusual planning. Each site will have its own difficult spots, but there will be many places where some splendid features can be created.

The answer to all these problems lies in careful planning and the first thing to do is to prepare a scale plan of the site. A large sheet of graph paper is ideal for this. A convenient scale is ⅛ in. to represent 1 ft. or 1 yd. Draw out the boundaries of your garden and include the position of the house or bungalow and any other outhouses. Remember to keep all measurements standard, either in feet or yards.

There are bound to be favourite features you wish to incorporate and a note should be made of these on a separate sheet of paper. The actual process of establishing a garden will depend on several factors. Time and money are important ones to consider. The styling must also blend with site, its contours and its immediate surroundings. Even the character of your dwelling must be taken into consideration.

The garden plan should be arranged so that your garden can 'grow' slowly or in easy stages. There are certain basic things which can be planned right away. First of all there are the paths which must be kept to a minimum and which will make the use of the wheelbarrow a much easier task during the development of the garden.

A lawn is perhaps the main feature, around which the remaining features are set. How big, how small should it be? As large as possible should be the maxim, for it will be a simple matter later on to extend it, or to cut in flower beds, etc. Lawns are discussed on *pages 271–274*.

You will want flowers for display and flowers for cutting. A colour scheme of your garden is a key-planning feature and the herbaceous and annual borders will provide this *(see pages 263–264)*. Tiny beds are silly, and bold masses of colour are to be preferred, especially where the herbaceous border is concerned. Flowers should be admired from inside the house as well, so don't forget to arrange the borders so that they can be seen from the main rooms in the house. Beds of fragrant flowers should be placed close to the house, especially near the windows.

Flower borders should provide colour for as long a season as possible and lists of suitable subjects will be found on *pages 264–265*. Shrubs are delightful in the well planned garden and even the smallest garden can accommodate a few well chosen specimens. They are also ideal for giving privacy and for screening ugly features. For lists of suitable shrubs see *pages 266–267*.

Where room permits, a plot should be reserved for a fruit and vegetable garden. This will not look very attractive during the winter months, so it is advisable to place it where it cannot be seen prominently from the house. An evergreen hedge screen across the width of the plot will divide it neatly from the rest of the garden. Fruit and vegetable gardens are dealt with on *pages 269, 288*.

The proportions or size of any of these features can be determined quite simply by drawing them out on a sheet of blank paper to approximate scale size. If they are placed on the scale plan of your garden it will be possible to adjust them to the most suitable size and proportion. At a glance you will be able to realise just where rearrangements of your original ideas will be necessary.

It is difficult to suggest a definite plan for the small garden, but the following design is a simple one to carry out and it can be added to over the years to form a most delightful garden.

The plan illustrates a method of planning a 'busy' garden which will incorporate as many attractive features as possible. Here is something for everyone — lawn, beautiful shrubs, fragrant flowers close to the house so that their perfume enters the open windows. The large herbaceous border is so placed that it provides a beautiful vista from the house and will also supply the housewife with masses of plants for cutting. For the man about the house there is ample room for his chrysanthemums and dahlias which will provide a display of colour also. The vegetable plot, fruit garden and greenhouse, etc., are effectively hidden behind the herbaceous border and top fruits. A private and cool seat is secluded under the shrubs and close to the colourful herbaceous plants. Crazy paving or plain slab stepping stones lead to the borders and bottom garden and will keep feet reasonably dry and clean in the bad weather. The patio, which can be used for family meals, entertaining, or just as a pleasant place to sit, is so situated that it provides the best view of all the most colourful aspects of the garden.

In the front garden there are more lawns which are restful and neat. Small borders can be cut out in the lawns to provide colourful plants in the form of roses or bedding plants. Specimen trees at suitable corners will add character to the house front.

NEW OR NEGLECTED GARDENS

WHAT DO YOU SEE as you stand on the site of your new garden? Masses of tall, vigorous weeds, heaps of rubble left behind by the builders and perhaps a few neglected bushes? A depressing sight certainly, but one which can be transformed into the garden of your dreams if the problem is tackled with a little thought and care.

Where does one start? The first thing to do is to have a preliminary clean-up of rubble and rubbish. If it is a new garden you are moving into, it is more than likely that your builders will have left some broken bricks lying about, not to mention pieces of concrete and mortar. These materials are quite useful and should be collected and stacked in a convenient part of the garden. They can be used for the foundations of paths, pools, garage or greenhouse sites a little later on.

A good bonfire will deal with miscellaneous rubbish such as dead vegetation and old pieces of wood. In the badly neglected garden, weeds and coarse grass may have grown quite tall. A small hand-scythe or a pair of shears should be used to cut down this growth to within a few inches of soil level. Cutting down weeds *before* they have a chance to cast their seeds is a very important job — not only for your own sake but also for your neighbours!

The cut-down weed growth and grass, provided the former is free from weed seed, can be put to good use. A compost heap can be started with this material which will slowly rot down. When fully decomposed, it will be valuable for digging into the soil. Weeds which have seeded must be placed on the bonfire at the earliest opportunity.

What are we left with now? In most cases the site will be covered with coarse grass. This may be of two types — the first ordinary grass with a mass of fibrous roots — the second masses of long white roots. This is known as couch or twitch grass. A sample piece of grass should be dug and the type of root examined. If the former, the grass can be buried at least 10 in. below soil level as the ground is dug over. The latter type of grass must *not* be buried but stripped off with the spade and placed upside down in a stack to rot down.

The actual cultivation of the site can now commence. Do not attempt to tackle too much at one time! Take small 'bites' at the work. It is far better to dig a small area well than to skimp over a much larger one. If the soil is light or has been cultivated previously then plain or single spit digging or forking will be sufficient. The term 'spit' refers to the depth of cultivation and is the full depth and width of the spade blade or the tines or teeth of the fork.

Heavier, neglected or 'stubborn' soil will require deeper working so that drainage and aeration are satisfactory. A trench is taken out as long as is convenient, 12 in. wide and to the full spade's blade in depth. The bottom of this trench is then broken up with the fork. A new trench is then taken out parallel to the first. The soil from this trench is thrown forward and into the first trench. The base of this trench is then forked over. Work proceeds in this way until the site has been completed.

Many weeds will be found during this cultivation *(weed identification is dealt with on page 299)*. Annual weeds can be safely dug and if they are buried at least 10–12 in. below soil level, they will rot down quickly. Deep-rooted perennial types must be pulled out and burnt at a convenient time. If they are buried many of them will grow again just as vigorously!

During the important preliminary or background work of preparing the site the question of drainage must be considered. If your soil is light or medium-heavy you are lucky, for these soils present no drainage worries. It is the heavy, clay soil which can be a headache!

Clay soils are composed of particles which are packed close together. If they are kept apart more or 'opened up', they will not hold moisture quite so readily and will not therefore, become so waterlogged. Sharp sand or well-weathered ashes, incorporated in the soil during digging, will open the soil quite effectively.

There is much to recommend the construction of simple drains. A main trench is dug out about 18 in. deep from the highest part of the garden to the lowest. The bottom 6 in. is filled with small rubble, topped with 2–3 in. of ashes. The soil is then replaced. Side-drains are also excavated in a similar fashion and these connect the main drain at an angle of 45°. The drains are usually spaced about 10 ft. apart.

The main drain empties into a sump or drainage hole at the lowest part of the garden. This sump is dug out as deep as possible and is filled entirely with all sizes of rubble topped with ashes. Make quite sure that no excess water drains away into neighbours' property.

This, then, is the plan for the initial attack on the new or neglected site. As work proceeds, note the quality or otherwise of the soil. Some parts are bound to be better than others and those where good pockets of soil are discovered may well be the ideal positions for your choice of shrubs or plants.

FLOWER GARDENS

ONE OF THE MOST EXCITING and delightful stages in the planning of a garden is the selection of flowers, trees and shrubs which will give colour and character to the site.

At first, the task may seem to be a very involved one, particularly when the aim should always be to provide colour for as much of the season as possible. Fortunately, nurserymen have made our task much simpler by the issue of their detailed plant catalogues, many of which have pages of illustrations in glorious colour. Plants are listed according to their heights and season of flowering and all these details make it possible for even the novice gardener to make a success of his planting schemes.

There are thousands of wonderful plants available and it is only possible to suggest a short list of plants. These, however, have been selected with the following points in mind:

1. To be easy to establish and cultivate.
2. To provide the best varieties.
3. To produce a flowering display over a long period.
4. To provide plants for as many purposes as possible.

The Herbaceous Border:

One of the mainstays of the flower display is the herbaceous border, which if planned carefully will provide flowers for display and cutting from early spring to late autumn. Planting takes place in the autumn in late October and in the spring in early April. The best time must depend on soil and weather conditions. The border should be fairly wide as many of the plants are bushy. It is also essential to plant in groups so that as one variety passes out of flower, another clump or group will take its place.

General attention consists of hand weeding during the early part of the season, but as the plants become established they should smother most weeds. An occasional light application of a general fertiliser in the early summer months will help growth and flower display. At the end of the season, when foliage has died down, the bed should be cleaned by carefully cutting off this foliage and the soil should be very lightly forked over. New beds are prepared by deep digging or forking in the early autumn, working in old manure at 1 barrow-load to 8 sq. yds., or composted vegetable waste at 1 barrow-load to 5 sq. yds. Add bonemeal at 4 oz. per sq. yd. at the same time. A general fertiliser should be raked or forked in about 10 days before planting takes place.

PLANTS FOR AN HERBACEOUS BORDER:

BACK ROW: *Anchusa,* Pride of Dover; *Aster,* The Prince; *Delphinium,* Blue Mist; *Helianthus,* London Gold; *Verbascum,* Cotswold Gem; *Sidalcea,* Rose Queen

MIDDLE ROWS: *Papaver,* Border Beauty; *Lychnis,* Chalcedonica; *Salvia,* vigata nemerosa; *Achillea,* Coronation Gold; *Lupin,* Serenade; *Anthemis,* Grallagh Gold; *Rudbeckia,* Goldsturm; *Phlox,* Torch; *Solidago,* Leraft; *Scabious, Clive Greaves*

FRONT ROW: *Pyrethrum,* Salmon Beauty; *Geum,* Princess Juliana; *Liatris,* Cobalt; *Erigeron,* Vanity; *Trollicus,* Goldquelle; *Aster,* Audrey

The length of the border is a matter of personal requirement, but 2 plants of each of the above varieties are suggested and this would produce a border approximately 30 ft. long and some 3 ft. wide. The border can be extended if necessary simply by including more plants of each subject or by adding to the above suggestions from a good catalogue.

Bedding Schemes:

For smaller beds, especially those in the front garden, a wonderful display of colour can be achieved if bedding plants are used. Flowers can be had from early spring and right through the summer. They are usually planted in early autumn for spring display and in the late spring for the summer show. Bedding plants can be annuals, biennials, or perennials. Some may be hardy, others half-hardy. Many can be raised from seed such as the annuals. The perennials, etc., are raised by rooting cuttings and it will be necessary to have a heated frame or greenhouse for this purpose. Old plants can also be divided.

The half-hardy annuals are usually sown in February — March in heat. The hardy types can be sown in April. Many of the perennial bedding plants are propagated by cuttings in the early autumn or spring.

A very wide range of summer bedding plants is usually available from your local shop or market. These are sold separately or by the boxful. They should not be planted out until danger of frost has passed which is usually at the end of May or early June.

The site for bedding display should be prepared a few days beforehand by forking over the soil and working in horticultural peat at the rate of 1 barrowload to 6 sq. yds. Rake in a balanced fertiliser at the rate of 2 oz. per sq. yd. General attention consists of weeding and watering frequently if the weather is dry. Pick off faded flowers regularly as this prolongs the display.

Suitable Subjects:

FLOWERING APRIL–MAY:

Wallflowers: Orange Bedder, Fire King, Blood Red, Carmine King, Golden Perfection

Primulas: Wanda, Denticula; *Bulbs,* such as Daffodils, Hyacinths, Tulips, etc. These are planted in the autumn of the preceding year.

FLOWERING MAY–JUNE:

Sweet Williams: Pink Beauty, Scarlet Beauty, Indian Carpet; *Pansies:* Mixed strains; *Canterbury Bells:* Mixed strains; *Forget-me-not:* Victoria; *Mixed Summer Display, Geraniums:* Paul Crampnel, Gustane Emich, Mrs. Lawrence, King of Denmark, Du Barry; *Begonias:* Double Bedding in mixed colours; *Petunias:* Superbissima Mixed; *Salvias:* Blaze of Fire; *Ageratum:*

Blue Mink; *Alyssum:* Royal Carpet, Minimum; *Antirrhinum:* Magic Carpet, Dazzler, Welcome, Nelrose, Choice Mixed; *Aster:* Mixed Ostrich, Plume, Queen of the Singles; *Lobelia:* Crystal Palace, Sapphire, Cambridge Blue; *Petunia:* Nana Compacta; *Stocks:* Ten Week Mixed; *Mesembryanthemum:* Criniflorum; *Nemesia:* Strumosa Nana Compacta Mixed

Plants for Walls, Paving and General Ground Cover:

Plants are very adaptable and a careful selection can provide subjects for the most unusual requirement. Often, there is the problem of making a crazy-paving path more interesting and attractive by planting suitable creeping plants. Walls can also be made more attractive by those plants which will either establish themselves in suitable cracks or planting holes, or else on the top of the wall.

Here is a selection of plants for any of the above requirements *(The month after the plant is the approximate flowering time)*

Alyssum Saxatile Compactum, yellow, May/June; *Aubretia,* purple/red, April/June; *Dianthus Deltoides,* rose pink, June/July; *Nepeta Mussinii,* blue, May/September; *Phlox Subulata,* blue, pink, red, May/June; *Sedum Coral Carpet,* bronzy foliage, pink flowers, May/June; *Sempervivum Comander Hay,* green and crimson rosettes, June/July; *Thymus Lanuginosus,* grey foliage, mauve flowers, June/August; *Ajuga Reptans Multicolor,* variegated bronzy foliage, blue flowers, May/June

When planting any of the above subjects, it is essential that they have a soil which has high organic or moisture-retaining properties especially where wall and paving plants are concerned. A mixture of 4 parts turfy loam and 1½–2 parts peat is ideal.

TREES AND SHRUBS

A COLLECTION of trees and shrubs should be included in every garden scheme. The small gardens need not be excluded as there are some delightful subjects which will not become a problem with regard to size of spread later on.

What have trees or shrubs to offer in the garden? Many are noted for the beauty of their bark and foliage. Some have distinct grace and charm of form and others are noted for their fragrance. A collection will provide colour and shade throughout much of the season and there is, therefore, something for everyone.

The site should be dug over as deeply as possible as drainage is very important. Old manure or compost will produce a vigorous root system and should be incorporated at the rate of 1 barrow-load to 8 sq. yds. for the compost. Rhododendrons and azaleas will not grow well on chalk and lime soils, but are excellent for any other soil type.

Very little pruning is required for trees and shrubs. Faded flowers must be removed regularly to prolong the flower display and diseased or badly placed branches should be cut right out.

Shrubs:

(E. denotes evergreen, figures denote approximate height followed by flowering date)

AZALEAS *(Ghent type which produce attractive tinted foliage in the autumn): Dr. C. Baumann,* 4–5 ft., June, red; *Bouquet de Flore,* 4–5 ft., May–June, pink; *Narcissiflora,* 4–5 ft., May, yellow

AZALEAS (MOLLIS TYPE): *Comte de Papodopoli,* 4–5 ft. May, pink; *Koster's Brilliant Red,* 4–5 ft. May, orange-red; *Golden Sunlight,* 4–5 ft. May, deep yellow

DWARF JAPANESE AZALEAS: *Favourite,* 2–3 ft. May, red E; *Sakata,* 2–3 ft. May, red, E

RHODODENDRONS (FLOWER APRIL–MAY): *Lord Roberts,* crimson E; *Pink Pearl,* pink E; *Purple Splendour,* purple, E; *Brittannica,* scarlet, E

General List of Shrubs:

(Plant at least 8–10 ft. apart to allow for later development. If more room can be spared, so much the better.)

JANUARY–APRIL DISPLAY: *Viburnum Tinus,* white 7–8 ft. E, January–March; *Viburnum Burkwoodii,* white, 5–6 ft. E, April; *Ribes Sanguineum,* red, 4–5 ft. March–April

MAY–JULY DISPLAY: *Weigela Conquette,* rose, 7–8 ft. May–June; *Philadelphus Belle Étoile,* white, 4–5 ft. June; *Fuchsia Riccartonii,* crimson/purple, 4–5 ft. June–October; *Escallonia,* C. F. Ball, rosy-crimson, 6–8 ft. June–July, E; *Berberis Venuculosa,* yellow, 5–7 ft. E, May–June

AUGUST–SEPTEMBER DISPLAY: *Caryopteris Clandonensis,* blue, 3–4 ft. July–September; *Ceratostigma Willmottiana,* blue, 2–3 ft. July–September; *Potentilla Farreri,* yellow, 2–3 ft. June–September; *Veronica Elliptica,* Autumn Glory, violet, 2–3 ft. July–September, E

CLIMBING SHRUBS *(D = deciduous. E = evergreen):* These are ideal for covering walls, fences and rustic work.

Clematis Contesse de Bouchard, rose, July–August, D; *Clematis Jackmanii,* purple, July–August, D; *Cotoneaster Horizontalis,* red berries in autumn, D; *Forsythia Suspensa,* yellow, March, D; *Honeysuckle Halliana,* white/yellow, June–October, E; *Jasminum Nudiflorum,* yellow, November–February, D; *Wisteria Sinensis,* mauve, May–June, D; *Pyracantha Rogersiana Flora,* yellow, June, E

Trees:

(Plenty of room should be given between specimens and 20–25 ft. is reasonable.) Prunus Amyzdalus Communis, pink, 15–24 ft., February–March; *Prunus Hisakura,* double pink, 25–30 ft., April–May; *Prunus Subhirtilla Autumnalis Rosea,* semi-double pink, 20–25 ft. November–March; *Laburnum Vossii,* yellow, 25–30 ft.

CONIFERS *(These are delightful subjects which add character to the garden. They are excellent as specimen plants and some are especially useful as features on either side of stems or to line drives and pathways.)*

Cedrus Atlantica Glauca, blue foliage; *Cupressus Lawsoniana Allumii,* blue; *Cupressus Lawsoniana Ellwoodii,* silvery green, dwarf habit; *Juniperus Sabina tamariscifolia,* green, low ground cover plant

Hedging Plants:

(A careful selection will provide attractive screens which will serve as wind breaks and which, in time, will give privacy to the garden.)

Beech, Common Green, green leaves in spring, dry brown leaves in winter. Plant 1½ ft. apart; *Berberis Thunbergii Erecta,* green leaves turn scarlet in autumn. Red berries in winter. Plant 12 in. apart; *Lombardy Poplar,* plant at least 15 ft. apart. Only suitable for larger gardens.

Roses:

No gardener would be without his rose bed! This is not surprising when one considers the wonderful colours and perfumes that roses provide in the garden. They are easy plants to grow, demanding very little attention. The soil must be well drained and deep cultivation is essential. Work in plenty of old manure or compost at the rate of 1 cwt. to 6 sq. yds. Planting time must depend on soil and weather conditions.

The first pruning of new roses is of vital importance otherwise poor results will prevail. Roses planted from late October to early January should be pruned in mid–February. Roses planted after February should be pruned just before planting.

First Pruning Requirements

BUSH ROSES: Cut back so that only 2–3 buds or eyes remain at the base.
CLIMBERS AND RAMBLERS: Shorten shoots to approximately half their length.

STANDARDS AND HALF STANDARDS: Prune as for bush roses. Weeping standards should have weak shoots cut back to about 4 in. and strong ones to 9 in.
SHRUB ROSES: Very little attention is required.

Planting Suggestions:

HYBRID TEAS *(These are ideal for beds and borders and will provide a riot of colour from early summer until late autumn. Prune when established in February to March. Remove weak shoots. Keep the centre open and cut back remainder to 3–4 eyes. X = suitable for poor soils, T = tall, L = low, M = = medium): Buccaneer, yellow,* X. T., scented; *Crimson Glory,* crimson, X. T., scented; *Eden Rose,* pink, X, scented; *McGredy's Yellow,* yellow, X. M., scented; *Mrs. Sam McGredy,* coppery-orange, M; *Peace,* yellow, X. T., scented; *Super Star,* gold shaded yellow, X. T., scented; *Virgo,* white, X. M. T.

Floribunda (Most have semi or double flowers. Prune when established as for Hybrid Teas.): Sarabande, scarlet, M; *Faust,* yellow, flushed red, X. M. T., fragrant; *Frensham,* rich crimson, X. T.; *Korona,* vermilion-scarlet, M. X. T.; *Masquerade,* yellow/salmon/orange, X. M. T.

DWARF POLYANTHA *(Excellent for edges of borders, paths, etc. Produce flowers, right through the season. Flowers are small and double in clusters. When established, prune by cutting back within a few inches of the ground in late winter and spring.): Ellen Poulsen,* cherry rose; *Little Dorrit,* coral-salmon; *Paul Crampel,* orange-scarlet; *Yvonne Rabier,* white

CLIMBERS *(Useful where walls, pillars or fences have to be clothed. Flowers are large and in clusters. When established, prune by cutting out dead wood and overcrowded wood. Do this in late autumn after flowering.): Crimson Glory,* crimson, scented; *Étoile de Hollande,* crimson, scented; *Shot Silk,* orange-cerise, scented; *Lemon Pillar,* pale yellow, scented

RAMBLING ROSES *(Also suitable for trellis walls, arches, etc. Prune when established by cutting out older growths and tie in new ones in their place. Thin out new growth where necessary in September or October.): Alberic Barbier,* white, X; *Albertine,* salmon, X; *Dorothy Perkins,* pink; *Emily Gray,* golden apricot, X; *Paul's Scarlet,* scarlet, X

ROSES FOR HEDGES *(Plant 1½ to 2 ft. apart. Trim lightly each spring. Height approximately 4–5 ft.): Buccaneer,* yellow; *Diamond Jubilee,* yellow; *Masquerade,* yellow, salmon; *Jiminy Cricket,* orange

FOR HEIGHTS OVER 5 FT.: —*Bonn,* orange-red; *Grandmaster,* yellow; *Kassel,* red; *Nevada,* pink; *Munster,* soft pink

SHRUB ROSES *(These are roses with a difference. They should be treated as shrubs – in other words they are specimen plants and should be positioned where they will give a bold display. Variations in flower, foliage and colours make these a most fascinating selection of plants for your garden): Amy Robsart,* deep rose, T; *Fruklingsgold,* semi-double yellow, T; *Hugonis,* single yellow; *Kassel,* red, very bushy; *Mermaid,* single yellow, T; *Wilhelm,* crimson, T.

FRUIT GARDENS

AGAIN, the amount and variety of fruit which can be grown will depend on the available space. In smaller gardens the soft fruits are to be recommended for large returns from a small number of plants. You must not forget walls and fences though! There are several subjects which can be trained against these to provide welcome fruit, particularly if they can receive shelter from cold winds and plenty of sun. The larger garden can, of course, accommodate quite a few top-fruits. This term refers to apples, pears, damsons, cherries, plums etc.,

Soil must be dug over well, making sure that there is good drainage. Apply old manure or compost at 1 cwt. to 8 sq. yds. To conserve this material it could be incorporated in the planting holes instead. A dressing of bonemeal or hoof and horn meal should be scattered and worked in at 4 oz. per sq. yd.

Planting time extends from November until late March. Pick your time when soil and weather conditions are suitable — that is to say when the soil is not frozen or wet.

The size of the planting hole will naturally depend on the subject which is being planted. The best guide is to take out the hole a little wider than the maximum spread of the root system. The depth of planting should be such that the original soil mark on the stem is level with the soil after planting.

It is wise to plan your fruit garden so that you can harvest for as long a period as possible. A careful selection of varieties will provide for this. Here is a selection of top and soft fruits which will form an ideal fruit garden for you:

Top Fruit:

APPLES: *Scarlet Pimpernel* is a dessert fruit which has a nice 'bite' to its flavour. Ready from August onwards. *Arthur Turner* has large fruit and is ready for eating September–October. It is a cooker. *James Grieve* has a most delicious flavour and should bear heavy crops when well established. Ready from September–October and is a dessert apple. It must have a pollinator and *Arthur Turner* would be suitable. *Ellison's Orange* is another wonderful dessert apple which is ready in September and will keep under good conditions until October.

A very reliable cooker for the household is *Lord Derby*. It can produce some very large fruits. *Bramley Seedling* is perhaps the best of the late cookers which, like *Lord Derby*, is ready from late November onwards. The only trouble is that it should be planted with two pollinators and *Laxton's Superb* and *Arthur Turner* would be suitable. A dessert apple for this ripening period (November onwards) is *Cox's Orange Pippin* which has a superb flesh. For the latest supply of apples, two are recommended — *Newtown Wonder* which is a cooker and *Laxton's Superb*, a dessert.

PEARS: For the first harvesting in August and September, *Williams Bon Chretien* can be recommended. It has a good quality flesh and flavour but should be harvested before it is fully ripened.

Beurre Superfin, *Conference* and *Doyenne du Comice* will provide fruit for October–December eating. The latter variety, if stored carefully, may last until January of the following year.

PLUMS: *Dennistons Superb*, *Early Transparent Gage* and *Laxton's Gage* produce crops in August. All are self-fertile — that is to say, they do not require a pollinating tree of another variety in order to set a crop of fruit. For cooking, The *Czar* is ideal and crops in August. A later crop, in September, is provided by the variety *Victoria* which is dual-purpose — it can be used for cooking or dessert. It is self-fertile.

CHERRIES: For cooking, *Morello* is very useful, particularly as it is self-fertile. *Governor Wood*, *White Heart Napoleon* and *Noble* are excellent dessert varieties. *Governor Wood* requires *Napoleon* as a pollinator, whilst this variety requires *White Heart*. *White Heart* requires *Governor Wood* as pollinator and *Noble* requires *Napoleon*.

Soft Fruit:

BLACKCURRANTS: A most valuable fruit to have not only for use fresh, but for bottling purposes. *Boskoop Giant* is ideal for this purpose. For late pickings, the variety *Daniel's September* is very reliable.

RED CURRANTS: One of the very best varieties to plant is *Laxton's No. 1*. It is a mid-season variety bearing large bunches of quality fruits.

RASPBERRIES: These take up little room and can be planted against a fence or can be used as a division in the garden. *Malling Promise* and *Malling Exploit* produce the early fruits and *Lloyd George* the late summer and autumn crops. This is a useful variety for jams and desserts.

GOOSEBERRIES: For early crops the variety *Leveller* is recommended with its yellow fruits. *Careless* has large white fruits and is mid-season. This is an ideal fruit for jam or dessert.

STRAWBERRIES: There is nothing quite like your own fresh strawberries! *Early Cambridge,* as its name implies, will provide the first outdoor pickings, to be followed by *Royal Sovereign. Talisman* is a very useful mid-season to late variety which should be found some room.

PEACHES AND NECTARINES: These must have a warm sheltered garden and do best planted against a sunny wall or fence. Of the PEACHES, *Peregrene* is very reliable, a good cropper and produces its crop in mid-August. *Dymond* produces its fruit a month later. For the NECTARINES, *Pitmaston Orange* is very delicious and fruits in August to be followed by *Pine Apple* in September.

LAWNS

Their Construction and Maintenance:

There are very few gardens which do not have a lawn. This is not surprising, since a well made and maintained lawn is a thing of great beauty and sets off other features admirably. If there is any secret of successful lawn making, it must be in the initial soil preparations. It is very difficult to correct any major faults once the lawn is well established.

The new lawn need not be perfectly level, but it is advisable to try to provide as 'smooth' a surface as possible so that you will enjoy your mowing later on! The site should be marked out with pegs and then dug over as deeply as possible without bringing up the poorer or heavier sub-soil as the case may be. Autumn or winter cultivation is ideal as the soil can be left rough to weather. This is important where heavy soils are encountered. Plenty of weathered ashes or sharp sand should be incorporated for heavy soils.

Organic matter is important as it helps to hold moisture during dry weather, it improves the physical condition of heavier soils and it encourages a vigorous root action. Horticultural peat or composted vegetable waste should be forked in a week or so before seed is sown or turf laid. The rate of 1 barrow-load to 4–6 sq. yds. will be adequate.

New sites contain a lot of weeds and it is quite a good plan to allow the ground to lie fallow or vacant for several months after it has been dug over.

This will give the weeds every chance to grow! The perennial ones which appear should be pulled out and burnt. The annual weeds should be tackled whilst they are quite small. All you need do is to use the hoe frequently and cut them off.

Base dressings of fertiliser are also required and should be made up as follows: —

$^{1}/_{2}$ oz. sulphate of ammonia

1 oz. bonemeal

$^{1}/_{4}$ oz. sulphate of potash

1 oz. superphosphate of lime

Apply each at the quantity stated per sq. yd. This is an ideal dressing for lawns established from seed. Where turf is used, the sulphate of ammonia should be left out.

The final sowing or turfing surface is achieved by thorough raking, first across the length of the site, then across the width. On light soils it is advisable to tread the area so that the soil is firmed and settled. This will do much to prevent sinking later on. The site is now ready for the new lawn. There are several ways in which the grass can be established, but seed and turf are undoubtedly the best.

A Lawn From Seed:

The use of cheap mixtures is not recommended. A quality lawn depends on the sowing of a carefully blended mixture to suit a particular purpose and soil condition. For general purposes, a hard-wearing mixture is best, especially if there are several healthy youngsters in the family! Finer grasses can be sown to provide a beautiful lush lawn, but this type will *not* stand up to regular hard wear. There are several leading seed establishments who sell different types of grass mixtures, and if you send them details of your own particular requirements they will be able to supply the right blend.

The best time to sow seed is in late August or early September, although the late spring is suitable also. Even distribution of seed is essential at $1\frac{1}{2}$ oz. per sq. yd. To facilitate this, small areas at a time can be marked out into sq. yds. with the garden line. After sowing the seed should be very lightly cross-raked in. To prevent bird damage, black thread or fine netting should be used. It is possible to buy specially treated seed which is distasteful to birds.

If weather conditions are dry after sowing, some water must be given and a fine perforated hose or sprinkler is ideal.

A Lawn From Turf:

This is the quickest way of making a lawn although the most expensive. The turf quickly bonds together and can be walked on within a few weeks of laying. Local grown and cut turf should be selected as it is growing in similar soil conditions to your own. Turf is usually supplied in yard pieces each measuring 3 ft. in length by 1 ft. in width. Prices vary considerably according to distance, but an average price would be about £4 per hundred delivered.

Start laying by placing whole pieces at the edges first, then fill in the centre afterwards. The turf must be bonded in the rows as bricks are in a wall: i. e. no joint in one row falls opposite one in the preceding one. It will be necessary to either add or take away a little soil as each piece is laid to ensure a reasonably level surface. The turf should also be firmed into position with the back of the spade as laying proceeds.

Some fine soil should be at hand so that the joints can be filled in. Unless this is done the turves will not knit together quickly and will dry out badly.

Maintenance:

When the new grass from a sown lawn is about 2–3 in. high it is ready for its first cut. Set the mower blades high at first otherwise a close cut may pull out the young grass by its roots. When established, lawns should be mown regularly each week, perhaps even twice a week if the growth is really vigorous. Little or no mowing will be required during the late autumn and winter months.

A good lawn is one which can 'breathe' easily. Aeration is of vital importance and spiking in the autumn (September to December) will more than repay the labour involved. A fork or special aerator should be used for this work.

A top dressing of fine soil at the rate of 4 lb. per sq. yd. will encourage good growth. This should be applied in the early spring, not deeper than ½ in., and worked in well with a stiff brush or back of the rake.

The control of weeds in the lawn is not the problem it used to be. Thanks to the rapid development of modern chemicals there are many first-class preparations which are available from your seed shop. These are simply scattered or watered on to the lawn. Many of these preparations contain selective weedkillers which attack the weeds but do not harm the grass.

A lawn which is given regular feeding and which is kept mown regularly should not be prone to too many weed troubles.

Lawn sand is a very effective way of controlling many common lawn weeds such as Creeping Buttercup, Ribwort, Pearlwort, etc. It is made up as follows:

3 parts sulphate of ammonia — *1 part calcined sulphate of iron* — *20 parts dry sand*

Apply at 4–6 oz. per sq. yd. three or four times during the year.

Rolling should be avoided if the soil is of a heavy nature as it will compact badly and the lawn will not be able to 'breathe'. Some of the lawns which have a light soil can be rolled in the spring using a roller which is not heavier than about 2 cwt. The roller should not be used in wet weather.

Lastly, remember those edges! A trim lawn is one which has neat, clean-cut edges which are easily maintained by the use of the edging iron and long handle shears.

PATHS

Design and Construction:

VERY FEW GARDENERS appreciate the way in which paths can play an important part in the design and beauty of the garden layout. By the use of carefully selected materials, and even mixtures of materials, some very attractive designs can be produced.

A path is as good as its foundations. This is an excellent maxim to observe, and whatever type of path is constructed it is essential that plenty of broken rubble or bricks are rammed well into the site. Usually a trench can be dug out, some 6–9 in. deep, and the rubble placed in this. Allowance must be made, of course, for the thickness of the surface layer when the foundations are being planned. For good drainage, the finished surface of a path should be slightly above the surrounding beds, etc. The exception to this rule would be if a path ran alongside the lawn. In this case its edge should be just *below* the lawn, so that the mower could be taken over the lawn edge.

The most popular path is the concrete one. To make it more attractive, colouring can be added as the cement is mixed and there are some very pleasant shades which can be obtained in this way. Concrete paths should be about 2–3 in. thick to ensure satisfactory wearing qualities. A suitable mixture is as follows:

1 part cement *2 parts sand* *3 parts shingle*

If mixed ballast is used, the mixture should be:

1 part cement *4 parts mixed ballast*

NOTE: All the above parts are by bulk — e. g. 1 bucketful = 1 part.

Pre-cast paving slabs are very popular and easy to lay. Although a sand or ash 'bed' for them is satisfactory under most conditions, a far better job is achieved if they are laid in an inch layer of concrete made up as follows:

1 part cement *4 parts sand*

This bed of concrete will prevent weed growth through the joints.

Crazy paving or broken pieces of paving is another popular material for paths. It is important for safety's sake to bed these down in concrete — not sand or ashes, as, owing to their irregular shape there is a possibility that odd pieces may tip when trodden on. Old bricks, laid on edge or flat produce a very 'rustic' effect and are very suitable for paths laid along a pergola walk.

The most attractive displays or designs are produced when mixtures of materials are employed. Large pebbles can be purchased, and if they are set in a thin layer of concrete, they will be safe. Occasional squares of pebbles set amongst the paving slabs will add interest and beauty to a path. Old bricks can be used in this way with slabs and pebbles.

Paths and drives can be made from tarmacadam which can be supplied in bags. The material is tipped out on to a firm foundation and raked level to an approximate depth of ½ in. Granite chippings supplied with each bag are scattered on top and rolled in. The path or drive can be used within a few hours of completion and the cost is extremely favourable.

No matter what type of paths are constructed, remember to keep their number down to a minimum. Too many paths are unsightly and serve no useful purpose. Wherever possible a path can wind or curve here and there. This is a graceful way of path construction and prevents the monotony of straight, uninteresting ones.

PESTS

How to Control the Most Common Varieties:

No matter how well we grow our plants, there is the chance that some pest or disease may attack them. Each year can bring its own particular trouble. Sometimes greenfly are particularly bad, another season will be remembered for blight disease on the outdoor tomatoes and potatoes.

Fortunately, horticultural scientists are keeping pace with these troubles and your local seed or sundries shop can usually supply the appropriate tin or bottle to deal with the situation! There are very many pests and diseases which *could* attack plants, but the following is a brief account of some of the more common troubles and the best method of dealing with them.

FLOWER PESTS: *Greenfly* or *Aphides* are very common during the summer causing curling and distortion of leaves. Nicotine, malathion, derris and B.H.C. sprays or dusts will control.
Capsid Bugs are troublesome on young shoots and buds which are eaten and become malformed. Dust with D.D.T. A liquid solution can also be used.
Earwigs often damage chrysanthemums and dahlias. Blooms are eaten as well as leaves. B.H.C. or D.D.T. sprays or dusts should be employed.

Leaf Miners cause tunnellings in the foliage. Pick off and burn badly affected foliage and spray or dust also with D.D.T., B.H.C., nicotine.
Leatherjackets feed just below soil level and stems are often cut through. Particularly troublesome in new gardens being developed from grassland. Aldrin, B.H.C. or D.D.T. dusts should be worked in.
Cutworms cause similar damage and the same control measures are advised.
Thrips feed on foliage and blooms producing the familiar streaked or silvered appearance. Particularly bad during hot weather. Malathion, D.D.T. or B.H.C. sprays should be used.
White Fly can be recognised by a black fungus which develops on sticky areas on plants. Leaves become spotted. Often found under glass — frames, greenhouses and cloches. Use malathion, nicotine or B.H.C. dusts.
Rose Sawfly (Slugworm) is a grub which skeletonises the leaves. Use a D.D.T. spray or dust with malathion.
Millipedes and Wireworms can seriously damage the roots of plants. Both are very troublesome pests, especially in new gardens. Work in B.H.C., aldrin or D.D.T. before and after planting.
Slugs and Snails are a common trouble in every garden, established or otherwise. Leaves, stems, fruits such as marrows and young plants in particular, are attacked. Make sure drainage conditions are improved as they like wet soils! Remove weedy corners and rubbish. Use proprietary slug baits or pellets frequently.

FLOWER DISEASES: *Rose Black Spot* shows as distinct black areas or spots on the foliage. Spray with Thriam and collect and burn all badly affected foliage.
Rose Rust is prevalent in mid-summer and causes orange-coloured spots to form on shoots and leaves in particular. Spray thoroughly with Bordeaux mixture or *colloidal sulphur*.
Rose Mildew appears as a white-grey powdery substance on foliage and stems. This mildew will also attack many other plants in the garden, particularly Michaelmas daisies. Cut out and burn very badly affected growths, particularly those on the daisies, and spray occasionally during the summer months with colloidal copper or sulphur.
Rust can affect chrysanthemums, wallflowers, sweet williams, hollyhocks, as well as several other subjects. Brown or yellow rust-like marks or spots appear on leaves. Particularly bad in damp, wet weather. Pull off and burn leaves and spray with colloidal copper or Bordeaux mixture.
Tulip Fire results in a scorched or burnt appearance on leaves and buds. It is wise to use different planting site and to spray with Thriam.
Damping Off attacks the seedlings of a wide range of plants. Most of these collapse at soil level and die. Bad watering, too thick a sowing and poorly drained soil can cause this trouble. Water with Cheshunt compound.

Aster Wilt rots and turns black the plant's stems. Area at ground level usually also rots. Try to use resistant varieties. No other control measure known.
Gladiolus Scab, as the name suggests, covers corms and leaves affected by black spots and scab. Soak corms before planting in a solution of calomel for 15 minutes made up from 1 oz. calomel in 1 gallon of water.
Gladiolus Dry Rot can be recognised by a yellowing of the foliage which generally starts at the top and gradually works down. Affected corms have black lesions. The only control is to burn affected corms and to plant in a new bed each season.
Honey Fungus can attack the roots of plants such as privet and flowering shrubs. Affected plants are killed. If the soil is examined it will reveal black threads. Yellow toadstools develop later in affected soils. Drainage must be improved and the area watered with sulphate of iron — 4 oz. in 1 gallon of water.

FRUIT PESTS: *Sawfly* affects apple fruits by the white maggots which eat into the fruitlets in early summer. Spray with B.H.C. a week before and after blossom falls.
Capsid can be recognised by punctures made by the small bugs in fruits, flowers and leaves. Russet scabs form on the fruits. Spray in February with D.N.C.
Apple Blossom Weevil is a small grub inside blossom buds which causes them to turn brown and they do not open. Remove affected buds as soon as they are noticed. Spray with D.D.T. at bud burst stage in early April.
Aphis and Woolly Aphis (American Blight) are a common menace. The former attack the young shoots and leaves. Leaves become badly curled owing to the sucking habits of the insects. Use malathion, lindane, derris or pyrethrum dusts. The latter trouble produces the cotton-wool-like growth or deposit which can be found on branches and trunks. A tar oil wash should be applied in January. Methylated spirits will remove the 'wool' if applied with a brush.
Bug Bud Mite on blackcurrants causes some of the buds to swell to many times their normal size. The mites are to be found inside affected buds. Pick off and burn affected buds. Apply lime-sulphur when leaves are the size of a halfpenny. The strength should be twice the usual winter strength.
Raspberry Beetle ruins the fruit by the small white maggot which is found inside. Spray or dust with derris 10 days before and after flowering.
Winter Moth appears in March or April. Buds and fruitlets are attacked by the caterpillars of this moth. Use a tar oil wash in January or a B.H.C. spray in early April. Whenever caterpillars are seen, they should be picked off and destroyed.
Codling Moth attacks fruit internally about June. The caterpillar of the moth tunnels right through the fruit. Early in January spray with tar oil. Apply D.D.T. in mid June and mid July.

FRUIT DISEASES: *American Gooseberry Mildew* produces a coating of white powder on stems and leaves. Bushes become stunted and fruit is malformed. Apply lime sulphur just before and after flowering.
Apple Scab is recognised by black spots appearing on the fruits. Areas become 'pitted'. Use lime sulphur sprays as follows: Green cluster — 2½%, Pink Bud 2%, Petal fall 1%; for sulphur-shy varieties such as Charles Ross, Lord Derby, Early Victoria, Grenadier, Monarch and Permain, use Bordeaux mixture instead.
Brown Rot affects several fruits such as plums, apples, pears, peaches. Pale brown tufts of the fungus bodies are seen on the skins of the fruits. The flesh eventually rots. No definite control available as yet, but affected fruits should be removed and burnt as soon as they are noticed. Stored apples must be examined frequently as storage conditions encourage the spread of the trouble.
Gooseberry Cluster Cup affects leaves and fruit, through a fungus which causes a series of raised spots to appear in early summer. Spray with Bordeaux mixture at green tip stage using a 1% solution; give a second application 10 days later.
Gooseberry Leaf Spot results in dark brown spots appearing on foliage. Spray with Bordeaux mixture when leaves are unfolding.
Peach Leaf Curl attacks young leaves in early spring and they become badly curled. A deep crimson colouring is typical at the latest stage. Spray with Captan just before bud burst.
Scab is a fungus which overwinters on fruit and attacks apples and pears. Leaves become spotted in the spring. Fruit is cracked at a later stage. Spray with Captan.
Raspberry Cane Blight makes canes and leaves brittle. Spray with Bordeaux and remove and burn affected canes.
Raspberry Mosaic mottles in a light green-yellow pattern. Plant's growth is usually weak. Spray frequently against aphis which can carry this virus. Burn affected canes.
Reversion is a virus which affects blackcurrants causing the normal 5 lobes to the outer edges of the leaves to become less than 5. Pull up and burn any affected bush.
Silver Leaf is a very serious disease of plums, cherries, peaches. Leaves become 'silvered' and at a later stage the fungus bodies or growths appear on the trunk and other branches. Very badly affected trees must be removed and *burnt*. A Government Order decrees that all dead wood from an affected tree must be burnt before July 15 each year.

VEGETABLE PESTS: *Pea Maggot* attacks the peas inside the pods and in a bad attack many of the peas cannot be used. Use D.D.T. at flowering time and give another application 10 days later.

Pea and Bean Thrips can be recognised by such signs as silver markings on the skins and foliage as well as distorted pods. D.D.T., malathion or B.H.C. sprays or dusts should control.
Pean and Bean Weevil results in the edges of the leaves becoming 'scalloped' or eaten out. Use regular dusts or sprays of D.D.T., B.H.C. or derris.
Onion Fly maggots attack the base of the bulb, causing eventual rotting. Burn badly affected plants, dust with aldrin before sowing or planting.
Flea Beetle attacks seedlings of turnips and other members of the brassica or cabbage family. Seed leaves are badly holed. Dust regularly with aldrin or D.D.T.
Celery Fly results in white 'blisters' appearing on the foliage. Leaves eventually die. Spray with lindane, derris or malathion.

POOLS

DIG A HOLE, line it with plastic, fill it with water — and there's your pool! Yes, it is as easy as that these days, thanks to the versatile plastic and fibreglass. It need not be too expensive either, as quite small pools can be made to look very attractive. The use of concrete can also be considered, but it does involve a lot of work and one has to bear in mind that such a pool is a very permanent feature. Whereas the plastic or fibreglass ones can be taken with you if you move, or transferred to another part of the garden if the layout is being reorganised.

Whichever method is used, there are one or two important points to be observed. The pool *must* be in an open part of the garden and away from trees, otherwise falling leaves will pollute the water. Wherever possible, the pool should be sited as close to water and electrical supplies as is feasible, or to a pump which you will find necessary to install if you are planning a fountain or waterfall.

Fibreglass Pools:

These can be purchased in a wide variety of shapes and sizes. Most are informal in shape, that is to say they have curving or irregular outlines and produce a most natural effect when installed. These pools have exceptional strength, and all that is necessary is to excavate the site to the depth and outline of the unit and then drop it into place. The fibreglass pools can be purchased in several pleasant colours, such as light blue or light green.

The large fibreglass pool is expensive and one some 6 ft. × 4 ft. × 18 in. deep would cost about £23–£30. This, however, is a sound investment, for fibreglass pools do not crack during frosty weather. They will also last a considerable time, and require no maintenance whatsoever. Most designs have 'shelves' which provide for different depths of water. This enables you to plant a wide range of aquatic plants, many of which require certain depths for successful growth.

PLASTIC SHEETING: This is probably the cheapest way to make your garden pool. Although the life of this material is limited, probably 5 years or so, it is cheap enough to renew. One of the best materials is an extremely strong, laminated flexible plastic sheet, consisting of ȷerylene coated with P.V.C. A reasonable amount of elasticity is present, and this enables the sheeting to mould itself reasonably well to the outlines of an informal pool with very few wrinkles or folds being noticed. In any case, these are generally hidden by the water and plants. Prices vary according to the size of the pool, but a sheet 12 ft. square would be about half the cost of fibreglass. The colour is a delightful light pastel blue.

POLYTHENE SHEETING: If this is of a heavy grade or gauge, it can also be used, but a pool of this type should be considered as a less permanent affair, and the material will probably require renewing every 2 years or so. To provide added stength, it is recommended that this type of polythene is doubled when laid. Pastel blue opaque sheeting costs well below £1 per yard and is 12 ft. wide. Black sheeting the same width is even cheaper.

With both types of pools, the site is excavated in 'steps' to provide for various water depths. These shallow are as should hold about 1–4 in. of water. A deeper section should be provided for a water depth of from 6–18 in. and the deepest section, 24 in.

NOTE: The life or duration figures quoted for these materials must only be approximate at present, as all the materials are comparatively new and have only been in use for a year or so.

Concrete Pools:

Formal or informal designs can be constructed. The latter is easier, as little or no shuttering or support for the concrete is required as it sets. Whatever design is contemplated, it is important that the base is well reinforced with rubble to a depth of 6 in. before concrete is laid. For best results the following concrete mix is recommended:

1 part cement *2 parts sand* *3 parts shingle*

If mixed ballast is used, the mixture is as follows:

1 part cement *4 parts mixed ballast*

All parts can be by weight or by capacity: i. e. 1 part cement could be 1 cwt. cement or 1 bucket of cement. All ingredients *must* be mixed together thoroughly and a waterproofing powder added. This can be obtained from a specialist pool firm.

The cement should be applied at least 3–4 in. thick at the sides and base of the excavated site. When dry, a final coat or rendering can be applied one inch thick. The mixture for this is:

1 part cement *2 parts sand*

To seal the cement finally and to render it harmless to fish it is essential that it is treated with a special sealing preparation which is very easy to apply before the pool is filled with water. This preparation can also be obtained from the pool specialist firm.

Concreting should *not* be undertaken during frosty weather as it will be affected. Slow drying is essential and a covering with thin polythene or damp sacks will ensure good setting.

Shuttering or wooden supports will be required when a formal pool is being constructed with concrete. This holds the concrete walls in place during the setting process and can be removed when the concrete has set. Shuttering will only be required for the sides and should be placed 3–4 in. away from the soil sides of the excavation and held in position with strong stakes.

Plants and Fish:

One of the easiest ways to stock your pool is to purchase a complete collection of plants and fish from one of the many specialist firms. These are specially prepared to suit various sizes and depths of pools.

There are, of course, very many delightful plants which can be selected individually and here is a short list of suitable ones to start your collection:

FLOATING PLANTS: One plant or portion should be planted for every 10 sq. ft. of water surface. *Azolla Caroliniana* or Fairy Moss which has a delightful fern-like leaf. It is green in the spring and turns bronze in the autumn. *Stratiotes Aloides* has star-shaped foliage and white flowers. *Lemna Triscula* or Ivyleaved Duckweed is another useful floating aquatic.

SUBMERGED OXYGENATING PLANTS: Very essential in order to oxygenate the pool and to supply a certain amount of food to the fish. The following should be planted, allowing 1 dozen for every 24 sq. ft. of water: *Elodea Canadensis, Callitriche Verna* and *Elodea Crispa.*

MARGINAL PLANTS *(The figure in brackets after each variety denotes the depth of water required.): Aponogeton Distachyum* (6–18 in.) heavy scent, (white flowers, oval floating leaves; *Zantedeschia Acthiopica* or Arum Lily 12 in.), *Calla Palustus* or Bog Arum Lily (2 in.), white and green flowers, most attractive; *Caltha Palustris Plena* or Double Marsh Marigold (bog conditions or in no water but very wet soil at edges of pool), yellow flowers; *Butomis Umbellatus* or Flowering Rush (4 in.) delightful rose-pink flowers;

Pontederia Cordata (3 in.) attractive, glistening foliage and blue flowers; *Scipus Zebrina* or Zebra Rush (4 in.), a 'must' for the pool, intriguing green and white banded foliage; *Typha Minima* or Reed Mare (2 in.), plant with very dainty, narrow leaves.

HARDY WATER LILIES *(Nymphaeas, as they are called, bloom from May to October and can be obtained in a wide range of colours. Various depths of water are required according to their vigour. The figures in brackets after each variety denote depth of water required.): Escarboucle* (12–18 in.), brilliant crimson and free flowering; *James Brydon* (12–18 in.), rose-red and free flowering; *Attraction* (18–36 in.) garnet red, flecked white; *Amabilis,* (12–18 in.) salmon-pink: *Marliscea Rosea* (12–18 in.) soft pink, easy to establish; *Candida* (7–15 in.) white and ideal for the smaller pool.

PLANTING: Most of the above can be planted from April to the end of August. Water lilies are best planted in May or June. Although plants can be planted in a good heavy loam (free from manure) placed in the bottom of the pool or on the shelves, it is far better to use planting crates of either wood or plastic. These can be obtained from the specialist firms and keep the pool much cleaner.

Fish:

Collections can be purchased for these, and the maximum stock which a pool should have is 6 in. of fish length, which includes the tail, for every square ft. of water surface area. Fish must *not* be introduced until at least three weeks have passed. The following fish are recommended: *Shubunkins, Goldfish, Comet Goldfish* and *Golden Orfe.* Water snails or *Mollusca* as they are called are the scavengers of the pool and must be included. Allow for 1 dozen snails for each 25 sq. ft. of water surface area. The best type is the fresh water snail *Limnaea Stagnalis.* *(For some further information on the care of fish in garden ponds, see page 251.)*

Careful planting will ensure that a really wonderful display will result later. Be patient, though, it will take a season before your pool will acquire that 'established' look about it. There is something very fascinating about water-garden life and you will find yourself spending many tranquil hours by the side of your pool.

ROCK GARDENS

ENDLESS HOURS of enjoyment can be had from a rock garden. Alpine plant life is fascinating, and offers many wonderful varieties and colours to admire as it nestles amongst the rock crevices.

The construction of a rock garden is in fact a modelling task. It is an attempt to construct in miniature the facsimile of a natural phenomena. The successful rock garden is one which has been assembled with great care, patience and thought. It is *not* a matter of placing a few lumps of rock haphazardly!

The best type of rock garden is constructed on ground which is either naturally uneven or which has a distinct slope. This does not mean, however, that a very successful rock garden cannot be constructed on level ground.

The first important point to bear in mind is proportion or size. The size of the completed garden should be neither too large nor too small in comparison with its surroundings. Once the size has been determined, the size and numbers of rocks which will be required can be calculated with reasonable accuracy. Avoid having too many small pieces — a few well-positioned large lumps will look far better!

The size and weight of the rock or stone will vary according to its type. This is a convenient spot to discuss the main types which are suitable. The best is undoubtedly weathered Westmoreland and is a grey colour. It is heavy and expensive and may cost close to £10 per ton.

Sandstone is delightful and blends in very well with most garden schemes, It is a lighter and softer stone and the harder grades should be asked for. Prices may be around £4–£6 per ton.

Other rocks which can be used include Kentish Rag (sand-grey colour). Mendip Mountain (red-grey), Devon Weathered (grey-brown) and Forest of Dean (grey). Prices range from £5–£10 per ton. In most cases, delivery will be charged extra, so it is advisable to order from as local a source of supply as possible. Most local nurseries or landscape firms can supply.

Now to the actual construction. Most natural outcrops of rock have 'steps' or stratas and between these there is really a track or 'path' of soil. This should be repeated in your construction. On the uneven site, rocks can be bedded into the face of high sides leaving the more gentle slopes for planting. On flat sites the rockery base should be built up by first applying a good layer of rubble for drainage followed by as much good loam as possible.

All rocks should be so placed that they slope slightly *into* the bank of soil. If you can visit a local natural outcrop of rocks you will see this most clearly. One or more pieces of rockery stone can be butted together so that a natural crevice or gap is formed, which makes an ideal planting spot for those trailing alpines. These pockets must be constructed in such a way as to provide plenty of soil for the plant's roots.

Rocks must be packed carefully where necessary so that they are completely firm. It may be necessary to use small pieces of rock for this purpose, and as the soil is replaced it should be firmed thoroughly with a blunt piece of wood. A suitable soil mixture can be made up from 4 parts turfy loam, 2 parts horticultural peat and 1 part sharp sand.

As each rock is placed in position, step back from your work and examine the rock garden as a whole. By so doing you will see at once the best position for every piece. A little time and patience will pay handsome dividends. Remember that each piece of rock has its best natural face, and this must be placed to the best advantage. Many rocks have strata lines, especially the sandstones, and these must run horizontally. If placed vertically there is the danger that frost will split the rock down its stratas.

Planting:

There are some wonderful collections available from specialist firms and a complete collection of alpines is one of the best ways of starting your rockery. Individual plants can be purchased also, although there are hundreds to choose from, and it is quite a task to make a decision from such tempting descriptions! Here, however, is a short list of alpines which, when established, will produce a really beautiful display on the rockery and which will form the basis of a well planned feature.

ALPINE PLANTS (ROCK GARDENS)

NAME	LEAF	FLOWER COLOUR	HEIGHT	FLOWERING PERIOD
Achillea Clypeolata	Silvery	Deep yellow	$1\frac{1}{2}$ ft.	June–Sept.
Achillea Tomentosa	Ferny	Golden yellow	6 in.	June–July
Alyssum Compactum	—	Bright yellow	9 in.	April–June
Anemone Pulsatilla	—	Purple blue	9 in.	April–May
Armena Corsica	Grassy	Brick red	9 in.	May–July
Aubretia (named varieties such as Barkers Double, Crimson Queen, Godstone and Lavender Queen)	—	Crimson, purple, deep red, violet	3 in.	April–June
Cyclamen Neopolitanum	—	White	4 in.	Sept.–Oct.
Crocus Asturiscus,	—	Violet-purple	4–6 in.	Aug.–April
C. Longiflorus	—			
C. Speciosus	—			
Dianthus Wisley var.	—	Bright rose pink	6 in.	June
D. Deltoides	—	Deep pink	9 in.	June–July
Gentiana Acaulis	—	Deep blue	3 in.	March–May
Leontopodium Alpinum (Edelweiss)	Felt-like	White, star-like	6 in.	June–July
Saxifrages	Rosettes	Yellow, pink, white, red	2–9 in.	May–June

SOILS

Types of Soils and their Maintenance:

'What's the soil like?' — That's the first question any gardener will ask you when you tell him that you have just moved into a new garden! The soil is so important, and its type will determine the manner in which it will have to be tackled in order to produce the best possible results from the garden. There are, of course, a very wide range of soils throughout the country, and each county will have its own particular characteristics. Soils can be conveniently divided into three main classes as follows — light, medium and heavy.

LIGHT SOILS: These are the easiest to work and can, in most cases, be cultivated in all weathers. They contain less clay particles and do not become heavy or waterlogged. Their drawback is that they tend to dry out rather quickly as their humus content is less than other types. Many light soils are often described as 'hungry' soils — that is to say, they require plenty of humus or organic matter as well as fertilisers to obtain the best results.

When these light soils are being prepared, the humus or organic matter must be supplied in the form of composted vegetable waste, spent hops, horticultural peat or farmyard manure. The latter should be incorporated at 1 barrow-load to 8 sq. yds. or any of the others at the approximate rate of 1 barrow-load to 4–5 sq. yds. A well balanced or general fertiliser should be worked in about 3–4 days before sowing or planting takes place, at the rate of 3–4 oz. per sq. yd. An autumn application of bonemeal or hoof and horn meal at 4 oz. per sq. yd. will also be required.

These light soils are delightfully easy to 'work' as they are so open. General cultivation such as raking or hoeing are very simple. These soils can usually be prepared in the spring as there is no need to enlist the aid of winter weather to break them down. Some soils are light enough for cultivation by the fork only. It is a most fortunate gardener who has this type of soil — but remember that regular applications of organic matter are vital to maintain moisture supplies.

MEDIUM SOILS: This soil is midway between the light and heavy types and can be considered the best 'general' soil to have. It presents none of the drying out problems the light soil could pose and it is comparatively easy to work, compared with the heavy ones. It is a soil which needs autumn preparation for the following season, and to keep it open and easy-to-work, humus or organic matter should be applied each autumn at the approximate rate of 1 barrow-load to 10 sq. yds. for farmyard manure and 1 barrow-load to 6–8 sq. yds. for the peat or composts, etc.

Attention should be paid to good drainage and the soil should always be cultivated as deeply as possible. The medium soils cannot be cultivated at any time of the year, as they hold water or moisture more readily and for longer periods than the light types. In most cases, however, they can be tackled when the weather is dry and bright and the soil itself is crumbly. Base fertiliser dressings are — 3 oz. per sq. yd. of general fertilisers and about 3 oz. of bonemeal or hoof and horn.

HEAVY SOILS: These can cause a lot of problems and there is no doubt that they involve a great deal of hard work. Nevertheless, they are a rewarding type of soil and one which usually has a fairly high amount of food nutrients locked up in it. The chief problem with heavy soil is that it can only be cultivated at favourable opportunities and it is usually poorly drained.

Heavy soils have particles which are very fine and which are closely knitted together. They hold water very easily and unfortunately are often reluctant to release the excess amounts! This leads to prolonged periods of waterlogged ground, particularly during a wet season.

This must seem a rather depressing picture, but it is possible to control this soil if the following procedure is adopted. The most important point to remember is that the soil should only be tackled when it is in as dry a state as possible, and preferably during bright weather. To trample over heavy ground when it is wet will consolidate it still further and make its cultivation a most difficult task.

The main or basic preparations should be carried out in the winter so that, when the soil has been dug over, it can be left to weather. During the digging, the clods should be left as rough as possible so that frosts can work on them. The expansion and contraction of water in the soil due to frost, does much to break it down.

As cultivation proceeds, plenty of sharp sand or well-weathered household ashes should be incorporated. These will keep the soil particles open and do much to improve drainage. Hydrated lime at 8 oz. per sq. yd. can be applied when digging is completed. This will also help break down the soil. Recently, gypsum has been recognised as being one of the best soil improvers, particularly for the heavy, clay soils. It is best applied before showery weather and must be worked into the soil. A dressing of 8 oz. per sq. yd. is advised. It is a product which cannot be too highly recommended for those of you who are confronted with a heavy, difficult soil.

The breaking down of the heavy soil ready for sowing or planting operations should only be undertaken when the weather is dry. There are usually many dry, crisp days in the early spring when the soil is friable and under these conditions even the heaviest of soil should respond. The first breaking down should be carried out by hitting the large clods with the back of the fork. The rake comes next and with it the smaller lumps can be broken down still further to produce the seed-sowing or planting surface. Be patient with this work and tackle it thoroughly and in easy stages. During the growing season, the surface soil can be kept stirred and loose by frequent hoeing and by the occasional use of the fork which 'pricks' over the surface to a depth of an inch or so.

TOOLS

Basic Equipment for Your Garden:

The purchase of garden tools should be looked upon as an investment. Pay a little more to obtain tools which are not only well-made, but well designed also. Many such tools should last practically a life time.

The initial expenditure need not be heavy, as a small collection of basic tools can be purchased as a start. These should include the following: a digging spade and fork, rake, dutch hoe and draw hoe, garden line, hand fork and trowel, pair of secateurs and shears, edging shears, a watering can and length of hosepipe. A wheelbarrow is an essential part of the equipment, especially if a new garden is taken over. Labels and twine should not be forgotten, and a mower with be needed for your lawn.

Later on, the collection can be added to from time to time. Aerators or spikers for the lawn will save a considerable amount of time and labour. Fertiliser distributors are also very useful and will apply the products much more accurately than can be done by hand.

In the greenhouse, shading blinds of wood or strong green polythene can be purchased as well as an ingenious automatic ventilator which works without the need for batteries or electricity. Plastic canes and wire-supporting material will also be invaluable, not only in the greenhouse, but outdoors also.

Pots and boxes will be required, especially if you have a frame or greenhouse. It is often difficult to ascertain the number and sizes which might be required. To start with, the following should be sufficient: 4 doz. 3 in.; 3 doz. $4\frac{1}{2}$ in.; 2 doz. 5 in.; 1 doz. $6\frac{1}{4}$ in.; $1\frac{1}{2}$–2 doz. seed boxes (15 in. × 9 in. × × 2 in. deep) and 2 doz. deeper boxes (3 in. deep). Pots can be either plastic or clay. The former are much more expensive, but are virtually unbreakable, and most of them retain warmth and moisture better. There are some very useful black polythene pots which are virtually gusseted bags. They are very cheap only a few shillings for 12–50 pots depending on size) and give excellent results. They can be used over and over again and when not required can be stored flat.

For those of you who are making a pool *(see page 279)*, there are several reliable and easy-to-install electric pumps available. These will produce a fountain or waterfall effect according to their size.

Although a cold greenhouse or frame can provide endless hours of pleasure throughout the season, the addition of heating will widen its scope and interest considerably. There are many different types available ranging from the modest oil-heater (paraffin) to the electric tubular and fan heaters. The latter are very versatile as they can be switched to air circulation only in the summer and heat distribution in the winter. Soil and air-warming wire are ideal for small propagation benches in the greenhouse, and especially for the outdoor frame.

VEGETABLE GARDENS

NOTHING is quite so rewarding as growing your own vegetables, especially when you have tested their exquisite, fresh flavour. The types of crops which can be grown must naturally depend on the amount of room available and, of course, on personal favourites. Where there is little room available it is perhaps advisable not to grow too many potatoes, as they do take up quite a lot of room. Crops which pay handsome dividends in such circumstances are the bean family, especially the dwarf French beans.

Nothing is more frustrating than to have a glut of one crop with nothing to follow it for several weeks afterwards.I t is important, therefore, that regular sowings are made of certain crops to ensure good continuity. Correct varieties must be used also, otherwise results may be disappointing.

The following is a list of vegetable crops with their full cultural requirements together with suggestions for varieties which will ensure the best possible returns from your labours.

Peas:

They require a well-worked soil which is enriched with either old manure or composted vegetable waste. Either of the ingredients will help to hold moisture which is so valuable to this crop. A vigorous root system will also be encouraged. Dig in at the rate of 1 cwt. to 10–12 sq. yds. Before sowing, distribute the following fertilisers along the drill and work them in with the rake: 1 part sulphate of ammonia, 3 parts superphosphate of lime and 2 parts sulphate of potash. Apply at 1–2 oz. per yard run of drill. All parts by weight. Seed is sown in flat drills, 10 in. wide and about 2 in. deep. Sow as evenly as possible along the bottom of the drill, spacing them 3 in. apart each way. Cover lightly with about 1 inch of soil. Keep the rows well-watered at all times, especially so when the pods have formed and are swelling. If you don't, you will have a poor crop.

Peas must be supported, even the dwarf varieties. The best material to use is brushwood which you can purchase from your local seedshop. String netting is also useful. Early training is very important.

VARIETIES: The first seeds you can sow are known as first earlies and they are usually dwarf-growing types. *Kelvedon Wonder, Gradus* and *Foremost* are excellent. The next sowings should use the second earlies such as The *Lincoln* and *Fillbasket*. Maincrop sowings follow with varieties such as *Alderman, Late Duke* and *Senator*. All these are tall varieties. The first sowings will be in March as soon as weather and soil conditions are suitable and a sowing every 3–4 weeks after this will ensure a good succession of pickings. The latest sowing can take place in June

Beans:

There are three types which are used — FRENCH, RUNNER and BROAD BEANS. All are valuable in the vegetable plot as they will give good yields from even a short row. All require the same soil preparation as that given for the pea crop.

FRENCH BEANS: Seed is sown as early in May as possible. Glass or plastic cloches placed over the earliest sowings will give protection against possible late frosts. Sow seed 8 in. apart in drills 1 in. deep. Rows should be spaced 18–20 in. apart.

RUNNER BEANS: Seed is best sown in deep boxes in a greenhouse or frame in April. From this sowing, plants will be ready for planting outside in their permanent rows in late May or preferably in June, when frost danger should have passed. It is essential, of course, that these plants are hardened off thoroughly before they are planted out. This is quite easy to do. The young plants should be placed in the frame from the greenhouse and more air is allowed gradually each week by either sliding the frame lights back gradually or by raising them an inch or so at a time. Eventually the lights are removed completely. Plant out 8 in. apart in a double row, spacing the rows 12 in. apart. Seed, of course, can be sown direct into the ground where the plants are to grow and the same spacings should be observed.

BROAD BEANS: In favoured or sheltered gardens seed can be sown out of doors, where the plants are to grow, in late October or early November. Spring sowings are from March to April. Sow seed in a double row, spacing seeds 8 in. apart in the rows and the rows themselves 10 in. apart.

All the bean family must have plenty of water, like the peas. Weak liquid feeds are invaluable when the plants have formed their pods. When the runner beans have reached the top of their training material, which can be strong string netting or bean poles which you can get from your local seedshop, the centres or growing points should be removed. Broad beans should be pinched also, usually when they have formed 4–5 clusters of blooms.

VARIETIES:

French Beans:	*Selected Canadian Wonder* and *The Prince. Hammonds Dwarf Scarlet* is a new type which is dwarf and bushy in habit and requires no staking
Runner Beans:	*Streamline, Goliath, Crusader*
Broad Beans:	*Seville Longpod* and *Aquadulce*

Carrots:

Not the easiest crop to grow in all gardens, but if your soil is well-worked or on the light side, they are well worth a trial. Fresh manure must be avoided at all costs as it encourages coarse roots. Use peat or composted vegetable waste at 1 cwt. to 6 sq. yds. Just before sowing, work in 4 parts superphosphate of lime, 1 part sulphate of ammonia and 1 part sulphate of potash at 3 oz. per sq. yd. All parts by weight.

Early roots, which are delicious for salads and which are best sown in a frame or under cloches, are sown in early February to mid-March. General outdoor sowings are from mid-March to mid-July. Carrots which can be stored for winter use are best sown in June.

Seeds must be sown as thinly as possible in drills $\frac{1}{4}$–$\frac{1}{2}$ in. deep. Space rows about 12–15 in. apart. Plenty of water is required during growth and where thinning is necessary the young roots which have been pulled will be ideal for salads.

VARIETIES: For the earliest sowings *Early Horn, Early Nantes* and *Amsterdam Forcing* are excellent. Main crop sowings should use any of the following: *Favourite, Scarlet Intermediate* and *Autumn King*

Beetroot:

A well-worked site is ideal, and manure or composted vegetable waste should be worked in at 1 cwt. to 10–12 sq. yds. Before sowing a dressing of 1 part sulphate of potash, 1 part sulphate of ammonia and 4 parts superphosphate of lime should be worked in at 3 oz. per sq. yd.

Early roots can be produced if seed is sown in early April, but this sowing must be kept well watered if good results are to be obtained. Main sowings should take place in late May. Sow the seed in 1 in. deep drills spacing them 15 in. apart. Seeds should be sown in small groups as the seed itself is in clusters. Beetroot is a crop which is ideal for winter use and roots can be left in the ground and pulled as required, or better still, they can be lifted before hard weather sets in and stored in dry sand in deep boxes in a cool, dry, frostproof place such as the garden shed.

VARIETIES: *Detroit Select Globe* and *Crimson Globe Improved* are two reliable varieties to use

Cabbage Family – Cauliflowers (Broccoli) Brussels Sprouts:

These are very important crops in the vegetable garden, especially as some of them provide valuable produce during the lean winter months. All will grow in a wide range of soil or cultivation conditions, although the cauliflowers and broccoli do better on richer soils.

The site should be prepared by digging as deeply as possible and old manure or composted vegetable waste should be incorporated at 1 cwt. to 5–6 sq. yds. Before planting bone-meal should be worked in at 4 oz. per sq. yd.

All the plants are best raised by sowing seed as thinly as possible in seed beds, or in the garden frame. When large enough and after they have been hardened off thoroughly, they are planted out with a good ball of soil attached to their roots.

Planting distances will vary slightly according to the type of plant, but the following distances will be adequate — Cauliflowers, broccoli and Brussels sprouts 2 ft. between plants and 2–2½ ft. between rows. Cabbages and sprouting broccoli 1½ ft. between plants and 2½ ft. between rows. Spring cabbage can be planted fairly close together and 1½ ft. between rows and plants should be sufficient in most districts.

The sprouting broccoli are excellent for the lean winter months as they will provide dozens of tiny cauliflower-like heads for regular picking. These are simply delicious when cooked! The sprouting broccoli are very hardy plants too.

Cauliflowers and broccoli are sown in March, April and May and are planted out from May to July according to variety. Brussels sprouts are sown in April and planted out in late May. Sprouting broccoli is sown in late April for July planting out. Savoy cabbage sowings are carried out in April and May for planting in late June and August. Spring cabbages are sown in July and August and plants go out in their permanent positions in late August and September.

VARIETIES:

Cauliflowers: Eclipse, All The Year Round, Early Giant and *Autumn Giant* are summer cauliflowers. This means that they should be ready for cutting during the months of June–September. Seed is sown from March to April and plants set or planted out from May to June

BROCCOLI: These are the hardier Cauliflowers and the following are excellent varieties: — *Veitch's Self-Protecting,* sow March–April, cut heads September–December; *Roscoff No. 2,* sow April, cut heads December–February; *Roscoff*

No. 4 and *Eastertide,* sow April and May, heads ready for cutting March–April; *Midsummer,* sow April–May, cut heads May–June

BRUSSELS SPROUTS: Seeds are sown from March to April. *Triumph* is a useful early variety and so is *Dwarf Gem* which, as its name implies, is a dwarf growing plant. *Fillbasket* and *Wroxton* are main crops of dependability

CABBAGES: *Favourite* is sown in the spring and should provide heads for cutting in June. *Christmas Drumhead* will be ready for cutting in November and December from a sowing made at the same time. *January King,* sown in May will be ready in January and February. *Savoy Cabbages* are sown in May to produce a crop from September onwards. A good variety is *Dwarf Green Curled*

SPROUTING BROCCOLI: The seeds are sown in April and plants are put out in late June. *Purple Sprouting* and *White Sprouting* are very reliable varieties

Potatoes:

Not a crop for the small plot as they take up quite a lot of room. Where space is at a premium a few earlies are worth while. Prepare the soil well by deep cultivation. Work in old manure or composted vegetable waste at 1 cwt. to 10 sq. yds. A base dressing of the following fertilisers should be worked in before planting: 4 parts superphosphate of lime, 2 parts sulphate of potash and 3 parts sulphate of ammonia. Apply at 3–4 oz. per sq. yd.

Tubers should be sprouted by placing them in shallow seed trays in a light, frostproof place. This is done in January. Reduce shoots later to the three sturdiest. Early varieties are spaced 10 in. apart in the drill with the drills 2 ft. 6 in. apart. Second earlies 12 in. apart in the drill and drills 3 ft. apart. The main crops need more room — 15 in. in the drills and 3 ft. between drills. All plantings are to a depth of 4–6 in. This is done by taking out a flat trench with a draw-hoe.

As the plants grow, soil should be drawn up on either side, using the draw-hoe for this task. The sign of maturity is when the foliage turns yellow and commences to die down. Lifting of the tubers can commence, using the fork carefully so that none are pierced. Late varieties can be stored over winter in sacks. Keep in a dry, frostproof place.

VARIETIES:

First earlies: *Home Guard, Duke of York and Ulster Chieftain*
Second earlies: *Olympic and Great Scot*
Main crop: *Majestic, Duke of Kent, Dunbar Standard and King Edward VII*

Turnips and Parsnips:

Site preparation is the same as that for the beetroots. Fresh manure must be avoided, otherwise coarse, misshapen roots will result — particularly with the parsnip crop.

Turnip seed is sown in March and can be repeated if desired in mid-July if storage roots are required. Young turnips are delicious and early roots can be provided if seed is sown in a frame or under cloches in early March. All sowings should be as thin as possible and hand thinning later will be necessary. Sow ½ in. deep and space rows 15 in. apart.

To obtain long, straight parsnips, bore a hole with a piece of wood and fill up with some fine soil. Sow a light pinch of seed in each hole and thin later to leave the strongest seedling to grow on. Space holes 12 in. apart with the rows 18 in. apart.

Plenty of water is required for both crops. If not applied during dry weather, rather coarse, tasteless roots may be produced.

VARIETIES:

Turnips: Snowball and *White Milan* are the best for early supplies
Manchester Market makes an excellent general crop

Parsnips: Offenham, Intermediate and *Magnum Borum* are suitable varieties

Onions and Leeks:

Both these crops must have a rich ground for good results. If a well-prepared site cannot be used, make sure that plenty of old manure or compost is incorporated into the new beds. Dig in at the rate of 1 cwt. to 6 sq. yds. Rake in 4 parts superphosphate of lime, 1 part sulphate of ammonia and 2 parts sulphate of potash. Use at 3–4 oz. per sq. yd.

There are two ways of raising the crops. Seed can be sown under glass in boxes in a temperature of 50–60° F. (10–14 degrees C.) in January. The seedlings are planted out later individually into deeper boxes and, after careful hardening off, are finally planted out in their final quarters. Spacings are — for onions, 8 in. apart in rows 12–15 in. apart. For leeks the measurements are 12 in. apart in rows 18 in. apart.

The second method is to sow seed outdoors in drills in March. Thin sowing is essential and seedlings must be thinned later to the distances advised previously.

General culture consists of regular feeding and watering. Leeks must be earthed up with soil or stems wrapped with black polythene or paper to blanch or whiten the stems. When onion tops yellow and die down they are ready for lifting. When dry, they can be stored in shallow boxes in the garden shed.

VARIETIES:

Onions: Premier will produce extremely large bulbs. *Bedfordshire Champion* and *Ailsa Craig* are two other varieties well worth growing
Leeks: The *Lyon* and *Prizetaker* should give large stems at the end of the season

Shallots:

The easy way to provide onion flavouring for your cooking! This is a very easy crop to grow and one which must be included especially if onions do not grow easily in your garden soil. Soil preparation is as for carrots.

Bulbs are planted in early March, pressing them into the loose soil to about half their depth. Space them 12–15 in. in the row with the rows 15–20 in. apart. As the clusters swell later in the season, draw a little of the soil away from them carefully so that the bulbs can swell and ripen. When foliage dies down treat as for onions.

VARIETIES: *Giant Red* and *The Aristocrat* are the best varieties to grow

Marrows:

There are two types which can be grown, the trailing and the bush. If you have not much room, don't grow the former! A rich position is vital for good returns and the best way to plant them is to dig out individual holes for each plant and fill with old manure or compost.

Seed can be raised under glass in heat in April, planting out later after thorough hardening off in June. Seeds can be sown in May where they are to grow, covering them with a jam jar until they are established. The strongest plant only is allowed to remain later.

Plenty of water must be applied throughout growth as well as liberal feeds. Pinch out the ends of the trailing growths of the trailing types when they are about 2–3 ft. in length. Hand-fertilisation of the female flowers should be carried out in the early part of the season. Fruits should be cut when about 12 in. in length. Rest on of board or even glass to prevent slug damage.

VARIETIES:

Trailing: Table Dainty and *Long White*
Bush: Tender and *True*

Cucumbers (outdoor):

Their culture is the same as for marrows. When the plants have made 6 leaves, the centres should be nipped out. This will encourage several laterals or side growths to form on which the fruits will be carried.

The cucumbers can be protected by growing them in a frame or under cloches. In this case the frame or greenhouse types should be used and all male flowers must be removed as soon as they are noticed, otherwise bitter fruits will result.

VARIETIES: For outdoor use the Ridge types should be grown: *Stockwood Ridge* is very reliable. For frame use, *Conqueror*, or *Telegraph Selected* will give good returns

Spinach:

Soil preparation is as for the root crops such as beetroot. Three types are grown — *Summer* or *Round* which is sown in March, *Winter* sown in late August, and *Perpetual* which is started in March.

All seed should be sown thinly with a little hand-thinning later on. Sow in drills 1 in. deep. Keep rows about 15–18 in. apart and thin plants to 12 in. apart.

VARIETIES:

Summer: *Goliath*
Winter: *Long Standing Prickly*
Perpetual: *Perpetual*

Salads:

Every vegetable plot must have a selection of vegetables which will provide salads for the summer months. The secret of success is to sow frequently and to use the correct varieties. Quick, steady growth is vital so that flavour is good and crisp.

Subjects which are the mainstay of the salad bowl are lettuce, radish and spring onions. Ground must be fairly rich and capable of holding moisture as long as possible. Horticultural peat applied down the drills at sowing time will be ideal for this purpose. It must be moistened thoroughly before use. Dig in compost at 1 cwt. to 8 sq. yds. Apply 2 parts sulphate of ammonia, 1 part sulphate of potash and 3 parts superphosphate of lime just before sowing at 2 oz. per sq. yd.

Lettuce is the most important salad crop. Seed should be sown at 3-week intervals. First sowing can commence in late March and the last suitable date is early August. Sow very thinly in drills ½ in. deep, spacing rows 12–15 in. apart. Thin plants later to 10–12 in. apart.

Radish can be sown either broadcast or in drills, spacing these 9 in. apart if more than one row is required. Sowing must be as thin as possible and the seedlings must be watered very frequently if the weather is dry.

Spring onions can be sown in mid-July to provide pullings from early April to May. A sowing can also be made in the autumn in August in sheltered warm gardens. This will provide a crop for midsummer the following year. Seed should be sown fairly thickly in ½ in. deep drill, spacing rows 12 in. apart.

VARIETIES:

Lettuce:	Early spring sowings — *Ideal, Favourite, May King* Main crop — *Improved Unrivalled, Supreme, Wonderful* Autumn — *Imperial.* Cos lettuce varieties — *White Heart* and *Paris White*
Radish:	For early sowings *Scarlet Globe* and *Tip Top* are very good. Main sowings during the summer should include *French Breakfast, Sparkler* and *Icicle*
Spring Onions:	*White Lisbon* is a variety which is usually used for this type of work

WATERING

How Water is Supplied:

Water — and plenty of it! That should be the rule, but how few gardeners carry it out. It is surprising what a difference to growth a regular supply of water can produce, and the aim should be to keep the soil just nicely moist at all times. It is far better to water lightly and frequently than to give a large amount only occasionally.

The surface soil of your flower beds, pots and boxes can be a little misleading. Quite often the top inch may seem quite moist, but a little farther down the soil may be quite dry. Pots are usually the worst offenders as they will dry out quite quickly. There is a way of telling whether they require water or not. If they are tapped lightly with a stick on the end of which an empty cotton reel is attached, a light or a dull ring will be produced. The former indicates dryness, the latter means that the moisture content is satisfactory. There are ingenious devices available now which are in the form of a probe which is inserted into the soil. Immediately a pointer indicates the condition of dry, wet or moist. It's quite fun to use and so very useful.

Methods of Supply:

There are no problems here as manufacturers have produced a vast number of gadgets which reduce time and labour with this important task. The simplest method in the garden itself is by the use of either perforated hose pipe or any of the ingenious sprinklers.

The perforated hoses are designed to produce a delightfully gentle fall of 'rain' over quite a wide area. It is an excellent method of watering young seedlings and plants as there are no heavy drops of water which could beat them down. A sprinkler should be included in the watering equipment. The rotating and oscillating models are ideal, especially those which can be adjusted to water over set areas or patterns. Some oscillating sprinklers can be placed right up to a boundary wall or fence and set so that the water does not fall on neighbours' gardens — a most useful feature in the smaller garden!

For the really lazy gardener and especially for the owner of a very large lawn there is a sprinkler which travels along the ground by itself and will follow the hose pipe, which can be laid out beforehand over the required 'route'. Only a low water pressure is necessary to motivate the gadget.

The watering problem becomes more acute in the greenhouse and garden frame, where, owing to the high temperatures produced, evaporation or drying out is accelerated. Many gardeners are away for most of the day and it is here that the problem lies. Fortunately there are several ways in which water can be supplied regularly to plants — and without supervision.

The first is an automatic device which, through adjustable jets on stand-pipes, supplies a mist or a fine spray of water overhead. It is possible to attach a length of perforated plastic pipe to the layout and this will water the tomato border. The layout is connected to the electricity supply as the control is through a solenoid valve. The basic cost is about £25 which includes one jet pipe.

Watering by trickle irrigation lines is another excellent method of providing regular amounts of water, and it is quite cheap also. For an outlay of a few pounds a complete unit can be purchased.

A length of tubing is provided with adjustable nozzles which are spaced a few inches apart. These can be placed alongside plants in the border or on pots or boxes where a regular drip of water is provided. The water is supplied to the tubing from a header tank of water connected to the mains.

An even simpler system and one which has a very promising future is as follows. Corrugated staging is used, down the centre of which a length of perforated rigid P.V.C. tubing is laid. Sharp sand is placed on top to a depth of 2 in. Pots are stood on the sand and by capillary attraction the moisture is drawn from the sand and up into the soil in the pots themselves. A header tank in the greenhouse supplies the water to the tubing.

Shading in the greenhouse will do much to prevent rapid drying out of the soil, and in the garden, mulches or top-dressings of peat, leaf mould, composted vegetable waste or old lawn mowings will conserve moisture during hot, dry weather.

How To Get Rid of Weeds:

One of the constant 'battles' which is waged in the garden throughout the season is that against weeds. Their severity will depend on local circumstances — an established garden, for example, will have its fair share, but nothing compared to a new or neglected site where weeds have been seeding and dispersing their seeds happily for several seasons.

Thanks to modern weedkillers the gardener's 'task' is a comparatively simple one in the fight against weeds. To obtain the fullest benefit from weedkillers it is necessary to appreciate the three main types available and the way in which they work. These are total, selective and pre-emergent (often known as residual). Each can help in its own particular way and much will depend on the severity of the weed growth and whether or not there are other plants already growing in the affected areas.

As its name implies, the total weedkiller is the most powerful and is most useful on vacant ground and where weed growth is particularly heavy and tough. Sodium chlorate is a total weedkiller. So powerful is it that ground treated must not be used for at least 6 months afterwards. It is an ideal preparation to use on the new sites where a complete clearance is required. It is also useful on neglected paths, particularly those which have masses of weeds growing through the joints etc. There are no weeds which this powerful weedkiller will not check or kill. It must be kept well away from neighbours' boundaries if they have any plants established in their gardens!

Selective weedkillers have certainly lightened the gardener's burden. These versatile preparations seek out the weeds but do not harm plants near by. There are two main types of selective weedkiller. One which will kill many plants other than grasses and another which works the other way round.

For lawn management, the former type is ideal as it can be watered on in dilute strength and left to weed the lawn whilst you are busy elsewhere in the garden. This is certainly a time and labour-saver. Weedkillers containing the chemicals 2,45T, 2,4D, and M.C.P.A. are used for this type of selective work. *Dalapon* is the chemical used in weedkillers which will kill grass but not other plants.

The third section includes the pre-emergent types. These are used on ground which has been previously cleared of weeds and where it is desired to keep the area clear of weeds for some time. *Simazine* is a typical chemical which is used in this type of weedkiller or suppressor. It is a most useful preparation for paths and drives.

There are very many plants which can be classified as weeds but in the average garden there are those which can be called common and which can be effectively controlled by one or more applications of a suitable commercial weedkiller. For convenience here is a list of weeds found in the garden starting with those which are troublesome in the lawn: *Selfheal, Ribwort, Broad Leaved Plantain, Cat's Ear* and *Creeping Buttercup* are easily dealt with by a selective weedkiller. The following weeds will need a little more attention and more than one application may well be required. *Dandelion, Mouse-eared Chickweed, Daisy, Pearlwort, Yarrow* and *Clover.*

Moss is often troublesome on a lawn. Poor drainage can be one cause. There are proprietary moss-killers available or lawn sand can be used as detailed in the chapter on lawns.

The most common of the other weeds which can be found in the remainder of the garden are *Dandelion, Broad Leaved Dock, Bindweed, Thistles, Horsetail* and *Ground Elder.* These are perennial weeds — that is to say, they die down each autumn but reappear the following season with renewed vigour. All are difficult to control as their root systems can either travel considerable distances along the ground or penetrate to considerable depths.

In most cases frequent spot or careful applications of selective weedkiller will check growth, although in bad infestations it will be better to clear crops if possible and give the drastic treatment of *sodium chlorate.*

Selective weedkillers will not kill the roots successfully and will only deal with the top growth. Control is made even more difficult when these weeds are growing amongst established plants, particularly when the weed has 'travelling' roots like *Bindweed*!

The annual types are easier to deal with as most can be pulled up by hand and placed on the compost heap to die down. Regular hoeing will also control well, especially if it is carried out whilst they are small. Choose a dry day for the work and the seedlings will shrivel up and die on the surface.

Don't forget to tackle all weed control before any of the weeds can produce their seed. If these fall to the ground there will be many thousands more to deal with later on. There is no need to despair even when confronted with the weediest site. Selective weedkillers, total weedkillers and the regular use of your trusty hoe will soon put you in control!

INDEX

H

I

J

K

L

M

N

O

P

Pests; Garden, 275–9; Household,